Praise for *Th...*

'Timely, essential, and thought-provoking, *The New Childhood* is the must-read parenting guide for raising 21st century, digitally driven kids. Instead of raising a white flag and giving in to social media and the Internet, Jordan Shapiro tells parents how to embrace technology, stay involved in their children's lives, and prepare them for their future. Read it! I promise you'll rethink your parenting. I couldn't put it down.'

– Michele Borba, EdD, author of *UnSelfie:
Why Empathetic Kids Succeed In Our All-About-Me World*

'For those who lament what the "app generation" may lack, Jordan Shapiro offers a timely, reassuring scenario.'

– Howard Gardner

'*The New Childhood* is a must-read for parents and educators! It's an incredible resource for developing healthy families and kids in today's technology-enabled world, and pushes us beyond clinging to rules, traditions, and practices developed for a different era.'

– Wendy Kopp, CEO and co-founder of Teach For All
and founder of Teach For America

THE NEW CHILDHOOD

Raising Kids to Thrive in a Connected World

JORDAN SHAPIRO

First published in Great Britain in 2019 by Yellow Kite
An imprint of Hodder & Stoughton
An Hachette UK company

First published in the United States of America in 2018
by Little, Brown Spark, an imprint of Little, Brown and Company,
a division of Hachette Book Group, Inc.

This paperback edition published in 2020

1

A CIP catalogue record for this title is available from the British Library

Paperback ISBN 978 1 529 30614 9
eBook ISBN 978 1 529 30763 4

Printed and bound in Great Britain by Clays Ltd, Elcograf S.p.A.

Hodder & Stoughton policy is to use papers that are natural, renewable
and recyclable products and made from wood grown in sustainable forests.
The logging and manufacturing processes are expected to conform
to the environmental regulations of the country of origin.

Yellow Kite
Hodder & Stoughton Ltd
Carmelite House
50 Victoria Embankment
London EC4Y 0DZ

www.yellowkitebooks.co.uk

Dedicated to my Mom and Dad.
You constructed my childhood so that I was
perfectly prepared for this moment in time.

CONTENTS

CONTENTS

Timeo Danaos et dona ferentes.
—Virgil

PLATO WOULD'VE BEEN A GAMER

I NEVER PLAY video games alone; I always sit on the sofa with my two boys, ten and twelve years old. We all thumb away at our gamepads together. Gaming is one way we bond—one way we engage in "family time."

You would probably imagine that anyone who dedicates as much of his energy to thinking about digital play as I do would want to sneak in some time with adult games like *Bioshock, Fallout,* or *The Last of Us* once the kids head off to bed. But I don't. Games do not actually interest me in and of themselves. I am concerned only with the ways in which they bring people together—families, friends, communities. I am interested in the cultural aspect of games—what it means to be a gamer, and how digital play influences the ways we think about the world.

Video game narratives are fascinating. In some ways, they are very much like interactive versions of the stories we enjoy on television or at the movies. They can be like theater, like novels, like tales told around a campfire. When you consider that almost every child in the United States plays video games, it is safe to say that they may even be the primary form of narrative for the twenty-first century. In other words, video games are the new bedtime stories, the new fairy tales, the new mythology, perhaps even the new scripture. They are the freshest form of written or recorded communication practices, which most scholars believe started around the twenty-seventh century BCE. That is when the earliest examples of literature appeared in ancient Mesopotamia. But long before that, way farther back than we could ever possibly imagine, stories were passed from one generation to the next by word of mouth.

Take a moment to consider just how mind-blowing the shift from oral to written storytelling must have been. It represented a complete change in the way ancient humans organized their communities, their societies, their civilizations. Those of us who lived through the transition to personal computers and smartphones think it was a big deal to see the world as we knew it completely disrupted when social networking and email became commonplace. But that was nothing compared to what it must have been like to live through the beginning of written language. It may have been the greatest technological shift of all time. The written word enabled people to remember and store information. It made it possible to send a letter to a loved one in a faraway place. It empowered folks to share expertise without ever having to meet in person. It allowed generations of humans to distribute knowledge across time.

Thanks to the written word, I am moved to tears when I take my children to visit the Plaka neighborhood beneath the ancient Acropolis in Athens, Greece. We walk along the same narrow market streets that Socrates and Plato once roamed. These philosophers died two and a half millennia ago, yet they are still educating the young adults in my college classroom almost every day. All because their ideas are preserved in writing. The ingenuity of the ancient people who first imagined symbolic language systems is astounding.

Long before the telephone, the internet, and video games, this was the trendy new technology that made it possible for people to collaborate and cooperate in ways that transcend both time and space.

Of course, written language — just like smartphones and tablets — had its critics in the beginning. Most famous among them may have been the great philosopher Socrates. He did not believe "anything certain or clear" could "come from what was written down." He compared writing to painting — what the artist presents may look like the actual thing, but it is really just an illusion, presented from a single perspective. According to Socrates, painting fails to represent experience because it is static and fixed. There is no room to probe. There is no space for empathy. It is not interactive. "Similarly with written words," Socrates said, referring to the elements of written language as if they were autonomous beings, "you may think they spoke as if they had some thought in their heads, but if you ever ask them about any of the things they say . . . they point to just one thing. The same each time."

Thankfully, Socrates's student Plato was a little more comfortable with technological change; he probably would have been a gamer. Plato recognized the importance of recording his teacher's thoughts. And because he did — because he wrote down the dialogues of Socrates — I have the good fortune of being able to teach the philosopher's ideas to undergraduate college students almost 2,500 years after they were spoken. Perhaps Plato understood that written language corresponded with a fundamental change in what it meant to live in the world as a human being. Perhaps he knew it would impact the ways we worked, played, and accomplished everyday tasks.

But was he right to ignore his teacher's wishes and put Socrates's words in writing? Maybe not. One could argue that history ultimately corroborated Socrates's concerns. As twentieth-century philosopher Alfred North Whitehead once said, "The safest general characterization of the European philosophical tradition is that it consists of a series of footnotes to Plato." In other words, for almost 2,500 years we have been scouring Plato's texts, trying to guess what, exactly, Socrates's words really meant. Nobody can ever be certain. Interpretation after interpretation is published; one PhD after another is granted. But Socrates's thinking remains evasive. Why? Because we cannot ask the man himself what he was trying to say. We cannot interact with the writing. Alas, all we have are words that "point to just one thing. The same each time."

Touché, Socrates.

The great gadfly-philosopher may have been correct about the limitations of writing, but he missed the benefits. Plus, his resistance was ultimately futile because the shift from oral to written storytelling was inevitable. Just like the printing press, the mechanical clock, the train, the telegraph, the radio, the camera, and many other transformative technologies: by the time the critics could articulate their objections, it was already too late. Society had changed in ways that necessitated new tools. That's generally how these things work. Human thinking changes; then, we build tools that help us interact with the world in ways that resonate with our new ways of thinking.

Tools do not use us, we use them. We are in control.

Still, we seem to have some primordial fear of our own creations. Robot uprisings. Clone wars. Time travel gone awry. There's nothing quite like a good sci-fi disaster movie expressing the fear that human ingenuity will eventually lead to the creation of tools that threaten our supremacy. It is a story as old as innovation itself. *Frankenstein* was *The Terminator* of the nineteenth century. Jewish mystics in sixteenth-century Prague told the story of *The Golem*, in which a clay man, brought to life, wreaks havoc on the community. The ancient Greeks had *Daedalus* and *Icarus*.

These stories all represent the same technophobia that currently surrounds video games and digital play. Journalist Mark Kurlansky calls it the "technological fallacy: the idea that technology changes society." To those of us living through a huge technological shift, it feels like machines are taking over our lives, dictating new behaviors, altering the ways we communicate with one another. But Kurlansky says, "It is exactly the reverse. Society develops technology to address the changes that are taking place within it... Technology is only a facilitator."

What are the new technologies of the twenty-first century facilitating? For one thing, it is a shift in how we tell stories.

Digital interactive media allows for new methods of storytelling. And when you consider that the majority of our narrative content is really just recycled material — reoccurring narrative tropes, such as Frankensteinian technophobia — it becomes clear that the method we use for transmitting that material is even more significant than the content itself. Marshall McLuhan suggested as much in the 1960s. He famously wrote "the medium is the message" in his book *Understanding Media: The Extensions of Man.* McLuhan was a scholar of communication theory who was interested in "the personal and social consequences" of a life lived with, and through, electronic media. He recognized that changes in communication technologies — written language, the printing press, the telegraph, the radio — always correspond with huge cultural shifts, not only in the way we think about our experiences in the world, but also in the way we organize our economic, social, and political structures.

It is from a broad cultural and historic perspective, like McLuhan's, that I initially became interested in the question of digital play and the future of childhood. I was sitting on the sofa, playing *New Super Mario Brothers* with my sons, when it occurred to me that digital play will make their childhoods drastically different from mine. Their formative years will be lived with screens — portable game consoles, tablets, smartphones. They spend enormous amounts of time in front of these devices. Therefore, they will reach adulthood with an entirely unique set of seminal experiences. They will eventually take the world's reins, thinking in ways that I cannot even comprehend. They will create a world that I can only barely envision.

So how do I prepare my children for a future I can't imagine? How can I get them ready for a life lived through new technologies? What does it mean for every individual, family, school — in fact, for all of humanity — that entire generations of children are now being raised on video games, a new kind of bedtime story?

These are big questions, without easy answers. But they're not new. Even when I was a kid, playing *Q-Bert* on my Atari 2600, almost every adult seemed to have an opinion about the way video games would impact children's thinking. Mostly, they were worried. They were concerned that too much exposure would affect children's fragile young psyches in negative ways. The grown-ups of the 1980s thought screens and games would rot kids' brains and corrupt our moral fiber.

I am pretty sure that they were wrong. Screen time didn't rot or corrupt anything. Still, the fear was understandable. It's basic technophobia. Changing tools disrupt our habitual ways of being. New devices shepherd us toward an unfamiliar and therefore frightening future. There will always be people who see what's new as a threat to the status quo. This is how ingenuity has always been greeted.

Consider Gutenberg's printing press, which made it possible to distribute Martin Luther's Bible, translated from ancient Greek/Hebrew into plain-language German. Looking back from our twenty-first-century perspective, we see the origins of modern media. We are grateful to Gutenberg for standardizing and democratizing the distribution of knowledge and information. We credit his invention as a critical pivot point in history, decentralizing power and leading to increased liberty and equality as well as the creation of modern democracy. But we completely overlook the negative consequences of print. We forget that the printed word led people toward a more private and isolated relationship with ideas. As cultural critic Mark C. Taylor explains, "Oral culture was of necessity more communal than print culture; with print and the advent of silent reading, people could wrap themselves in their own cocoons." Folks living in the sixteenth century resisted the change. "Commenting on the solitude and isolation of the reading experience, some early critics of print sounded like today's parents worried about their kids sitting alone in front of computer screens or mobile devices playing video games and texting with friends they rarely, if ever, see." It's almost funny how much twenty-first-century parents have in common with Gutenberg's detractors.

Today's grown-ups panic and fret about Snapchat, Twitter, Facebook, Discord, YouTube, or whatever digital platform-du-jour manages to capture preteen, tween, and teen imaginations. Almost every morning, when I open the news app on my smartphone, there is some fresh study, op-ed, or interview with an expert speculating on the impact of digital screen technology.

I have been that specialist. As a guest on hundreds of radio talk shows, I've listened to concerned parents, teachers, and caregivers call in and ask questions. Sounding exactly like the worried technophobes of centuries past, they are vexed about how digital play is defiling childhood, causing neurological damage, ruining eyesight, creating an obesity epidemic, triggering depression, and keeping our kids indoors. Are our kids losing the ability to reflect and be introspective? Does the speed and ease of digital communication prevent them from learning how to be good conversationalists? Are they learning to just log off rather than constructively resolving everyday conflicts? Will emoticons and 280-character tweets corrode literacy?

Will easy, ready-at-hand access to constant interactive stimulation hinder the next generation's ability to cultivate critical thinking skills?

The simple answer to all these questions is no. These concerns are predictable and clichéd. But still, I understand why some grown-ups worry. The entire encyclopedia, the arcade, the movie theater, and the telephone have all been smooshed down and crammed into a handheld device that kids can carry around in their pockets, and adults feel helpless. They see that learning, playing, entertainment, and dating have all changed, and they blame the technology. But the truth is that there is no need for blame. Childhood is just reconfiguring itself and adapting to new contexts.

The only problem is that grown-ups don't know how to make sense of it, and therefore don't know how to guide their children.

They have found themselves at a crossroads — worse, a multidirectional, nonlinear intersection. There is no road map, little precedent, and the traffic patterns are unfamiliar. Busy, overburdened parents and teachers end up navigating in all the wrong directions.

I get it. As a parent, I am constantly nervous. I recognize that changes in technology represent even larger cultural, economic, and political changes. But deep down, I also know that my kids will be just fine. In fact, without any help from me, they are already unconsciously preparing themselves for a very different world. They come home from school in the afternoons and the first thing they do is grab their laptops. They adore these machines with the same sense of pride that I once felt for my dirt bike and my Nike Air Jordan sneakers. And who can blame them? Computers are doorways that open up into a magical, limitless, connected world. My boys plop themselves down on opposite sides of the kitchen table, laptops between them. They log on to multiplayer online games like *Roblox*, *Minecraft,* and *Fortnite*. Then their afternoon adventures begin.

Soon I overhear them planning the next few hours of their lives: "Do you want to do a role-play?" "Can't we just play *Hunger Games*?" "Let's call Dylan and Orion." I hear familiar musical chimes as soon as Skype boots up. And in less than a minute, there are six or seven high-pitched preteen voices blasting through underpowered laptop speakers. My children are not outside goofing off with the neighbors' children. They are not around the corner hitting a ball across the local sandlot. Instead, they are with their closest friends, inside the bezels of their devices, playing on virtual playgrounds.

This shift away from skateboards and scooters toward keyboards and touchscreens provokes anxiety. But for my children's sake, I need to set aside my own knee-jerk fear of change and disruption. I need to recognize that most of us parents, teachers, caregivers — even politicians — are thinking about it all wrong. Despite being perfectly aware that every generation can and should play in unique ways, grown-ups are easily seduced by the nostalgic fantasy of a childhood that mirrors the one *we* remember. From our kids, we had hoped to see our own youth reflected back. As evidence, just think about the ongoing success of *Star Wars, Super Mario Brothers,* and every one of the Disney princesses. Entertainment companies know that we want our children to adore the same things we once loved, so successful legacy brands like LEGO and Nintendo thrive by updating products to make them feel fresh enough for a new generation, without losing the nostalgic familiarity that will stir the emotions of the grown-ups who carry credit cards. Lucasfilm and Disney both profit enormously from licensed toys, clothing, and video games that appeal to every adult's desire for a second chance — a desire to provide our children with the coveted objects and experiences that we missed out on.

But some gifts can be curses in disguise.

As the great Swiss psychoanalyst Carl Gustav Jung once said, "The greatest burden a child must bear is the unlived life of its parents." He recognized one of the eternal truths of child-rearing: in every generation, grown-ups unconsciously pressure children to live a life that mimics their own past but rectifies any and all shortcomings. When you consider Jung's statement, thinking about how many of our parenting practices are more about the grown-ups' egos than they are about kids' well-being, it is hardly surprising that we get so worked up about new digital technologies. Laptops, tablets, and video games seem to seduce our impressionable children with mediocre replacements for what we considered to be the true golden artifacts of youthful joy.

How could today's kids prefer JeromeASF's *Minecraft* YouTube videos to *Ren & Stimpy*'s animated adventures? How could they choose video games like *Madden, NBA Live,* and *FIFA* over bubble-gum trading cards or tabletop foosball?

Are you ready for the hard-to-swallow truth? The new toys are more engaging because they involve a different way of interacting with the world, a different way of thinking, a different way of living, learning, and loving. They are preparing kids for a connected world.

Believe me, I know that most grown-ups don't want to accept it. We would rather resist the new childhood, defending and protecting our precious memories. Embracing the childhood of the present can seem like a betrayal, as if we are turning our backs on the childhood of the past. If you are anything like me, you probably feel caught between an unconscious desire to safeguard your own imaginary inner tweenager (the memory of your own wounded prepubescent self) and a deep yearning to safely propel your real, present-day, flesh-and-blood offspring into the future. Moreover, you want to bond with your children, but the generational chasm between their interests and your own seems wider than ever.

This tension and confusion manifests as paranoia and fear about new media and technology.

It is an understandable and ordinary reaction. But if you let that anxiety consume you, soon you will hear yourself saying things you swore you would never say: "When are you going to grow up and stop staring at screens all day?" You will discover that you have become a lame killjoy, the old guard, a troll beneath the footbridge. Just like the grown-ups who always seemed to block your youthful ways, you will find you've taken up the antagonist's role in the cyclical drama of youthful heroes battling ogre-kings.

Sons against fathers, daughters versus mothers, Jedi Knights slaying Sith Lords.

Just like Socrates, your words will end up bringing on the very thing you set out to prevent. You will become a limiting factor in your own children's heroic lives.

Please don't let that happen.

I know parenting is hard. Especially when you don't really understand the game. There is no rule book describing what it is supposed to look like in the twenty-first century because digital play — like all the other transformative technological shifts that came before — is changing the very nature of child-rearing.

Parents, teachers, and caregivers all need to think critically and intentionally about how they can and should adjust their habits, expectations, and customs accordingly.

This book can help.

PART ONE

SELF

CHAPTER 1

THE NEW STORY TIME

DURING MOST OF recorded history, humans have shared ideas in more or less the same way. We tell stories.

Almost everything we do has a storytelling component. Every account of the past is just a story that we hope frames the present day in the context of history. Each scientific paper is a story that offers an empirical description of the natural world. When your accountant finishes your tax return, she signs a story about your income, earnings, and expenses. A mathematical equation, a line of computer code, a grocery list, and a recipe can all be broadly understood as types of stories.

The technology we use to distribute these stories has changed many times. We've gone from telling stories orally to writing cuneiform on clay tablets; from using animal-skin parchment to using wood-based papers; from monastic scribes to the printing press; from scrolls to books; from feather quill to fountain pen; from the graphite pencil to the typewriter, to the word processor. But on a foundational level, the content of our stories has barely changed.

Narrative has mostly remained linear. Novels. Lab reports. Complex equations. They always had beginnings, middles, and ends.

Until a few decades ago.

Now, multithreaded silicon processors and fiber-optic cable suddenly allow us to record and share knowledge differently. On the web, information no longer has the narrative arc that Aristotle laid out more than 2,000 years ago in his *Rhetoric* and *Poetics*. There is no reversal, no climax, no conclusion. Instead, queries open, they hyperlink endlessly around a digital web. Then, they hover permanently in the realm of networked possibilities. It's nonlinear. And for all we know, this could represent another monumental shift for humanity. It could be as big as the transition to the written word or the printing press. It has already opened up new ways for us to interact with information and knowledge. It will continue to transform the way we think — the way we express ourselves.

How should we understand this shift to nonlinear storytelling? What does it mean for our kids? How does it change the ways in which we should prepare them for the future? What skills will they need to be successful adults? What behaviors will they need to comfortably contribute to society? To answer these questions, first we need to understand how digital interactive media works.

Don't worry, I am not going to explain how monolithic integrated circuits (a.k.a. microchips) send signals across billions of tiny transistors. But if you engage with children — if you're a parent, a teacher, or a caregiver — you do need to think about how digital play affects the kids for whom you are responsible. That means asking about a lot more than just what's good and what's bad. It means moving beyond the on/off-switch mentality that ordinarily accompanies conversations about "screen time." It involves thinking critically about what is happening intellectually and emotionally when people engage with digital devices.

Rhetoric and Reading

Let's start with video games. How should grown-ups think about them? How does gaming impact kids? One answer comes from Ian Bogost, a researcher at the Georgia Institute of Technology. He coined the term *procedural rhetoric* to describe how the process of going through a video game's motions can persuade players to think in certain ways. It has to do with the way gamers embody particular ways of being. Unlike a traditional linear story — which is delivered by a storyteller or an author to an audience or a reader — Bogost argues that video games teach certain habits of mind by requiring players to act out specific procedures. It is the rules of the game that do the storytelling.

"While we often think that rules always limit behavior," Bogost says, "the imposition of constraints also creates expression." Think about the way that video games automatically enforce their rules. There is no need for the honor system, no need for an umpire. The game itself only allows certain kinds of play. In fact, because video-game rules are mechanically imposed, we sometimes cannot even identify them. We take the rules for granted. We think of them as part of the play space. For instance, we forget that only certain moves are permitted in *Mortal Kombat,* that players are allowed to take only a certain number of hits before they are eliminated, or that the dimensions of the play space are constrained. We hardly notice that the water into which *Frogger* plunges is just an area that is off-limits — the equivalent of stepping out of bounds. We do not think about the fact that Donkey Kong cannot leave the top level. Nevertheless, even when the rules seem invisible, they are always there. And we're usually paying a lot of attention to them because playing well always involves learning to understand constraints that are mostly unseen. It requires that we shape our actions in ways that adhere to the design of the game.

Bogost's concept of procedural rhetoric acknowledges the possibility that a game's author, or developer, can use the gaming experience — created through the implementation of rules — to persuade players to think and construct meaning in certain ways. The word *rhetoric* may sound fancy, but it literally just means persuasion. "Just as verbal rhetoric is the practice of using oratory persuasively and visual rhetoric is the practice of using images persuasively," Bogost writes, "procedural rhetoric is a general name for the practice of authoring arguments through processes." He wants us to realize that games do not just create experiences; they also make arguments.

It works subtly, the same way a novelist like J. K. Rowling can manipulate our emotions by determining how much she wants us to know, and how much she wants to conceal, about Harry Potter and Hogwarts at any given time. It is also similar to the way Steven Spielberg builds cinematic tension. At first, his camera reveals only Jeff Goldblum's face; then, slowly, it pans to reveal the Jurassic dinosaurs. Like a novel or a movie, a video game always limits players' perspectives. It forces them to view digital spaces in certain ways. Unlike a novel or a movie, video games can also limit players' actions, forcing them to solve problems in specific ways. Thus, a game is always pressuring us to think and make certain kinds of decisions — reinforcing thought patterns that, presumably, impact the way we make decisions even outside of the game world.

At first, this may sound like the same argument that angry politicians, activists, and critics often make against video games — that going through the motions of violence, in a procedural and immersive way, encourages violent behavior. Kids who play first-person shooter games like *Call of Duty,* so the theory goes, will get used to watching graphic visualizations of murder and homicide. They become accustomed to engaging in gruesome, unethical simulations of killing. Then, because they are desensitized to violence in the game world, they become desensitized to violence in the life world. They lack the wherewithal to behave ethically, to stop themselves from committing random violent crimes, such as mass shootings. It might sound logical at first, but there is no evidence suggesting that things are this simple. Ian Bogost knows this; his concept of procedural rhetoric refers to much more nuanced types of impact and persuasion. He is looking at how the rules and the mechanics of a game, experienced in context, influence our thinking. Shooting your way out of a tight game situation *is* teaching players something, but not necessarily something about real guns.

From a neuroscience perspective, the research suggests that first-person shooters cultivate "more accurate attention allocation, higher spatial resolution in visual processing, and enhanced mental rotation abilities." These are all complex ways of describing the cognitive functions we use to identify, track, and hit a moving target. They are also skills we use in a variety of other, nonviolent situations throughout the course of our everyday lives. "Attention allocation" describes one's ability to focus on any task. "Spatial resolution" refers to the way we make sense out of the stimuli we receive through our eyes. And "mental rotation" is how we can recognize an object as itself from multiple perspectives. Just through repetition, gamers hone the neural pathways involved in using these cognitive skills.

When it comes to procedural rhetoric, however, it's not about the way these skills are strengthened, but rather the way they get put together into a meaningful order. For example, first-person shooters generally encourage us to be stealthy as we scan our surroundings, pinpoint particular targets, and eliminate them using the tools at our disposal. "But the meaning of individual first-person shooters vary [*sic*] based on the way those processes are used rhetorically,"

Bogost explains. "Doom is about saving the world from hell-spawn; Waco Resurrection is about the politics of religious fanaticism." The meaning depends on the context. And this is why nobody has ever discovered a reliable correlation between video-game violence and real-life violence.

To drive this point home, James Paul Gee, a linguistics scholar who has studied video games, once wrote, "If playing violent video games leads to a statistical increase in violence we should see a rise in violent crime, say, after QuakeCon each year, an event which draws thousands of players to play violent games." We don't. Unlike a video game, real life generally does not adhere to straightforward cause-and-effect patterns. There are certainly some good ethical reasons to keep your kids away from überviolent video games; but fearing that immersive M-rated (for "mature") game play will turn them into sociopaths is not one of them. Human behavior is rarely so algorithmic.

Gee is one of the most influential researchers in the world of video games. In 2007, he wrote a popular book called *What Video Games Have to Teach Us About Learning and Literacy*. You would be hard-pressed to find a game developer who hasn't read it. The book looks at video games from the perspective of Gee's field of study: theoretical linguistics. That is just a fancy way of saying that he studies the way languages work — how they came to be, how they are learned, how they inform our lived experiences.

Gee's research shows that each and every video game works according to a systematic logic that is very similar to the logic of a language. Learning to play *Space Invaders,* according to Gee, is a kind of literacy — players master the ability to *read* the game, to decode the system. "Video games are like an external version of the mind," Gee once explained to me. "When we understand things and plan actions, we run gamelike role-playing simulations in our heads. In a sense, our mind is a game engine. We can combine elements from disparate experiences and create fantasies and think through complex problems." Gee's ideas may sound complicated. But just think, in the simplest terms, about the process through which babies learn languages.

All spoken languages — English, Spanish, Mandarin, Arabic — are complex. But babies learn them naturally and easily. How? First, through trial and error. Baby hears the sounds her parents make and experiments with making the same sounds herself. What happens with each utterance? How do the adults in her life react to each sound? Baby watches her parents' responses and catalogs that feedback in a mental filing cabinet, noticing patterns, making associations. Soon, she begins to understand the relationship between certain sounds. Some scientists describe this process as one through which the baby calculates simple statistics, running basic data analytics: How often do particular sounds occur together? In what order?

Next, Baby experiments. She tests her new hypotheses about the relationship between sounds. She pulls noises and phonemes from her repertoire and pieces them together to form words, phrases, and sentences. Before we know it, Baby is talking. In fact, Baby is probably talking a whole lot. As anyone who has ever raised a child knows, a two-to-three-year-old can become just as passionate and obsessive about talking — about asking "Why?" — as my twelve-year-old is about playing *Minecraft*. Who can blame the two-to-three-year-old? A few months ago she was a helpless baby; now she has mastered the ability to navigate an extremely complex language system.

We can even say that she's become *literate* because, according to Gee, there are other types of literacies besides reading and writing. For example, you've probably heard folks talk about "digital literacy" and "financial literacy." Both of these concepts are derived from an academic framework called "multimodal literacies" that Gee applies to video games. He sees games as perfect little self-contained complex systems that need to be learned the same way we learn a language. To win, we need to be "literate," we need to be able to speak and read the language of the game. We need to comprehend how all the interrelated rules, components, and elements work together. We do that in a way that is very similar to how a baby learns to understand speech. We recognize obstacles, platforms, weapons, and power-ups in the same way a baby recognizes how sounds like *mom, food, poop,* and *play* relate to one another to form a language with grammar and syntax. So, if you have beaten the classic Nintendo side-scrolling platformer *Super Mario Brothers,* you have mastered a new literacy; you know how to read the Mushroom Kingdom. Congratulations!

Ritual, Religion, and Play

Ian Bogost understands games as narratives with procedural rhetoric. James Paul Gee sees them as complex systems that require specific types of literacy. But games can also be understood as a type of ritual.

Johan Huizinga, an influential cultural historian from the first half of the twentieth century, wrote, "There is no formal difference between play and ritual." He sees religious rituals, political rituals, and social rituals as a form of play. To understand what Huizinga means, think about when you go through a rite of passage. Consider that you are actually role-playing. For instance, when you participate in a wedding ceremony, there are certain lines you're supposed to say, places you are expected to walk, specific manners of behavior. You are playacting within a set of boundaries. You are following the unseen rules of a game. In fact, when any of us participates in a ritual — jury duty, the Pledge of Allegiance, a baptism,

Thanksgiving dinner, a school dance, and so on — we are going through the motions of a specific narrative; we are acting out a story.

The same is true when we play video games.

These days, children play an awful lot of video games. According to Common Sense Media, in 2017 teens and tweens spent, on average, a little over two hours a day with screen media. That means my own children probably engage in video-game rituals more than in any other sort of ritual. They do it repetitively, playacting their way through the same *Minecraft* scenarios over and over again. While rituals of digital play may not lead directly to life-world behaviors like inflicting physical violence, they certainly do influence the way children think about their lives, just as other kinds of rituals do.

Let's consider religious rituals.

Some people love organized religion. Others find it boring and repetitive. When I was a kid, I was in the latter category. I hated going to synagogue. My mother would force me to dress up in uncomfortable clothing — a wool suit and a button-down shirt that felt too scratchy. The clip-on tie made me feel like I had a lump in my throat. Was the purpose of that tie to remind me not to talk? After all, that is mostly what happened in synagogue: I was *sssshhhh*ed. I stood up when the adults stood up and I sat back down again whenever they sat down. I did not understand the words they were saying in Hebrew; it all sounded like gibberish to me. Over time, however, I internalized the order of things. I knew when to bend my knees and when to bow. I learned the melodies, the sounds of the words, and the expectations. I knew how the different components of the service interacted with one another. James Paul Gee might say I became *literate* in the rituals of synagogue, in the beliefs of the Jewish religion. The fact that I was uninterested did not matter. Rituals do their work whether we want them to or not, whether we believe in them or not. They all have their own *procedural rhetoric*.

Ian Bogost might say that the rules of synagogue are just as expressive and persuasive as they are restrictive. They taught me intellectual processes. They taught me to be fluent in the language of Judaism. They taught me how to use Judaic ideas to interpret the world around me and then to articulate my perspective. As a kid, I always wondered why my mother forced me to go. But as an adult, I see that she was trying to preserve a culture, to anchor me in a tradition, to instill a way of thinking.

Now, I understand that those boring synagogue rituals were similar to playing a game. The first time this idea really made sense to me, I was in Denmark at the LEGO Foundation's Idea Conference. It is an annual event where some of the smartest people working on issues around children, learning, education, and play gather to share information and ideas. (Of course, we also spend a lot of time building with all the colorful bricks in and around LEGO's headquarters.) At the conference, Jack Shonkoff, the director of the Center for the Developing Child at Harvard University, gave a talk on early childhood brain development. He said that all over the world and in many different historical epochs, children play slightly different versions of very similar games: jump-rope games, chase and tag games, hopscotch games, circle games, ball games, and many more. While each variation is unique to its geographical region, it is still easy to recognize them as similar because they share the same characteristics. Certain types of games all have certain types of rules. Likewise, there are analogous boundaries, limitations, and restrictions across all the games played by kids in a particular age group. Just think about the way they all involve the same sorts of back-and-forth interactions among players.

Shonkoff explained that these games are universal because they are the most effective way for children to develop important social skills: the ability to *focus and sustain attention*, to *set goals, make plans, and monitor actions*, to *adapt to changing conditions*, to *solve problems*, to *follow rules*, to *control impulses*, and to *delay gratification*. In his book *From Neurons to Neighborhoods: The Science of Early Childhood Development,* Shonkoff gets even more specific. He writes about classic childhood games like Red Light, Green Light and Simon Says. "Doing well at these games requires paying sharp attention for a long time, keeping track of the rules of the game, and interrupting actions you are all set to perform." Furthermore, players must learn to resist the temptation to cheat. They must learn not to throw a temper tantrum each time things don't go their way. If they want to keep having fun, they have to actively preserve the order of the game; they need to make sure it does not dissolve into chaos. To do so, they need to understand, at least intuitively, how the game system functions: Which parts of the game are flexible and which are not? How do the different parts work in relationship to one another? Which boundaries are rigid and which are porous? Players always need to be *literate* in the rules of the game.

Children develop this kind of literacy through a process of trial and error, always ultimately aiming to maintain the fun and avoid fights among their peers. "Conflict, arguments, and outright physical aggression disrupt the flow of play, indicate that something is wrong, and challenge children to figure out what needs to happen to get play back on track," Shonkoff explains. When all goes according to plan, the children not only have fun, they also learn how to interact with one another. They practice and learn acceptable behaviors through direct experience as they become acculturated to social customs.

The games are like little rituals. They work in the same way that synagogue does — rigid in their expectations, but without the uncomfortable formal clothing. Just like all the other rituals, stories, and games, they exist to instill, maintain, and reinforce certain thought patterns, ways of behaving, types of expression, ways of relating to one another, and methods for sharing experiences with the people around us. Digital play works the same way. Video games blend role-playing and narrative together and then deliver their messages into our living rooms. They teach our children ideas, values, concepts, and manners — whether we want them to or not. The actions, sounds, stories, music, characters, and procedures shape the way our kids will live in a connected world.

Takeaways

Avoid the digital/analog binary. Teach kids how to integrate new modes of play into a holistic twenty-first-century play space.

Many grown-ups worry about how much time children spend playing video games, and therefore they adopt the problematic "on/off switch" mentality. They buy into a false binary, believing that digital play can be understood in opposition to all nonelectronic activities. As a result, kids' lives get divided into screen time and nonscreen time. It's unfortunate because a lot of the play that happens in the game world can offer developmental benefits similar to what's gained through the play that happens in the life world. For example, all games can be understood as little rituals. Participants act out scenarios within a set of boundaries; they follow unspoken rules. The rules limit players' perspectives and actions, encouraging them to solve problems and make decisions. In this way, digital play is just like all other forms of play; through ritualized action it reinforces thought patterns and strengthens certain neural pathways. Of course, that doesn't mean it's an adequate replacement for physical activities and tangible toys. But it can be a valuable supplement, offering an appropriate twenty-first-century addition to a child's everyday toybox.

Video games are great teachers. Your kids learn lots of things while playing.

All video games work according to a systematic logic that is very similar to the logic of a language. Players master the ability to "read" the game. They learn to understand how all the interrelated rules, components, and elements work together. They learn to recognize obstacles, platforms, weapons, and power-ups. How do they learn so much, so fast? Because great video games share a lot in common with great teachers: both are rigorous, responsive, reflective, and real (what I call, the four *R*s).

- **Rigorous:** Great games feature just the right amount of challenge. They're not too hard and not too easy. They keep players in the "Zone of Proximal Development." That's the term Lev Vygotsky, a Russian psychologist from the mid-twentieth century, coined to describe the ideal learning environment: a theoretical space where individual students encounter obstacles that can be overcome only with the support of external or social guidance. Likewise, good video games always provide players with the necessary power-ups at just the right time.
- **Responsive:** Great games always offer clear, concise feedback. Imagine how frustrated you'd be if you didn't understand why Pac-Man died. If you don't know why your strategy failed, how could you ever hope to improve your space-ghost-chasing skills? Good teachers know that the same principle applies to learning: assessments

are only useful if they provide the learner with the feedback necessary to iterate his performance.

- **Reflective:** There's a clear difference between the gamer and the character she controls. Therefore, the player is able to reflect on her in-game performance without internalizing the disappointments that come from failure. Similarly, educators often talk about "metacognition," the ability to think about your own thinking. Metacognitive reflection is what enables a learner to have what psychologist Carol Dweck famously called "a growth mindset"—the recognition that intelligence is not "fixed."

- **Real:** Games are obviously not real; but they are immersive enough that they often feel real. Players learn the rules of video games through hands-on exploration and experimentation. This is the same principle that makes project-based learning so effective in the school classroom. The best learning is always experiential. Otherwise, it would be like trying to understand a video game by reading the user's manual but never actually playing.

Encourage your kids to play; it's the best way to learn social and emotional skills.

All kids, everywhere, play similar kinds of silly games, like Simon Says, Telephone, jump rope, marbles, and jacks. Why are these games so universal? Because playful rituals cultivate social skills. Through play, children learn how to interact with one another. For example, they discover that to keep having fun with friends, they must follow certain rules. They need to constantly be deciphering and responding to the complicated language of the game system. Otherwise, everything dissolves into chaos. And that's no fun. Kids hate conflict because it disrupts the game. The more they play, the better they get at mediating the tension between their own playful desires and the boundaries that create a space for fun. Eventually, all the practice they get on the playground prepares them to abide by the complex social contract of adult interaction. Digital play may sometimes seem like it's isolated and antisocial, but even video games are preparing kids to react and respond thoughtfully to external and social stimuli. Let your kids get the practice they need!

CHAPTER 2

THE NEW PLAYTIME

WE SOMETIMES MISTAKENLY think of what happens among children as merely superficial. For instance, I think about the way my own children spend time sprawled out on the living room rug with action figures or toy cars. Sometimes they are on the sofa, clutching game controllers and fighting off the invaders who approach Hyrule castle (in Nintendo's *Zelda* series). They laugh. They giggle. They get swept up in imaginary, silly, and impossible worlds.

At these moments, I enjoy my "free time." I send emails. I write articles. I review research. I pay bills. I text Amanda, my girlfriend. I think, "I'm glad the kids are distracted. I'm glad they don't need my attention right now." I suspect that most parents feel the same sense of relief whenever their children are absorbed in independent play. We all need a break sometimes. We deserve it. We should wholeheartedly embrace these moments of serenity.

However, we should also be careful not to think that the work on our laptop screens is more important than the imaginary play in which our children are engaged. Instead, we should think of play — digital and otherwise — as the work of childhood. Imagine it as a kind of innovation incubator in which the cultures and societies of the future are actively designed. Our adult workaday responsibilities have short-term stakes; children's imaginary worlds have long-term impact. Their play worlds will produce the real worlds of tomorrow. It may sound a bit like an overplayed Whitney Houston song — *I believe the children are the future.* But when you consider what the science says about child's play and cognitive development, it becomes more than just cliché.

Learning by Playing Together

There is a plethora of definitive research, just like Jack Shonkoff's, that shows how children develop social skills through games and play. They learn to share experiences with others. They learn to collaborate, to resolve conflicts, to read social cues, to build competence and confidence. All the lessons that children learn from the tiny little rituals in games that they play all over the world constitute the so-called *soft skills.* That is an unfortunate term that minimizes their importance. In fact, these soft skills — the ability to focus and sustain attention, to set goals, make plans, and monitor actions, to adapt to changing conditions, to solve problems, to follow rules, to control impulses and to delay gratification — are the foundation of all learning, all social interactions, all the life skills children need to become successful adults.

You have probably heard the terms *self-regulation* and *executive function.*

Self-regulation describes the ability to manage one's behaviors and emotional reactions in ways that are socially acceptable. It would not be appropriate, for instance, if you were to burst into tears every time something unexpected happened — when you heard a loud noise like an ambulance's siren, when you'd been accidentally bumped by a stranger while walking down the street. Imagine how hard it would be to keep a job, to maintain a romantic relationship, even to go grocery shopping if you did not know how to regulate your emotions and behaviors. At a very young age, through playful experiences with family and friends, children learn the socially acceptable ways to express their feelings, their ideas, and their desires. Eventually, self-regulation becomes essential for participation in the grown-up world.

Executive function is at work in a similar set of soft skills. It provides us with mental flexibility and resilience. It allows us to multitask, and to manage and utilize cognitive abilities like memory and attention. Executive function helps us find the best strategies to get what we want or need. For instance, I suspect that when you feel hungry, you do not just sit at your desk completely debilitated by the burning feeling of emptiness in your belly. But you also don't drop everything and stuff your face the way Cookie Monster might. Instead, you keep focused on your job, while considering simultaneously where and when you will be able to grab a snack. Almost without realizing it, you quickly devise a time-management strategy, identifying the best possible point at which to stop the task you are currently engaged in so that you can satiate that rumbly tummy. Sometimes your initial strategy does not work — maybe the vending machine is out of order or the phone rings and keeps you busy for another forty-five minutes. If you have strong executive function, you can modify your plan on the fly.

Your self-regulation and executive function skills started to develop before you were six years old. Think about how a child reacts when she wants a ball that is out of reach or a toy that is being used by someone else. Does she scream and cry? Shut down and stop playing altogether? Or does she know how to wait patiently, to delay gratification? Does she know to ask a teacher for help, or think to suggest sharing or playing together? These are everyday situations that cultivate the self-regulation and executive function skills needed throughout life. When you watch children in the preschool classroom, their actions may seem inconsequential, but they are enormously important. Each game they play is like a mini-rehearsal, a practice run for taking care of themselves while living in society with others. This is where children start to construct tomorrow's communities, build tomorrow's businesses, and stimulate tomorrow's economies.

When I pick up my kids from school, I sit on a bench in the yard and watch them on the playground. They are absorbed in ongoing imaginary scenarios with their friends. One corner of the yard becomes a small city, a restaurant, a grocery store, a castle, or an alien planet.

A child places a rock atop a log, announcing its significance: "This is the supercomputer that can destroy the galaxy. We need to protect it at all costs!"

The others react, "Oh no, it's been hacked! Quick, get into the rocket before the zombie apocalypse."

"No. Use this rocket. It's better. It moves at light speed."

"Watch out! I think I see galactic bandits up ahead."

"Grab the supercomputer, let's take it with us!"

It sounds like nonsense. Kids can be silly and overly enthusiastic. Their fantasy supercomputers, rocket ships, zombie apocalypses, and galactic bandits are frivolous. But the method by which they act out the story matters. Remember, "The medium is the message." It is the ritual of the game, the process of learning to read the system, that is significant. Together, the children experiment with new ideas, new concepts, new ways of relating to one another. Together, they derive meaning and create rules associated with each prop, each rock, each stick. Their collective narrative emerges.

Jean Piaget, the famous Swiss psychologist, recognized that a process of adaptation, which he called *accommodation,* was happening in these playful scenarios. Writing in the 1950s, he described how children imitate their peers and adjust their behavior to the circumstances of the game. They make tiny accommodations for one another. They learn to be flexible, abandoning existing ideas and replacing them with new information. Nowadays, we know exactly which parts of the brain are activated while children practice adaptation skills. We also recognize adaptation as a component of executive function.

Some experts label the kind of schoolyard fantasy my kids are regularly involved in "pretense" or "sociodramatic play." The game itself has no objective, no winners or losers. Instead, it is an experiment in designing rules, creating customs, and organizing systematic worlds of their own. If developmental psychologist Lev Vygotsky had seen my children in the schoolyard, he would have noticed that they interact with the object on the log as both supercomputer and rock simultaneously. It means something in both the real and the fantasy contexts. The kids pretend to type on it, but they don't worry if it falls into the mud. In one context, it's a fragile piece of technology; in another it's just a rock. They also relate to their friends as both school chums and space cowboys, applying different rules to each circumstance simultaneously. Vygotsky thought this kind of sociodramatic play was one surefire way for a child to develop self-regulation skills, since moving between the different contexts involves suppressing impulses (not calling the rock what it is in reality) and also following social rules (addressing friends in character).

Presumably, the same skills are developing when kids engage in digital pretense and digital sociodramatic play. Each time children play make-believe—whether on the playground or online—they are practicing fundamental social skills that require self-regulation and executive function.

Kindergarten and the Sandbox

Success in the adult world depends on one's ability to follow the rules, to acknowledge that other people have perspectives different from your own, and to interact constructively with others. In a way, then, play is the beginning of civic participation. It is the place where kids receive their first lessons about how to live in community with others.

One early American researcher who wrote about the social and civic nature of play was the preeminent child psychologist G. Stanley Hall. In 1897, he conducted a study on how children played in a "sand pile" that was located outside Boston. Hall wrote an account of his observations in a little book called *The Story of a Sand-Pile*. He described how children built "wells and tunnels; hills and roads like those in town; islands and capes and bays with imagined water" as well as "mines of ore and coal, and quarries of stone." All in an oversized pile of sand.

Studying sand play might sound like a strange thing to do. But think about it in the context of the late nineteenth century. Back then, there were no sandboxes. Child's play, the way we think of it, was a new development. Sure, kids played those universal games: jump rope, chase and tag, hopscotch, and so forth. But school playgrounds did not exist. There were no public slides or swing sets. The psychotherapists who would eventually recommend sand play therapy had not arrived. Those colorful plastic shovels and pails we are all accustomed to had yet to be manufactured.

Everything about a child's life in the nineteenth century would look unfamiliar to a time traveler visiting from the present day. The moment you stepped out of your DeLorean, you would be surprised to discover an extremely different kind of childhood. Most of the kids you'd see would be working. Working really hard. And those too small to labor in fields, factories, or mines might be assisting adults in menial household tasks.

Remember that the first U.S. federal child labor law — the Keating-Owen Act — was not passed until 1916, and even that restricted only interstate commerce of goods produced by kids who worked more than eight hours a day. If the kids worked fewer than eight hours, the fruits of their labor were fair game. By today's standards, that may sound shocking. But at the time, the United States was still pretty orthodox when it came to the Puritan work ethic. Mainstream morality judged a person's inherent worth according to his or her labor, output, and productivity. "Good American citizens" would have objected to idleness in both children and adults. The values parents wanted to instill in their children were obedience, devout prayer, and a strong work ethic. Historian Steven Mintz studied the history of American childhood and discovered many seventeenth-century complaints about "children playing ball or flying kites in the street." Play was considered "a sinful waste of time."

But when G. Stanley Hall chose to study sand play, a shift was already under way. Attitudes about work, family, and child development were changing. He wrote *The Story of the Sand-Pile* for the same reason I wrote the book you hold in your hands right now. Sand-play was the digital play of the late nineteenth century. Like screen time, it was new, controversial, and represented radical economic, social, and cultural changes. Therefore, if we want to figure out how best to respond to a digital childhood, we should first acquaint ourselves with the history of how we came to think of the sandbox as just an ordinary part of growing up.

Childhood, as we know it, begins with Friedrich Froebel's nineteenth-century Kindergarten Movement. Froebel was a German educator who argued that young children would thrive if their formal education began early and featured an intentionally playful and nurturing atmosphere. His Kindergarten Movement pioneered the use of lively activities and colorful manipulatives to build social and motor skills. Wooden cubes and balls of yarn were among "Froebel's Gifts" — a collection of objects that the educator recommended presenting to children in a precise sequential order. He invented many of the learning toys that have now become commonplace, probably many of the objects you remember from your own preschool and kindergarten days.

In 1840, Froebel coined the term *Kindergarten* to refer to his school in Prussia, which he had previously called *The Child Nurture and Activity Institute*. The word *Kindergarten*, which literally translates as "child's garden," had a double meaning. First, Froebel envisioned it as a garden in which educators tend to children in the same way a gardener tends to plants: nurturing them so they can grow autonomously and blossom into their full potential. "Children are like tiny flowers," he famously said, "they are varied and need care, but each is beautiful alone and glorious when seen in the community of peers." Second, Froebel's curriculum — which would later influence philosopher and educationalist John Dewey — prioritized outdoor play. He believed children had an "indefinable longing" to "seek the things of nature, the hidden objects, plants and flowers."

The garden itself was a critical component of his kindergarten vision. So, Froebel urged German politicians to include mounds of sand in public parks. They were called "sand bergs" (or "sand mountains"). And they quickly spread around the developed world. Most scholars credit this movement in European city planning as the genesis of all public playgrounds. Sand bergs reached the United States around 1885, when a physician named Marie Elizabeth Zakrzewska visited Berlin and saw children frolicking, building, and socializing in the sand. Upon her return to Massachusetts, she reproduced them as Boston's "sand gardens." New England must have been ready to abandon the old Puritan condemnation of idleness, because the sand gardens were just as popular in the United States as they had been in Germany. Within just a few years, twenty-one sand gardens had been created in Boston.

That's where G. Stanley Hall encountered them. And they fit his vision of child-rearing perfectly. He wrote *The Story of a Sand-Pile* to help promote a new perspective on childhood and learning. He argued for freedom of expression and spontaneity. Indirectly, he was contributing to the Kindergarten Movement, helping to transform how adults came to think about children. His book describes sand play as more than just superficial silliness, because he saw imagination as a necessary expression of "a child's soul." Sand play was also an impactful way to cultivate a new generation of American citizens. "Life is for service," he wrote, "this idea should be implanted deeply in the heart of every child." Hall thought the sand pile had the potential to be a critical part of how children developed the capacity for ethical and moral reasoning. And therefore, he argued, it was more important than hard work or rigorous labor. Needless to say, kids loved the idea that having fun was becoming the work of childhood.

Parents of video gamers will immediately recognize what Hall meant when he described the way children became completely obsessed with the sand world of their own making: "The 'sand-pile' at once became, as everyone who has read Froebel or observed childish play would have expected, the one bright focus of attraction, beside which all other boyish interests gradually paled." Did the sand-pile parents of the nineteenth century worry about addiction, conflict, or violent fantasies? Probably not. But that's only because few people, at the time, were accustomed to considering children's experiences. In the 1890s, even the mainstream education establishment wanted nothing to do with what they considered to be the "pseudoscience" of child psychology.

It would take quite a few more years before thinkers like Freud, Jung, Klein, Winnicott, Vygotsky, and Piaget could successfully reconfigure our view of childhood.

Finding a Sense of Self

You've probably heard the expression "sense of self." It is grounded in the idea that identity is, in some ways, a product of the culture that surrounds us. Our social settings provide context and therefore limit the potential lenses through which we can see what it means to be a person. Philip Cushman, a cultural historian and family therapist, puts it nicely. He says that "each era has a predominant configuration of the self, a particular foundational set of beliefs about what it means to be human." Of course, we all have personal thoughts, feelings, and emotions, too. They are molded by our unique experiences and genetic predispositions. But the way we derive meaning from those experiences is shaped by a collection of explicit rules and implicit expectations that are the product of the time and place in which we live.

You need only consider differences between yourself and your parents or grandparents to understand how sense of self changes over time. Think about the kinds of emotional responses you value that they do not. Humor in television sitcoms often highlights this generational disconnect. Archie Bunker in *All in the Family,* Marie and Frank Barone in *Everybody Loves Raymond,* Jay Pritchett in *Modern Family.* Grandma doesn't understand why we celebrate preschool graduation or give a trophy to every kid who plays in the game. Grandpa doesn't get why today's parents encourage their kids to talk to bullies about their feelings—in the good ol' days these things were solved with a knuckle sandwich! Our values and customs shift because our understanding of what it means to be human shifts. Likewise, our understanding of what it means to lead a dignified, fulfilled, and empowered life changes.

Cushman explains that the essence of the self "is always a product of a specific cultural frame of reference." He wants us to see that who we are as individuals is shaped by the narratives, activities, and social structures that surround us. Our conception of identity is informed by community and culture. Our sense of self is created by the procedural rhetoric of the world in which we live, the everyday rituals in which we engage. In other words, as we become literate in the habits and customs of our surroundings, we simultaneously learn to embody a version of the self. A culture's educational, medical, and child-rearing conventions all create the rules of the game that inform to a child's developing sense of self.

Today, we take the twentieth-century concept of individual identity for granted. The sort of play that happens in a sandbox seems commonplace; we don't see it as a self-configuring social force. Most parents just assume that free play helps their children cultivate confidence and creativity. We are so removed from the origins of the Kindergarten Movement that we barely recognize the playground as the social, emotional, and cultural teaching tool that Froebel and his contemporaries intuitively intended it to be. We forget that, in the late nineteenth century, the idea that childhood was an opportunity for freedom, exploration, and creativity was revolutionary. When Hall was writing about the sand pile and Froebel was starting the Kindergarten Movement, very few people acknowledged that the individual had an inner life—hopes, fears, dreams, phobias, neuroses, and so on.

It wasn't until the turn of the twentieth century, as new developments in industrialization led to economic, political, and social shifts, that an individual came to be imagined as a "container of a 'mind,'" Cushman writes, "and more recently a 'self' that needs to be 'therapied,' rather than, say, a carrier of a divine soul that needs to be saved." Why did our sense of self suddenly change? Because in order to participate and thrive in a secular, industrial world we had to see the individual — as opposed to the household, the tribe, or the Paleolithic band — as the primary socioeconomic unit. Our children needed to learn how to imagine themselves as something separate and sequestered. They needed to be aware of the boundaries that separated them from other people. They needed to know that they were always responding to, rather than co-created from, their immediate contexts. They needed to learn how to think of a person as a unit divisible by hours worked, dollars saved, and products consumed.

They learned this through play. And oftentimes, it started in the sandbox.

Takeaways

Play — digital and otherwise — is not frivolous or superficial. It's the work of childhood.

Playful fantasies prepare kids for a future reality. That's why it's good when children immerse themselves in make-believe scenarios with no objectives, no winners, and no losers. Experts call this "pretense" or "sociodramatic play." It is how kids experiment with designing rules, creating customs, and organizing systems. Eventually, it's the experiences they have in imaginary worlds that produce the real worlds of tomorrow. And the playground itself makes little difference. Kids can make up the best games on both life-world monkey bars and in game-world sandboxes. In both settings, when grown-ups let them be, kids tend to immerse themselves in positive and prosocial creative fantasies. Therefore, parents, teachers, and caregivers should let children play in as many kinds of spaces as possible. Provide kids with diverse opportunities to reap the benefits of both physical and virtual sociodramatic play.

Through play, kids hone their self-regulation and executive function skills. They master the basics necessary to become successful adults.

More play is always better because every game provides kids with opportunities to practice their self-regulation and executive function skills. Children imitate their friends and adjust their behavior to the circumstances of the game. They make tiny accommodations for one another. They learn to be flexible, abandoning existing ideas and replacing them with new ones. Success in the adult world — personal and professional — depends on one's ability to do many of the same things kids do naturally while playing. Even grown-ups need to follow the rules, acknowledge that other people have perspectives different from their own, and interact constructively with others in order to keep the peace. Whether on the school playground or on an online server, kids receive their first lessons about how to live in community through the games they play. So, parents should encourage as much social play as they possibly can — and make sure it happens in diverse physical and virtual settings. Don't forget that digital play can also be social. There are multiplayer games with both cooperative and competitive modes. There are online games where players interact in a virtual sandbox together. And even when two kids sit next to each other, taking turns on a tablet or a computer, they are still engaged in the kinds of social negotiations that help children learn and thrive.

Play is the beginning of civic participation. And like culture, it changes over time, adjusting and adapting to new economic and technological realities.

In the late nineteenth century, kindergarten and sand play were both radically new and controversial additions to child-rearing and education. Today, we just assume that the sort of play to which we're all accustomed is good for children. But that wasn't always the case. We forget that many of our most beloved childhood traditions are products of a particular time and place. The original sand piles helped kids develop a new set of social skills for a changing world. Kids cultivated the "sandbox sense of self" that enabled them to live a fulfilled and productive life within an industrial economy. The digital sandbox has the potential to do the same thing for kids who live in a connected world. And while today's grown-ups are wise to recognize that video games alone won't adequately furnish kids with all the skills they need for the future, they should also be wary of too much Frankensteinian technophobia. Don't deny your kids the necessary opportunities to learn connected social skills in hands-on, experiential, and creative ways.

CHAPTER 3

THE NEW SANDBOX

TODAY'S GROWN-UPS WORRY that kids don't play outside as much as they did in past generations. But their concern is not really about the well-being of young children. Instead, I suspect that they are unconsciously nervous about the well-being of cultural customs that have become well established and comfortable. Intuitively, adults understand that most ritualized child's play was used throughout the twentieth century to cultivate kids into adult selves that fit snugly — like cogs — into the economic, social, and political machines.

Nowadays, the old children's games are threatened by digital alternatives. In addition to the public parks and sandboxes that grew out of Froebel's Kindergarten Movement, we have virtual playgrounds that exist only in an online world. That's disconcerting to parents, teachers, and caregivers because they do not yet know how to make sense of the kind of play that happens here. Governments do not yet know how to regulate it. Consumer advocates do not yet know how to evaluate it. Neither religious nor secular cultural institutions can figure out how to interpret, direct, or control the meaning-making that happens in the digital sandbox.

Most of us do not even know what goes on inside the bezels of our own children's digital devices.

What Do You Want to Be When You Grow Up?

A 2015 Pew survey asked grown-ups about video games. They found that a quarter of adults in the United States "think most video games are a waste of time." But almost the same number "think most games are *not* a waste of time." Another third "think *some* games are a waste of time while others are not." And the remaining adults are "unsure what to think about this issue." They all sound very confused. Asked if video games "help develop good problem solving and strategic thinking skills," the results are even more mixed: "17% think this is true of most games, while 16% think this is *not* true of most games." The largest group (47%) "think this is true of some games but not others." The rest (20%) are just not sure.

With so much confusion, it is hardly surprising that many people are paranoid about digital play. It leads noisy curmudgeons to scapegoat the game world. They see it as a site of unhealthy passive consumption. They describe it as if it were an immoral temptation. But digital sandboxes are playful, experiential, and creative; they feature all the ingredients that more than a century's worth of educational research tells us make for quality learning. They provide the opportunities for identity exploration that are an essential part of developing a healthy sense of self.

Of course, the idea of a "healthy sense of self" is complicated. If identity is always, to some degree, a product of one's historical and cultural context, then the notion of something being "healthy" is thorny. It means that standards of good health are partially the result of cultural bias. The standards represent our collective definitions of "normal" and therefore they often include inadvertent social and political agendas, inherently biased ideals that are tied to a particular set of technologies.

I hope that doesn't sound like some sort of conspiracy theory; I really don't mean it that way. Certainly, a lot of what we mean when we say "good health" has to do with objective measures of biological longevity and sustainability. But oftentimes, when we use the term "healthy," we are actually concerned with whether or not our bodies are fit enough to function within the economic, social, and technological realities of the time and place in which we live.

Mental agility and focus are markers of good health during the postindustrial information age — an era in which the best jobs require long periods of intense engagement with the analytic data on a computer screen. But in agrarian times, when farming skills led to prosperity, physical strength and endurance would have been considered the pinnacle of good health. In the Spartan era of ancient Greece, where warriors held all the power, "health" was associated with traits that modern humans would consider socio- or psychopathic: wielding bronze weapons and engaging in merciless competitions to the death.

Take a moment to think about all those times you've wondered why we've suddenly seen so many instances of psychological and emotional disorders that were relatively rare in the past. It has nothing to do with the evils of modern technology; it is a result of these ever-changing notions of health.

Attention Deficit Hyperactivity Disorder (ADHD), for example, is probably no more prevalent now than it was fifty years ago. And it is certainly not caused by too much screen time. In fact, most of the research suggests that ADHD leads to excessive screen use, not that excessive screen use leads to ADHD. The reason attention disorders seem to be more common is because they are diagnosed and identified more often. Why? Because of simple infrastructural changes that have happened over the past few decades. Under the Individuals with Disabilities Education Act (IDEA), for example, public schools in the United States are now required to identify and evaluate students who may have disabilities. Also, some economists suggest that financial factors have played a part in the increase: an ADHD diagnosis can make a family eligible for Supplemental Security Income (SSI) benefits.

I suspect, however, that the most substantial reason ADHD seems more prevalent has to do with our changing definitions of the healthy self. We want more children and adults to be able to focus for longer periods of time. We recognize that things are changing and that the economic and social marketplace of the future will demand a different skill set. Tomorrow's jobs require a different kind of worker. And therefore, our collective prosperity is dependent on our ability to prepare a generation of kids who feel happy, healthy, and fulfilled while working in new ways.

Could it be that in the same way sandboxes and kindergartens cultivated "health" in the twentieth century's industrial era, digital sandboxes — in which our children already prefer to spend their time — will cultivate a different kind of "health," one that's better suited to the twenty-first century's connected economy? I think so. And if that's the case, then adults need to start seeing the digital world not as a scary space into which kids escape, but rather as a primary location in which children receive lessons in living together. Only then can we do the work of child-rearing in the most effective and responsible way possible. Only then can we have a thoughtful discussion about how digital play impacts our children. Only then will we start to notice the significant positive and negative ways that the virtual playground differs from the play spaces of the past.

The Tools of the Time

Consider the megahit video game *Minecraft*. It belongs to what is called the "sandbox" or "open world" game genre. In games like these, players can roam freely through a virtual world. There are plenty of other sandbox games besides *Minecraft*. *Fortnite* belongs to this genre, as well as most of the LEGO and *Zelda* games. But few are as popular as *Minecraft;* as of January 2018, the game had sold more than 144 million copies.

Minecraft is an open-ended creative sandbox featuring virtual pickaxes. In it, players can dig, build, and explore. The game generates a world — made up of different elements and resources — as players move through it. The possibilities are literally infinite; it will just keep generating new virtual terrain for as long as players are willing to continue exploring. On popular servers like *Mineplex,* there can sometimes be more than twenty thousand players connected simultaneously.

In my house, almost every day after school, my kids call their friends on Skype and they play on *Realms* together. A Realm is a *Minecraft* world that is hosted on a web server. It is a semipublic virtual space in which a group of players can meet up, create, and play together. When I watch my kids and their friends interacting in these networked block Realms, I see the same sort of role-playing and make-believe that my friends and I engaged in when we were kids.

Growing up in Center City Philadelphia, I remember how back alleys and empty lots were transformed into battlegrounds, medieval castles, and secret spy lairs. In epic games of freeze tag, we used our neighbors' steps as safe zones. Hiding behind Dumpsters, we experimented with both positive and negative behaviors. But most important, we all learned to cooperate creatively as we were forced to navigate social dynamics among headstrong friends. We designed rules, created customs, and organized worlds. We practiced and honed our self-regulation and executive function skills while we did whatever we could to maintain an atmosphere of fun among friends.

Nowadays, in a world where children are no longer permitted the freedom to wander along urban sidewalks the way I did, I think it is encouraging to see that they have used the tools of the times to expand the space in which they can practice their social interactions. Immersed in *Minecraft*'s block world and connected to their friends on Skype, my kids go on grand adventures. They build schoolhouses and courtrooms, dungeons, labyrinths, and pirate ships. Then they act out fantastic all-consuming scenarios in these networked virtual realities. They participate in everyday rites of passage similar to the ones dramatized in classic movies like *Stand by Me* and books like *The Adventures of Tom Sawyer*. Their *Minecraft* sociodramatic play looks just like a digital version of mine.

Nevertheless, it's frustrating that my kids often seem detached from the life world. I sometimes struggle to convince them to look up from their laptop screens. They are wrapped in a cocoon of single-minded focus. They won't stop gaming long enough to make eye contact with the people immediately around them. They don't say hello when others walk into the physical room. They forget conversations we had just a few minutes ago, making me feel like I offered dinner to a couple of zombies. When the game is on, they seem completely isolated and disengaged from physical reality. And it makes me worry about whether I am effectively promoting a sense of etiquette and social decorum.

But I also recognize that they'd behave the same way no matter what was capturing their attention. Construction paper, toy cars, *Dungeons and Dragons,* and LEGO bricks can also tempt them to ignore me. Age-appropriate obsessiveness is not unique to the digital world. Moreover, we ought not equate being single-minded with being antisocial. My kids are focused, not isolated. In fact, most of the time, when they are staring at screens, they are connected to a community. They're not ignoring everybody — just the grown-ups with whom they share physical space.

As a parent, I need to be patient and empathetic. Today's kids are struggling to learn how to use social and emotional skills in two different worlds simultaneously. It can't be easy. The physical world and the digital world are separate arenas with different rules, customs, and habits.

When you were a child, your parents probably spent a great deal of time teaching you subtle behaviors. You may not have noticed it, but each time they told you to stand up when an adult came into the room, to shake their hands and make eye contact, they were preparing you to navigate the social customs of the adult world. Likewise, they taught you appropriate manners for using the technologies of the time.

I remember when my brothers and I started to answer the phone. At first, we just said, "Hello." But once we discovered how much fun "reverse prank calling" could be, things quickly got out of hand. Grandma would call and she'd be very confused when we answered the phone, "Shapiro's Funeral Home and Bakery, a crematory for your dead *and* your bread. How can I help you?" Needless to say, my parents were embarrassed when important calls came in. They taught us to say, "Hello, Shapiro residence. Can I ask who's calling?" We all learned an important lesson about proper ways to mediate social interactions through the networking technology of the time.

When I think about my own children, it's clear that an enormous amount of their adult social interactions will be mediated through a specific set of networked technologies. They will grow up and work in a world full of emails, text messages, video chats, and instant messages. How will they learn appropriate behaviors and skills for a life lived through digital tools? How will they become literate in the habits and customs of a digital world?

They will do so in precisely the same ways children always have: through play.

A Global Playdate

Minecraft provides my children with a digital sandbox in which they can cultivate appropriate behaviors that are tailored to a globally connected world. That's clear. But let's take a moment to consider what it means that G. Stanley Hall's sand piles were local, while *Minecraft* is global. The significance of this distinction became clear to me while I was visiting classrooms in Northern Ireland. There, all of the schools use *Minecraft* as a teaching tool. They recognize that twenty-first-century education requires learning through digital play.

I visited classrooms in Derry/Londonderry where students were using *Minecraft* to re-create the country's landmarks. The setting was almost too perfect. Driving from school to school across the emerald countryside, I noticed that the physical terrain of Ireland resembles the greenery of *Minecraft*'s block world. At the famous Giant's Causeway, bizarrely perfect hexagonal rock formations sprawl out geometrically into the sea as if they were spawned by an algorithmic game engine.

In the classroom, students were discussing history, geography, and culture. I sat down beside a ten-year-old girl in a crisp blue school uniform and asked her what she was building in her *Minecraft* sandbox. She clearly articulated the goals of the assignment, described her objectives, and told me how she was meeting them. I was impressed.

"Do you also play *Minecraft* at home?" I asked.

She smiled. "Yes. I do, all the time. More than my mum would like."

"On which servers?"

"*Hunger Games. Mineplex.* Some others," she answered without hesitation.

Back in Philadelphia, if I were to ask my boys that question, they would answer in the same way. Here I was, across the Atlantic Ocean, interacting with one of my children's potential playmates. Of course, there is nothing particularly profound in realizing just how easily the internet allows us to connect with people around the globe. But when you think of *Minecraft* as a limitless giant international sandbox, things get interesting.

In that physical sandbox near Boston, G. Stanley Hall discovered a community of boys who were, in effect, practicing local civics. They were applying and experimenting with the sorts of cognitive, social, and emotional skills that we teach in schools. They were cultivating perfectly configured identities, a sense of self necessary to succeed in the industrial economy of the twentieth century. What's more, they were using academic content and hands-on skills to practice how to be meaningful contributors to a local democratic society. I suspect that those children eventually grew up to live in a community that was just as regional as the sand pile. Today's kids, alternatively, are growing up in a world that demands they participate in a global economy mediated through microchips and fiber-optic cable. Our twenty-first-century children's civic responsibility, their ability to contribute, and their capacity to collaborate and regulate their behavior and emotions among a diverse group of people requires the kind of learning that can happen only in a globally networked digital sandbox like *Minecraft*.

The only problem right now is that because grown-ups are so

afraid of an unfamiliar future, our children are playing without responsible mentorship. They are playing without guidance, without coaching. They are figuring out how to navigate a new world on their own. Generations of recorded best practices around living and thriving—human wisdom transmitted from one era to the next through oral, written, and now video game storytelling—is being ignored. Meanwhile, children are internalizing their parents' misplaced guilt around screen time and they will eventually recognize it for what it actually is: an entire generation's disdain for a future they don't understand.

Our resistance to digital play is just like Socrates's resistance to writing. It is futile. Your kids need your help. And it's easy to provide. Parents, children, and families just need to start playing in the digital world together.

Takeaways

Everyone needs a sense of self, and kids develop it through social play.

The way kids learn to think about what it means to be a person is about a lot more than just biology. It depends on culture. Social settings provide context, defining the possible ways that one can conceive of the self.

To participate and thrive in any particular era requires having a sense of self that's aligned with the current economic and technological trends. For example, if you can't imagine yourself as an entrepreneur, you can't be one—and if you had been raised in a feudal economy, you'd never even consider the possibility of founding a start-up. Likewise, for anyone raised during the industrial era, it would be almost impossible to imagine working as a Vestal Virgin, always tending to the everlasting flame in the ancient Roman temple. This means that a "healthy" sense of self is not absolute or objective; it's a product of one's historical and cultural context. It always represents our collective definitions of "normal" and includes biases that often are tied to a certain tool set. Good health is just like a good technology: the definition never stays the same; it changes over time.

Children need to develop a sense of self appropriate for the present era. And they'll do this through games, routines, and customs that mimic and reinforce the conventions of the society in which they live. Unfortunately, grown-ups often get in the way because they're seduced by nostalgia. They try to push their own childhood experiences onto their kids. Of course, we all have fond memories of the quintessential moments that shaped our lives — camp, school dances, Little League games, science fairs, ballet recitals, first dates — and our kids will have similar occasions. But their transformative memories won't necessarily happen under the same circumstances (unless parents pressure kids to make meaning in exactly the same ways they do).

So, grown-ups should be more open-minded to new and diverse kinds of play. It's important to let kids discover their own experiences, so they learn to situate a sense of self within the social and cultural era in which they live.

Embrace the toys of the time.

Sandboxes helped cultivate healthy child development during the twentieth century's industrial era. Digital sandboxes will cultivate a different kind of healthy child development, one that's better suited to a connected world.

Each time a group of kids logs on to a game server, they're engaged in the same sort of role-playing that their parents remember. It may start in the sandbox, but eventually it transitions to more complex settings like parks, playgrounds, diners, and dance halls.

Likewise, the way kids play make-believe changes in accordance with the large social and cultural shifts happening around them. That's why coming-of-age stories are always a product of the times, shifting to reflect the new narratives that kids use to make sense of their lives. You can see this clearly in literature. For example, in *Little Women,* Jo March is an outspoken tomboy navigating the rigid gender expectations of nineteenth-century New England. A couple of decades later, Tom Sawyer took Huck Finn to search for stolen gold in McDougal's Cave. In 1951, Holden Caulfield gets fed up with the "phonies" at the Pencey Preparatory School and takes the train to New York City. By the end of the twentieth century, *Stand by Me* tells the story of Gordie Lachance and his friends wandering alone through suburban outskirts to find a dead body. These stories all follow a similar psychological and narrative structure, but the contexts are very different. Why? Because coming-of-age stories are about the way that children grow into adult members of society — the way kids integrate context into a sense of self.

Therefore, I suspect that today's kids will find their stories of transformation in video games. It's through digital play that they'll make the transition into a connected adult world. Don't think of your kids' gaming habit as an escape, but rather as a site for the healthy exploration of self and other.

Being single-minded is not the same as being antisocial.

Today's kids are usually focused, not isolated. They're almost always connected to a community, a play group that's immersed in sociodramatic play together. They act out fantastic all-consuming scenarios in networked virtual playgrounds. They participate in everyday rites of passage.

It's hard to overstate the importance of this digital play. When they're online, your kids are actively — albeit unconsciously — preparing themselves for an adult life full of emails, text messages, video chats, and Slack discussions. Therefore, they need safe opportunities to experiment with these types of interactions. How else will they learn the appropriate behaviors, habits, and customs? Every online game represents a chance to try out new ways of being with digital tools. That's a good thing, because the future is already here. We're all living in a connected world. And today's kids will need to be prepared to participate in a global economy that mediates transactions and communications through microchips and fiberoptic cable.

Cultivating our children's ability to contribute to society, and developing their capacity to collaborate with a diverse group of people, requires the kind of learning that can only happen in a globally networked digital sandbox. It's actually a matter of civic responsibility. Parents need to let their kids play online.

PART TWO

HOME

CHAPTER 4

THE NEW FAMILY

I COOK FOR my children every evening, then I call them to the table. "Dinner's ready!"

They don't move. They just keep staring at the Xbox, the iPad, or their laptop. I've tried everything: screaming, counting to ten, threatening with ultimatums. Nothing changes.

I understand why; I can even empathize. Video games feel like a job to kids. They are preoccupied with mastering the skills involved, focused on leveling up. They are experimenting, exploring, iterating strategies. Just like adults who become absorbed in their own work, my boys don't want to stop right when they're on the brink of achieving their goals. Would you want to be interrupted in the middle of a task after investing hours of your time? I wouldn't.

The problem is that when I've been cooking, I don't care what is going on in my kids' minds. The temperamental chef in me operates on a purely emotional level. I have been working hard in the kitchen and I want them to appreciate the meal while it is still hot. Plus, I feel a lot of pressure. Television sitcoms and parenting books have made it unequivocally clear that perfect families always have perfect dinners.

"Come on. Don't make me repeat myself!" I call them again.

"Dad! Just let me finish this life. Please."

"What?" I am shocked that my son thinks this is a reasonable response.

"I'll stop as soon as I die."

"But isn't the goal of the game *not* to die?" I ask. "You're basically saying you want to take as long as you possibly can." He doesn't respond. I don't even know if he hears me. He bangs the space bar a few times, then shrugs.

"You distracted me. Thanks a lot."

Slamming down his laptop screen, he mopes toward the dining room table. Soon his brother also takes a seat. This is how our routine begins; this is the pattern. Like so many folks around the world, we almost always eat family dinner together. It is a tradition I inherited from my mother, and one she likely inherited from hers.

In a way, the family dinner is sort of like a video game, especially if you understand video games the way I have been describing them: as instances of procedural rhetoric through which we become literate in cultural attitudes and values, forming a sense of self. Dinner may not always be playful, but combine prescribed behaviors and actions with rules and limitations—do it within a designated space—and you've got the recipe for a gamelike ritual.

My family's dinnertime ritual has lots of rules. They are not especially strict. We don't say grace. We don't dress up in our best clothes. But there are clear physical limitations nonetheless. I regularly remind my kids to sit up straight, plant their bottoms on the seat, keep their elbows off the table, and chew with their mouths closed. There are also intellectual expectations. Every day it's the same routine. I ask, "How was school?"

They both shrug. "Fine."

They push the food around on their plates or shovel it mindlessly into their mouths. It takes a while before I can get them talking. But after ten minutes or so, we connect the ideas they are learning to the games they play and the movies they watch. The other night, my older son compared his social studies lesson about Nazi Germany and fascism to *The Hunger Games* and the *Wolfenstein* video game franchise. I immediately launched into a mini-lecture about Orwell's *1984*, the *Trials of Socrates,* and a brief history of dystopian literature: "Utopia means 'no place,' it comes from Thomas More..."

I am sure they will forget most of what I said. Both boys rolled their eyes and barely listened. That's okay. The important thing is that we went through the motions. I modeled a habit of drawing intellectual connections. We practiced polite dinner table conversation. After a while, it all eroded into pretend shooting anyway. Index fingers were pointed across the table. Spit flew from my sons' lips as they made explosion sounds. *BANG! PICHOO! POW!*

I put a stop to that immediately.

Some types of play are not acceptable at my dining room table.

#DeviceFreeDinner

During the 2016 Summer Olympics, NBC aired a public service announcement promoting #DeviceFreeDinner. The TV spot featured athletes using smartphones and tablets during key moments of competition. A gymnast answers the phone in the middle of his ring routine. A soccer player reads text messages when he should be blocking an opponent's free kick. A swimmer is distracted by a video on her tablet during the starting moments of the 50-meter backstroke.

Cue the sound of a woman's voice. She is cheerful, articulate, and well-spoken. Presumably, she is meant to signify the perfect middle-class mother.

"There are some places where devices just don't belong," she says. Apparently, the family dinner is chief among them.

The commercial was produced by Common Sense Media, a non-profit organization that has been helping grown-ups navigate issues related to digital media since 2003. In their mission statement, they describe a commitment to empowering "parents, teachers, and policymakers by providing unbiased information, trusted advice, and innovative tools to help them harness the power of media and technology as a positive force in all kids' lives." Founded and led by Jim Steyer — a civil rights lawyer, children's advocate, and Stanford University professor — the organization has funded and published an impressive amount of research on how digital technology impacts kids and families. I rely on many of their studies to support the ideas in this book.

In 2016, they polled U.S. families with children between the ages of two and seventeen for a report entitled *The Common Sense Census: Plugged-in Parents of Teens and Tweens*. In that survey, almost half (47 percent) of parents said, "they or a family member used a mobile device at dinner in the last week." Just over a third reported leaving the television on during meals. Thirty-five percent said that "mobile devices at dinner caused an argument."

Findings like these are meant to shock you. They were released to support the #DeviceFreeDinner campaign. The statistics communicate a narrative that warns us that the traditional family dinner is under attack. The villain in this story is digital devices. They encroach on sacred space. Their touchscreens are blasphemous. Their interactive games are an affront on the well-ordered bliss of a perfect meal, and therefore, the perfect family. Common Sense Media wants grown-ups to "commit to putting devices away" and make the "healthy" choice instead.

The irony is that the perfect dinner they are trying to protect — in which kin come together at the end of a hard day at work or at school, carve a golden-brown bird, and pass green peas and creamy mashed potatoes — went mainstream just as mass media was laying its earliest foundations. Dinner's origins are linked to the origins of the devices themselves. Established in the early 1800s, dinner came into fashion along with factories and office buildings. It rode into rural life with the steam engine, plowing right through old agrarian customs. The meal became a part of everyday life because it ritualized a sense of stability in a world of rapidly accelerating travel and ubiquitous telecommunication. Just like Froebel's kindergarten, it introduced and reinforced conventions for a new model of childhood, a new model of parenthood, a new model of family, and a sandbox sense of self.

Nowadays, dinner feels like the cornerstone of family values and an iconic part of a healthy childhood experience. But the notion that perfect families have perfect dinners was, from the very beginning, more about Industrial Age social conditioning than it was about health.

There was a time, not too long ago, when humans didn't eat dinner at all. "The poor ate whatever and whenever they could," writes historian John Gillis. "Even the middle classes, which could afford an adequate diet, had no notion of the 'meal' as we have come to know it. Meals arrived in the early 1800s, dividing the day into clearly defined sections. It was the dawn of the Victorian era, and for the first time, people stuck to a schedule — breakfast, lunch, and dinner. Each was to be eaten at a specific time, and anything out of order was considered sinful.

Today, in the twenty-first century, almost all the parents I know constantly make sure their children have enough to eat, even between meals. On school days, I pack extra snacks in my kids' lunch boxes — dried fruit, cheese crackers, or peanut butter pretzels.

On moderately long drives, I take along granola bars, grapes, and juice boxes. One of the only times my kids ever stop playing video games of their own volition is when they want a snack. But my family would look dysfunctional to parents from the Victorian era. In their time, snacking was considered a sign of weakness. It demonstrated a lack of restraint and a propensity for overindulgence. Those were bad personality traits. Morality was associated with order and moderation; things weren't to cross categorical boundaries. Good people resisted and repressed all their urges. And well-behaved children always ate on schedule and never spoiled their appetites. They never gave in to temptation.

At the time, doctors, scientists, specialists, and experts were just beginning to get involved in the business of child-rearing. Psychoanalysts and pediatricians reframed morality and obedience as "health." According to historian Abigail Carroll, they insisted that "failure, by snacking, to 'observe all family regulations' revealed a character weakness that might, if not corrected, translate to a future social liability of a more serious nature." Today, we may be relaxed when it comes to snacking, but sanctimonious remnants of that Victorian commitment to dinnertime morality are still everywhere you look — especially when it comes to digital devices.

Today's parents are nervous because their children find devices as irresistible as chocolate cake. Like the Victorians who worried about overindulgence, twenty-first-century grown-ups fret about the instant gratification kids experience while playing video games. Does the on-demand pleasure of YouTube or Netflix prevent kids from developing the restraint necessary to deal with boredom? Will kids come to always expect the constant stimulation that video games can provide?

Parents have hundreds of questions. They fear the internet will spoil their children, leaving them ill-prepared for an adult life that demands moderation, prudence, and temperance. They frame it as an issue of biological health, using words like "addiction." They tell me stories about trying to get their kids to come to the dinner table. They complain that smartphones and tablets are keeping an entire generation of children from experiencing real human connection. And unfortunately, it is easy for them to find research that purports to validate their fears.

Sherry Turkle, for example, is an MIT professor who wrote a best-selling book called *Alone Together: Why We Expect More from Technology and Less from Each Other*. She studied what happens when people have smartphones beside them during a meal. She found that it "changes both what they talk about and the degree of connection they feel." I'm sure that's true — it is obvious, even. The smartphone exists so that it can transform the way we engage with the world around us. That is the purpose of all technology. That's what tools do.

Turkle, however, sees the new tools as evil temptations. In her mind, their mere presence is an affront to the accepted social order. Along with many like-minded grown-ups, she seems to forget that change, by itself, is neither good nor bad; but it is inevitable. Worried that we're moving away from well-established communication habits, she writes, "Even a silent phone disconnects us." She seems completely unaware that what we currently consider to be a healthy form of positive interpersonal dinnertime connection is just a long-standing fad that did not come into fashion until a few hundred years ago.

It was the mid-1800s when family members began to face one another during mealtime. Before then, they ate side by side, quickly and quietly. "Food was fuel," according to Abigail Carroll, "socializing was secondary — if it happened at all." Dinnertime conversation did not become "a standard expectation and eventually a carefully cultivated and highly prized art" until the nineteenth century. Our current way of talking may feel like it is just the way things are, but the truth is that habits of communication are always changing. Think about Shakespeare's Elizabethan English, and how it can be difficult to understand. Even dialogue from early-twentieth-century movies can feel unfamiliar. That is because the ways we talk to one another are connected to current cultural values, attitudes, technologies, and social norms. Interpersonal communication is always tied up with etiquette, customs, and habits that shift and transform over time.

It seems to me that it is a fear of change that lies at the heart of Turkle's work and Steyer's #DeviceFreeDinner campaign. They both want to keep things the way they are now — maybe they even want to go back to the good old days; they want to make dinner great again.

Certainly, there is strong scientific evidence that the family dinner, and the conversations that happen at the table, have a positive impact on child development. It has been linked to a lifetime of healthier eating habits, better grades in school, fewer behavioral issues, and a lower risk of substance abuse. I cannot dispute the accuracy of these claims. But could it be that modern scientists have only empirically proven what the Victorian moralists already knew? Dinner is great for teaching children how to fit into society. It shows them how to be civil and polite. In a ritualized way, it exposes them to common vocabulary and teaches them current conventions around conversation and communication. It builds lifelong habits, such as eating three meals a day, that grown-ups still associate with healthy adjustment.

We talk about "well-adjusted" children all the time. It is a concept that became popular after G. Stanley Hall (yes, the sandbox guy) wrote a two-volume book on adolescence in 1904. But "adjustment" is just a fancy way for psychologists and medical practitioners to discuss whether children abide by current social conventions. Adjustment is all about conforming to established patterns, structures, and expectations. Yes, dinner gives kids a chance to practice following the rules. But which rules? The dinnertime rules with which we are so familiar — the forms of interpersonal communication to which Sherry Turkle and the #DeviceFreeDinner campaign are so strongly committed — were designed at a precise moment in history. They exist to help children become well-adjusted to living within a specific economic, technological, and social paradigm.

That paradigm has already changed. So, shouldn't our customs change along with it? I think so. But before we can figure out exactly how they should change, we need to understand how the perfect family dinner came to be.

The Home/Work Split

It was the beginning of the Industrial Age, and middle-class men — specifically those who were living in parts of the world that rapidly embraced factory manufacturing, the office building, and new kinds of work — suddenly spent most of their day away from the places where they slept. Businesses moved to cities, where telegraph lines could easily transmit data to and from faraway places. The farms on which every member of the household worked to maintain economic viability were vanishing, and the residential communities that would eventually become "the suburbs" began to pop up in their stead. People redefined men's and women's roles in ways that responded to the current technologies and customs. A new distinction between "home" and "work" took hold.

For the first time ever, work was considered a place: the location to which men commuted by train to earn a living. The term "commute" literally refers to the discounted railroad fares men were charged when traveling between cities and suburbs in the 1840s.

Commuting is a concept that did not exist before the locomotive appeared. Likewise, the *Oxford English Dictionary* reports that the first written example of the word "work" as used to describe "one's employer or place of employment" did not appear until 1966! Certainly, before that, it was normal to name early industrial factories "works." Think of London's famous Thames Ironworks and Shipbuilding Company. But it was not until the train and the telegraph jump-started a commuter economy that people started "going to work." Work life and home life became separate realms.

It was also around the mid-nineteenth century when the family dinner ritual became popular. Why? Because it emphasized Industrial Age divisions, such as the split between home and work. Dinner happened at home. And home was no longer the primary location in which all of life was lived by all members of the household — as it had been in the age of the family dairy, neighborhood blacksmith, or local tailor. Home was a specific place now managed by Mom. Home became women's territory: the bosom to which men returned after a hard day of earning wages, the nest to which children returned after studying in school. As such, it took on new significance. Home became a sanctuary in which families were protected from the machinery, efficiency, profit, and immorality of the industrial world.

Historian Stephanie Coontz explains, "Emotion and compassion could be disregarded in the political and economic realms" precisely because these traits were celebrated and ritualized in the home. The separation worked because "the cult of the Self-Made Man required the cult of the True Woman." The True Woman, or the perfect mother, was representative not only of a place called "home," but also of a whole slew of nurturing, caring behaviors that had been intentionally excluded from urban factories and industrial office buildings.

In the same way that experts and specialists defined Victorian expectations around children's behavior as "healthy," Industrial Age gender roles were now considered to be "natural" and "biological." All the sentimental, emotional, and empathetic qualities that make home comfortable, safe, and nurturing became associated with the women who managed the households. And the family dinner was established as a nightly celebration of this new perspective on gender and industry. Like all rituals, the meal served to remind people — every night — exactly what they believed in. Families became literate in the procedural rhetoric of the home/work split.

Dinner has functioned in this way ever since, and people still do not take it lightly. A 2017 Organization for Economic Cooperation and Development (OECD) report included the family dinner among their measures of children's well-being. They said that eating dinner as a family can improve students' academic achievement, boosting test scores by "at least 12 score points in science." Relatedly, a 2013 Gallup poll found that the majority of U.S. families with young children (53 percent) report eating dinner together an average of 5.1 times per week. But historian John Gillis says that every time researchers actually observe families, the results tend to be strikingly different. Only a third eat together every night. Which, he explains, means that "As in so many things having to do with family, people tend to report more togetherness than is actually the case." Why? Probably because they feel pressure, shame, and guilt. Most likely, they have seen the sitcoms I've watched and read the magazine articles I've seen. They are familiar with the idea that perfect families eat perfect dinners together. And they feel anxious to conform. Even in private, they need to demonstrate to themselves that their children are well-adjusted. They want to perform the nightly ritual correctly because, according to a 2010 Pew Survey, 76 percent of adults in the United States say that family "is the single most important element in their lives."

That statistic shouldn't surprise anyone. We are living during an era in which the nuclear family is very important and our commitment to spouses, children, and siblings is considered a moral imperative. But that wasn't always the case. Before home and work split, it would have been shameful for family to play such a primary role in people's lives. Our current dedication to family would have seemed bizarre to our ancestors. Why? Two reasons. Historically, child mortality has been the norm rather than the exception, so it would have been foolish to get attached to offspring who were likely to die. Also, traditional religious doctrine instructs people not to put much stock in ties to biological kin. Just think of Genesis: God literally asks Abraham to demonstrate his willingness to sacrifice his son Isaac. Abraham is expected to prove his commitment to the divine. In the early days of the Judeo-Christian West, God was considered the only legitimate father, and heaven the only real home. Contrary to popular belief, the earthly family, as we imagine it, has very little to do with traditional religious values. Instead, it owes its existence to the modern rise of secularism, technological innovation, gender divisions, the suburbs, and the split between home and work.

Likewise, most of the familiar activities we do with our kids are only a few centuries old. Like the sandbox and kindergarten, they exist to reinforce the individualistic sense of self that powered the Industrial Age. The family traditions that we take for granted exist to cultivate children into well-adjusted adults who can easily participate in a specific kind of society. These customs are neither sacred nor essential to the human experience. It's all just fashion; and fashion changes with the times.

Times have already changed. But my family still eats dinner together every night. Like a Victorian patriarch, I demand that my kids put down their devices and come to the table quickly. I expect them to behave respectfully while they are eating. However, I also acknowledge that in a rapidly changing world, the etiquette of the family dinner might not serve the same purpose that it once did. It may need to be transformed, supplemented, or replaced with new traditions that are better suited to the cultural and technological shifts that are now well under way.

The dominant labor, economic, and gender paradigms are all in transition, yet most of our everyday family rituals — which were established to reinforce the worldview of a bygone technological era — remain the same. Ultimately, it is unrealistic to expect one realm of our lives to change without completely disrupting the others. Home life *must* catch up with work life. Twenty-first-century grown-ups need new ways to interact with our kids. We need to establish opportunities to model positive behaviors for living an always-connected life. We need to create rituals — other than dinner — that inherently promote good values for a constantly networked world. We need to reimagine our family lives with intention. And we need to do it at a magnitude that mirrors the size of the shifts that have already irrevocably changed the rest of our lives.

In my home, dinner remains device-free. But it is not the center of our family life. We all spend much more of our time in front of screens, sometimes with game controllers in hand.

Family Screen Time

On afternoons when I have custody of my boys, the three of us sit near one another in the living room. They focus on their laptops — gaming, watching YouTube videos, writing stories. I sit at my desk, in front of my computer, answering email and tying up the day's loose ends.

If the sanctimommies walked in, they would cringe. They would see three individuals sucked into three different screens. They would complain about what appears to be a lack of interpersonal communication. Why aren't we playing together? Why do we seem so disconnected? Why are we all focused on our individual devices?

Ours may not look like the kind of family time to which most of us are accustomed. But it does resemble something that experts call "parallel play." The term comes from a 1929 study by sociologist Mildred Parten Newhall. "Parallel play" refers to an early stage of child development during which toddlers play independently, right alongside their peers. Walk into any preschool and you will see it. Two-to-five-year-olds sit together at tables or on the floor. They engage in the same activities but pay very little attention to one another. Whether finger painting, digging in the sandbox, or building with LEGO bricks, it seems as if they have no interest in friends.

In fact, for almost half a century, psychologists watched parallel play and saw it as evidence that toddlers lacked the capacity to have real social experiences. They theorized that young children saw one another as objects rather than people — that kids had encounters rather than interactions. But these experts may have been biased. They wanted to see kids play in a way that resembled the polite face-to-face exchanges that the Victorians had perfected for the dinner table. They understood that the patterns of play — cemented in childhood — eventually become skills and behaviors for the grown-up world. So, they framed their ideas about child development to mirror the common narrative of cultural progress. They described "healthy adjustment" so that it moves in the same direction as polite dinner table etiquette: from "primitive" side-by-side to "civilized" face-to-face.

It wasn't until the end of the twentieth century that scientists realized what any preschool teacher already knew: try to separate the

kids and you invite temper tantrums. Parallel play is not as sequestered as it looks. Babies as young as two months are already intensely
focused on their peers. Even when immersed in parallel play, they
are interacting with one another through imitation and other subtle
means of communication.

Likewise, in the afternoon, my kids and I may be focused on separate digital tasks — we look disconnected — but we are very much
together. Like an old married couple reading the paper over Sunday
morning coffee, we call out interesting tidbits to one another. Notifications ding from our devices as we instant-message web links, sharing the memes that make us laugh. We tell stories and boast about
our online accomplishments. We're not abiding by the etiquette and
customs of the dinner table, the Victorian parlor, or even afternoon
teatime. But nevertheless, we're communicating and interacting. I'm
modeling behaviors, introducing vocabulary, and thereby encouraging them to think about the world in which they live.

Sometimes, after a while, my older son moves into his bedroom.
He wants to be alone at his desk. Without fail, the younger one
always ends up there, too. He curls up on the corner of his older
brother's bed and focuses on something separately. They both swipe
away at their respective screens. It is a peaceful sight — true affec-
tion among siblings. Both boys prefer to be in each other's company
even if they are not directly interacting. They choose parallel play
because they know that coordinated fun is often fragile. In Jack
Shonkoff's words, "A brief distraction, someone bumbling into your
play area, a few miscues, and the pattern is broken." He is describing
toddlers, but all parents know that, among siblings, play is tenuous
at any age. It can last only for a limited amount of time before dissolving into chaos. Debates, arguments, and sometimes even physical brawls happen because keeping playtime stable is hard work. It
requires awareness and focus.

Cooperative play certainly looks more like face-to-face communication — which is why we tend to privilege it — but it is hard work for kids. It involves complicated emotional multitasking. It tests a person's ability to concentrate on the game at hand while simultaneously managing interpersonal relationships. To play with his brother, my son must read social cues and practice empathy. Sometimes, to keep the peace, he is even forced to sacrifice his own playful desires. He also needs to stay fixated on following the rules of the game. It's not easy. Video games, board games, and action figures can all lead to conflict. And that's okay, because when cooperative play collapses, kids are still learning. In fact, they are honing essential self-regulation and executive function skills that they will continue to use in their adult lives. Likewise, mastering the ability to shift between solitary, parallel, and coordinated play is an underappreciated competency that directly translates to the workplace.

Grown-ups, in any job, need to know how to be productive when alone, how to accomplish their work while sitting parallel to someone else, and how to deal with a team on a project that demands cooperation. Mature grown-ups assess every situation and then identify the appropriate type of interaction. Whether kids play on screens or with physical toys, they're gaining opportunities to practice these skills. And as telecommuting becomes more common, as massive co-working spaces replace offices and cubicles, and as cooperative work is increasingly done on networks rather than at conference tables, the ability to shift between styles of interaction becomes more important.

My kids and I practice these transitions every day. We have learned, through trial and error, that we each need some alone time at the end of the day. Solitary play is the way we ease into being at home together. And parallel play is how we adjust to one another's company. It is our strategy for managing the stress of shifting from one part of the day to the next. But after an hour or so, I usually decide that family time should also include some direct coordinated play. I power up the Xbox or the Nintendo. That grabs my kids' attention. They close their devices and join me almost immediately. I don't even need to ask. They start hooting and hollering. "Dad, go over there! Get that guy! Jump! Now!"

We first started gaming together when my wife and I separated. The boys were four and six years old, and they used the Nintendo Wii as a kind of security blanket. It provided a sense of stability in their newly chaotic and confusing lives. Games aren't like divorce; they have consistent rules. They are made up of dependable systems. They are predictable and steady.

At the time, I hadn't played a video game in twenty years. I knew very little about them; and what I knew, I didn't like. I thought games were a time-suck, something that less productive people did in the evenings when they could be reading or writing, something for lonely slackers and lazy people. But I wanted to spend time with my boys. I wanted to help them through this difficult patch in their lives, and they wanted to play video games. If I'd told them to stop, put down the controller, come outside to hike through the woods with me, they would have perceived it as punishment.

Instead, I plopped down on the sofa next to them and before I knew it, we were all spending hours each day playing *New Super Mario Brothers* together. Whenever I picked them up from their mother's house, they would immediately start screaming from the back seat of the car, "Can we play *Mario* when we get to your house?" We argued over who gets the best magic mushroom. We high-fived when we leveled-up. We laughed. We hugged. It was a great bonding experience.

However, I knew that just because my kids enjoyed it didn't

necessarily mean it was good for them. They would also be happy if I gave them gummy bears for breakfast and let them stay up all night watching zombie movies. My conscience nagged at me. I wondered if I had become the stereotypical overly permissive bachelor-dad. To ease my anxiety, I picked up some books about video games, about cognitive development, about play theory. I learned that my kids were, indeed, escaping into the game world. But that was not necessarily a bad thing, especially if I was playing with them.

I learned that when I got involved, it showed my kids that I took their imaginative play seriously. It subtly sent the message that I acknowledged the strategies they were using to cope. It told them that I appreciated the things that mattered most to them. And it offered a fun and safe space in which I could help them cultivate sophisticated social and emotional skills.

When we played together, I took on the role of father, mentor, teammate, and therapist. I asked, "What emotions go with jumping high enough onto the flagpole that you get a free life?" "How do you feel when you lose?" "Don't you think it's interesting that you get better at winning by losing over and over again?" I pointed out how difficult some adversaries seemed to be. I observed how crazy the game's graphics were. Together, we guessed what future levels would look like. Then, after we put down our controllers, we headed to the dinner table. There, the game world provided the analogies I used to ask them about difficult situations. "How would you describe the game world solution to a playground fight? To a hard math problem? To a conflict with a classmate? To feeling alienated from your friends?" This line of questioning gave them the benefit of a bird's-eye view. The comparisons made it easier for them to experience the emotional roller coaster of their school-day social interactions separate and compartmentalized from the melancholy pall that my divorce had cast over their lives. It gave them the distance they needed to find a new perspective on their life-world problems. Most important, it helped them reimagine everyday scenarios in ways that felt empowering. It put the metaphorical game controller in their hands.

Unbeknown to them, I was conducting a simplified version of play therapy.

Digital Play Therapy

The famous psychoanalyst Melanie Klein was one of the first advocates of play therapy. She derived her theories about kids from discoveries Sigmund Freud made while working with adults' dreams. Klein observed that, during play, children act out the unconscious narrative dramas that shape their everyday lives.

When your children are on the floor making cars, dolls, action figures, and trains talk to one another, they are performing scenarios that could correlate to deep anxieties and intense desires. If you pay close attention, there is a lot you can learn from listening. That is why Klein and her followers practiced something that would eventually come to be called nondirective psychodynamic therapy. It is nondirective in the sense that the doctor doesn't tell the client how or what to explore; the client just plays. It is psychodynamic in the sense that it helps a client familiarize herself with the way feelings, thoughts, and emotions move through her mind. Today, when you walk into most child psychologists' offices, you'll still see a menagerie of figurines somewhere in the room. They are used to facilitate nondirective psychodynamic play therapy.

Swiss psychologist Carl Jung developed a similar practice called active imagination. Jung asked individuals (both children and adults) to engage with the images, characters, and stories that inhabit the unconscious. It is only by taking seriously what is ordinarily dismissed as superficial fantasy that one can become "individuated."

That is Jung's term for a version of healthy adjustment that is not defined by one's ability to conform to social pressures.

His research suggested that people needed help learning how to give equal airtime to a bunch of conflicting internal voices. He imagined the psyche like a sandbox in which a cast of unconscious characters struggle to play nicely together. If you were his patient, Jung might ask you to close your eyes and return to the world of your dreams. Then, he'd suggest ways to modify your in-dream behavior, and you would tell him how the outcomes of the fantasy changed when you made alternative decisions. What if you interacted differently with those internal playmates? What happens if you don't run away from that monster? What if you're only falling because you haven't tried flying yet? Can you just ignore the fact that you're only wearing underwear and finish presenting that book report anyway? Active imagination is like playing a video game based on your dreams: play it enough and you not only become literate in the language of your psyche, you may also become the author of your own internal dramas.

Of course, video games are not internal dramas. They do not arise from my children's unconscious. They are about as far from being nondirective as play can possibly be. Most games are big-budget interactive media productions created by huge teams of artists, writers, and programmers. The scripts are set, and playing usually involves solving puzzles or performing feats that simply unlock the next chapter in a prescribed story. Games are fixed rituals, with procedural rhetoric. Still, that doesn't negate their psychotherapeutic potential. Stories can be powerful even if you are not the author; we've known that since ancient times. Plato's student Aristotle coined the term "catharsis" to explain the phenomenon. He was writing about theater, the most popular form of entertainment in ancient Greece, but the concept is relevant to any medium. When you cry during a tragic dramatic movie, belly-laugh at a television sitcom, jump out of your seat to celebrate beating a game's final boss level, you are experiencing what Aristotle called catharsis.

The term literally has to do with cleansing or purging. It describes the positive sensation that comes from any sort of emotional release. It applies equally to moments when tears flow uncontrollably as to when the corners of your mouth give way to even the slightest smile. When your best friend pats you on the back and consoles you — "It's okay, let it out" — she's taking Aristotle's lead. He gave us the idea that an emotional purge is therapeutic, and the concept has been widely accepted ever since.

In 1975, Bruno Bettelheim published an influential book titled *The Uses of Enchantment: The Meaning and Importance of Fairy Tales*. In it, he explained why some stories are more cathartic — more emotionally therapeutic — than others. Specifically, he was interested in classic bedtime stories. How have folk tales, such as those collected by the Brothers Grimm, remained relevant to small kids for so many generations? Why don't they feel dated? They somehow continue to entertain and enlighten even as customs, habits, and experiences change.

"Jack and the Beanstalk," for example, has nothing to do with modern life. Few twenty-first-century children can relate to selling the family cow for just a few beans. Yet the story continues to be told. Why? Because, according to Bettelheim, it offers an opportunity for children and their parents to symbolically address serious inner conflicts together.

It works like this: All kids know that sometimes, when you disappoint a parent, an angry giant seems to awaken — fee, fi, fo, fum. Parental rage can arise from even the smallest of seeds. And for a child, that provokes anxiety. It is excruciatingly hard to be comfortable with the idea that Mom and Dad can sometimes be frightening. To feel safe, you need to know that the giant can be conquered and put to rest. But the giant you fear is also the same person who protects you and makes you feel safe. Talk about tension!

Of course, the fairy tale does not provide an explicit solution to the problem — there is no beanstalk to chop down in real life. But the storytelling experience, shared between parent and child, can be cathartic. By telling the story to our kids, Bettelheim explains, we "give them the most important reassurance of all: that we approve of their playing with the idea of getting the better of these giants." When we read them these stories, we help our children release their feelings of anxiety. We give them a symbolic pat on the back.

Notice that Bettelheim does *not* say that the transformative power of fairy tales resides in the content of the narratives themselves. Kids don't get the same benefits from reading alone. Parents and kids need to go through the ritual of storytelling together. It is all about the process. Likewise, when it comes to integrating digital play into the family experience, it is all about the process of kids and grown-ups playing together.

Most grown-ups recognize the benefit of reading to kids. They also play family board games, they build wooden Thomas the Tank Engine tracks with toddlers, and they toss balls around the backyard. Unfortunately, parents and caregivers are likely to leave kids alone with screens; they use screens as babysitters. Why? How can the screen-as-babysitter phenomenon be such a common practice if every grown-up I talk to seems to agree that it is a bad thing? Is it because adults are selfish? Do they value time for themselves more than healthy child development? I don't think so. Instead, I suspect that grown-ups intuitively realize there is nothing inherently wrong with using the screen as babysitter. The issue has just been framed the wrong way. It has nothing to do with the screens or with how the kids engage with them. The real problem is that the screen is often used *only* as babysitter. There's absolutely nothing wrong with solitary and/or parallel screen play—by all means, let your kids play on your smartphone while you make dinner! But don't forget that for today's kids to be well-adjusted, they also need coordinated family screen play.

"Joint media engagement" is the term experts use to describe the way kids and grown-ups engage in media together. Originally, researchers studied television and wrote about "coviewing." They discovered that when families watch television together, the potential that children will learn something from whatever it is they are watching increases. Those early studies focused on *Sesame Street,* so it was less about catharsis or managing internal emotional conflicts than it was about cultivating literacy and numeracy skills. But the same principles still apply. It was the late 1960s when Joan Ganz Cooney established the Children's Television Workshop, and, according to the original press release, *Sesame Street* was going to "stimulate the intellectual and cultural growth of young children— particularly those from disadvantaged backgrounds." The show was created around the time that President Lyndon B. Johnson was introducing his Elementary and Secondary Education Act, the equality-in-education component of his War on Poverty. Back then, preschool was considered elite, but *Sesame Street* aimed to provide all young children, regardless of their socioeconomic status, access to a basic early academic curriculum.

Test studies made it clear, however, that if this ambitious project were going to make a difference, young children and their caregivers would need to watch the show together. That is why Jim Henson's Muppets were so perfect. Kermit, Grover, and Big Bird's brightly colored silly faces appealed to small children, while their edgy parodies of mainstream media entertained parents. International celebrities also helped ensure that every episode of *Sesame Street* operated on multiple levels of content sophistication. The kids were learning phonics, while the parents enjoyed performances by Johnny Cash and James Taylor. Everything about the show was designed to keep toddlers and their parents sitting *together* in front of the television. And therefore, families who watched together developed a shared vocabulary — making it easier for caregivers to help their kids learn and grow.

Every time a grown-up reacted to one of Kermit's jokes, it sent a message about what parents valued. Later in the day, when Mom mimicked the way Muppets sounded out spelling, it reinforced lessons in literacy. Coviewing was the perfect way to integrate the television into the whole picture of family life. But it has been more than forty years since the first episode of *Sesame Street* aired. The television is no longer the primary screen in our lives. So, in 2007, the Joan Ganz Cooney Center at Sesame Workshop released a report entitled *The New Coviewing: Designing for Learning through Joint Media Engagement.* Led by a literacy expert, Dr. Michael H. Levine, the center updated the concept of coviewing to include screens other than the TV. The report addressed all the new types of interactive content that computers, smartphones, and tablets offered. But more important, it acknowledged that parents, teachers, and caregivers needed a new model for child-rearing in the twenty-first century.

Family life had changed, but few people — parents, mentors, caregivers — felt comfortable engaging with the new technologies that threatened to dislocate the center of our homes.

Takeaways

Home life needs to catch up with work life.

Grown-ups need to acknowledge that most of our beloved everyday family traditions became commonplace only because they helped cultivate children into well-adjusted adults who were prepared to participate in an industrial economy. The split between home and work made it easier to live a meaningful life within a specific technological reality. But we no longer live in the Victorian era; the current world requires us to interact with a very different tool set. And while work life has changed many times to accommodate new technologies, home life remains stuck in the distant past.

Twenty-first-century grown-ups will need to figure out new ways to model positive behaviors for living an always-connected life. We need to create rituals — other than dinner — that inherently promote good values for a constantly networked world.

Embrace family activities that have technological components. Play with your kids!

- **Legacy** video-game franchises, like *Pac-Man* or *Super Mario Brothers,* are a great way to start. Parents will get the pleasure of nostalgia. Kids will just be happy to get their parents' attention. When you're ready for something newer, try a game like *Shovel Knight;* it's one among a cohort of indie games that use old-fashioned platformer mechanics and 16-bit graphics. One of my family's favorite games is *Overcooked,* a cooperative multiplayer simulation game that often keeps the three of us laughing for hours.
- **Robotics** kits can function like the new garage mechanics. There's a whole slew of simple robot toys that combine with a smartphone or tablet to teach coding skills. Check out Sphero or Dash and Dot. LEGO also makes a variety of different sets that combine tangible brick building with digital programming. These are perfect for kids and parents to use together. Then, as kids get older, a programmable quadcopter drone can be like a space-age alternative to flying a kite.

- **If** you check out the toy aisle, you'll be surprised to discover a lot of products aimed at getting kids to understand how computers work. Think of these as the new build-your-own electric transistor radio or chemistry sets. littleBits is a collection of interactive modular electronic building blocks. The Kano Computer Kit is a build-your-own Raspberry Pi set. Neither of these requires any soldering, but you and your kids will learn all about how computers work while playing with them together.

Playing video games with your kids can have psychotherapeutic value.

Just like bedtime stories, digital play can facilitate catharsis. But it only works when parents and kids interact with media together. This is called joint media engagement. And if you approach it like traditional play therapy, playing together can help your kids develop confidence, self-esteem, and social-emotional wellbeing.

Ask your kids about the games they play and try to play along with them. This demonstrates that you take their sandbox rituals seriously. It tells them that you value the identity-forming experiences, and it encourages them to feel positive about their emerging sense of self.

It's also good to use the metaphors of the game world to describe the life world. When parents and children have a shared vocabulary, it's easier to have conversations about difficult topics. It provides families with a set of metaphors with which to bridge the gap between digital and real-life activities. When we can talk about both realms with our kids — transitioning seamlessly between online and offline ways of being — we're all better prepared for living together and making sense of a connected world.

Start staring at your own screen.

All kids need to master the ability to shift between solitary, parallel, and coordinated modes of play. This is an underappreciated competency that directly translates to the workplace. As telecommuting becomes more common, as massive co-working spaces replace offices and cubicles, and cooperative work is increasingly done on networks rather than at conference tables, the ability to shift between styles of interaction will become even more essential.

Unfortunately, the conventions of the nineteenth century have taught us to privilege coordinated play above all else. But that's only because it resembles the kind of face-to-face communication that happens at perfect family dinners. Parents shouldn't get caught up in the inaccurate binary between social and isolated play. Don't always expect your kids to be having fun with friends or siblings. Remember that there are also good things about solitary and parallel play styles. It's the ability to participate in the appropriate style of play at the right place and right time that matters most.

CHAPTER 5

THE NEW HEARTH

"SCREEN TIME" ONCE referred to the amount of out-in-front exposure a Hollywood celebrity had in a picture show. It measured how many frames of film included an actor's face. For an aspiring star, the goal was to be in the camera's focus and the audience's gaze as much as possible. Getting more screen time was a good thing.

The term didn't become pejorative until 1991, when journalist Tom Engelhardt used it in an article for *Mother Jones* magazine. At the time, almost every kid in the United States was begging for action figures inspired by the *Teenage Mutant Ninja Turtles* television program — the little plastic toys earned the Playmates company $1.1 billion between 1988 and 1992. Likewise, the Saturday morning cartoon, *Captain N and the New Super Mario World,* encouraged kids to covet Nintendo's Game Boy — the handheld console that turned the Soviet game *Tetris* into an American household staple.

Pop-culture fads like these were pervasive in the 1990s. And Tom Engelhardt felt uneasy about the way entertainment, advertising, storytelling, playtime, and retail were all blending together. From his perspective, there was something nefarious about it. Family life and screen life were becoming one and the same. Children were being turned into customers. Consumerism was becoming the foundation of childhood. He reported that 40 percent of American households had two television sets in 1991, and a quarter had three or more. But Engelhardt's issue wasn't the screens; it was the content, which was almost entirely funded by "toy companies, ad agencies, theme-park-based entertainment conglomerates, TV and movie production companies, fast-food chains, and other business enterprises." Because of licensing deals and crossover promotional campaigns, children's playtime seemed to be dissolving the well-established Victorian era split between home and work, between family and commerce.

It used to be that children spent most of their time buttressed within the bounds of the compassionate, pure, and nurturing household. Either that or they were stimulated within the intellectually wholesome academic classroom. They were safe and protected from retail and trade. The scary economics and industry of the outside world were intentionally kept at a distance — shoptalk was left on the doormat, finance was forbidden at the dinner table. But by the 1990s, advertisers, marketers, and toy manufacturers had completely burrowed into the home. Storytime, shopping time, and even mealtime were mashed together. Cartoon characters, video-game images, and pop stars were printed onto underwear, T-shirts, frozen foods, placemats, cereal boxes, and more.

In response, Engelhardt used the term "screen time" to signify three things. The first was the most obvious. It had to do with the duration of time kids spent in front of screens. The second was a little trickier. It acknowledged that children had become sought-after like the Hollywood starlets of the past: "screen time" now designated the corporate world's marketing gaze, fixed on children's lives. Screen advertising was focused on children as much as children were focused on screens. Companies wanted kids' attention, and viewers-as-shoppers were now the real stars of the show. Giving them as much screen time as possible served consumerism well; it meant higher sales and bigger profits.

The third way Engelhardt used the term was as an abstract philosophical observation about the nature of time itself. He observed the quick-cut rhythm of film editing and the race-against-the-clock urgency of a video game "preprogrammed to run at more than human speed." He worried that these things were transforming the way kids experienced the movement of time. "The speedier the screens, the more inert, ultimately, the viewers," wrote Engelhardt. In other words, screen time is different from clock time because it changes the way kids experience being in the world: they sit still, while images on the screen flow hurriedly. He concluded his article sarcastically, "This is commercial Zen, the deep stillness our society holds out to its children."

Remarkably, in just two thousand words, Engelhardt had already hit on all the screen-time trigger points that would worry parents for the next few decades.

Right Place, Right Time

Today, managing kids' screen time remains one of the most difficult struggles parents face. A 2017 survey by Common Sense Media found that 76 percent of parents agree that "the less time kids spend with screen media the better off they are." But oddly, 68 percent also say their kids spend "just the right amount of time with screen media." And 7 percent say their kids need more exposure, not less. Clearly, parents are confused. They're worried, but also satisfied. How can that be?

Maybe it is because despite all the hand-wringing about a changing media landscape, today's kids actually get roughly the same amount of screen time as their parents did in the 1990s. The types of screens have changed. Their parents watched cartoons on television while today's kids spend most of their time on mobile devices like smartphones and tablets. But the statistics on total screen time remain mostly flat. Depending on the study, it still averages somewhere between ninety minutes and three hours per day.

Most of the ill effects parents agonize over have also barely changed. Specifically, today's grown-ups worry that screen time disrupts the virtue of the family home and contaminates the essential purity of childhood. Of course, they don't say it that way; those are my words, my interpretation. They say they are concerned about sexual or violent content, too much advertising and materialism, depictions of substance abuse or other unhealthy behaviors. They brood about how hard it is to protect their children from cyberbullying and data phishing. They posit fantasies about how video games and social media have led to narcissistic attitudes, shortened attention spans, obesity, lack of physical activity, declining capacity for empathy, and an inability to appreciate nature. But ultimately, they are just pointing toward all the same attributes of well-being that Engelhardt lumped together with a nod to Zen Buddhism's mindfulness and presence.

The screen-averse attitude is about values, principles, and cultural customs. It's a moral and ethical position. It's grounded in beliefs about proper and improper ways of living a good life. It may be framed as if it were objective, as if it were about physical or mental health; but the real problem is that grown-ups are resistant to change. They are anxious about their kids' adjustment.

They should be. After all, today's parents aspire to the impossible: adjusting their kids to old-time habitual norms that no longer characterize the predominant social experience. This is the root cause of their screen-time anxiety—it is not the technology, but rather discomfort with the increasingly ambiguous boundary between home and work. Like Engelhardt, parents don't like it that the private world of the controlled family home fraternizes with the frightening unpredictable chaos that is supposed to happen elsewhere. Connected digital devices exacerbate their stress because, paradoxically, they facilitate deeply private encounters with a wildly public world. Parents see attention streaming away from the household. The lines between inside and outside, private and public, isolated and connected become ambiguous. And grown-ups become confused. This is why most of the screen-time advice offered by experts, practitioners, and journalists advocates for drawing clearer boundaries and achieving better balance — these are misguided attempts to bring what's blurry into focus.

For example, the American Academy of Pediatrics (AAP) recommends what I call "the on/off switch approach." They suggest limiting quantities of screen time for kids under six: none for kids to eighteen months, and one hour per day for kids two to five years old. After that, parents are told to create a customized plan for their child. In an interview with CNN, Yolanda Chassiakos, lead author on the AAP's *Children and Adolescents and Digital Media Report,* explained that an average child's day should include "school, homework time, at least one hour of physical activity, social contact, and sleep." After that, Chassiakos says, "whatever's left over can be screen time." But I'm a little confused as to how she defines "screen time." It seems like she's living in a very different technological age than I am. My kids' homework almost always involves online engagement, physical activity includes a connected fitness tracking wearable, and social contact is very often digital. The only thing clear about Chassiakos's guidelines is that what matters most — what constitutes the AAP's notion of healthy adjustment — is that things move back into clearly defined categories, divided and organized into a family model without uncertainty.

A similar example comes from my friend Anya Kamenetz, National Public Radio education writer and author of *The Art of Screen Time*. She connects her golden rule of twenty-first-century parenting directly to the dinner table. Borrowing from food writer Michael Pollan, she offers screen-time advice as if it were a diet system: "Enjoy screens. Not too much. Mostly with others." I like that she promotes joint media engagement, but I'm wary of a perspective that sees digital devices as a temptation and imagines that parents are responsible for managing their kids' ability to exercise restraint. Like the AAP guidelines, it's Victorian-era thinking at its best: moderation and temperance! The problem, of course, is that we no longer live in the Victorian era. Balance and boundaries no longer make sense as the organizing principle of child-rearing. Lifestyle compartmentalization — which once aimed to avoid the temptation of cross-contamination — may have made sense for the world of commuting and family dinners, but it doesn't necessarily make sense for a connected world. Webs are nonlinear. Clouds are indeterminate. Machine learning depends on swappable data. Therefore, child-rearing in the twenty-first century will require parents to move beyond the clarity of binaries. The split between home and work will no longer be useful; it won't help our kids prepare for the new adulthood.

Grown-ups seem happy to accept the way that work life is changing — industry cranks along, adapting to new economic models and embracing network technologies. But when it comes to home life, they're ready to do everything they can to make sure it stays old-fashioned. Frightened by new gadgets, which beget new routines, they resist anything that disrupts the traditional rites of the family home. But the ideal home life that they imagine is not nearly as traditional as it seems. It's linked to the technologies of the past.

Gather Round the Mantelpiece

Telegraph lines gave way to radio waves in the 1890s, and by 1922, the British Broadcasting Company was producing a few hours of programming daily. The technology was originally used to communicate where cables could not go: to military ships out at sea. But people quickly recognized broadcasting's potential. In 1926, Westinghouse and the Radio Corporation of America established a network of twenty-four stations, called the National Broadcasting Company. Soon after, wooden cabinet radios replaced the hearth as the focal point of the household. It is no accident that the first popular consumer radios looked more like furniture than like gadgets. They were designed for home life and family time.

By the 1930s, 90 percent of households in the United States owned a radio, which is why Franklin Delano Roosevelt's famous Fireside Chats were so effective. Roosevelt delivered thirty of these evening broadcasts between 1933 and 1944 — all from the White House diplomatic room, which has no fireplace. So, where did the name come from? CBS reporter Harry Butcher originally wrote it in a press release. It stuck because the fireplace had been the center of life for millennia. The Latin word for hearth is "focus," and Roosevelt wanted families focused and assembled around their radios, the same way they once gathered around the mantelpieces in their parlors.

The president began his first chat on March 12, 1933, in a casual tone: "My friends, I want to talk for a few minutes to the people of the United States about banking." Remember, conversations about money and commerce had been banished from the "feminine" household since the beginning of Victorian times. But Roosevelt crossed the boundary between home and work to promote a sense of order. It was the middle of the Great Depression, and families did not trust the finance industry. They were hoarding cash savings under their mattresses. Roosevelt needed to create the impression that family stability depended on people's restored faith in the power of bank deposits.

At the time, family life was in turmoil. The Depression kept millions of men from commuting, and the suicide rate was at an all-time high. Parents were unemployed or underemployed. Extended families were moving in together to save on rent. Marriages frequently dissolved. And many children were abandoned. Still, the struggle helped establish some new family traditions. Because there was so little money available for parents to spend outside the home, and barely enough food to maintain the dignity of those ritualized family dinners, folks thought up imaginative ways to keep themselves feeling fulfilled. They played board games and listened to the radio. It was the beginning of family life the way we currently imagine it. The social, emotional, and even spiritual parts of life took a step away from cathedrals, temples, town squares, and dance halls; they moved inside the sacred and private wainscoted walls of the family room.

President Roosevelt had helped transform the radio into the new American hearth. In just a few decades, it would even flicker like a real flame as cathode-ray images accompanied sounds, and television "screen time" became the new focus of family life.

Today, in my Philadelphia home, two small sofas sit on either side of an ornate red rug. A 4K digital flat-screen smart TV is mounted on one wall. Directly opposite, you will find the fireplace. In winter and fall, both glow throughout the evening and into the night. Our furniture is midcentury style — imagine tapered walnut legs on a

boomerang-shaped coffee table. It has this 1950s-split-level suburban vibe. The look has become trendy lately, perhaps because it
evokes a nostalgic sense of *Brady Bunch* family stability.

Like most Americans, I enjoy watching sitcoms and dramas with
my children, soaking up the wistful fantasy that times were once
simpler and home life was more stable. Each week, we watch episodes of *Modern Family*, *This Is Us*, and *The Simpsons*. It is not so
much that we care about what happens to these fictional television
families; it is because my kids and I feel especially close, after dinner,
when we snuggle by the warmth of the fire and laugh at the TV
together. This is our private time.

If you had known me in my twenties, before I had children,
you would be shocked to visit my family room today. I was much
more cynical in my youth. Back then, I gave up watching television
because I thought it was trying to brainwash me. I would have been
quick to propose a Marxist or Orwellian conspiracy theory. Television is the opium of the people, I thought. Big Brother uses it to
hypnotize us. The shows exist only so we know what to buy — they
want to keep us watching the commercials.

Now, I see things differently. I understand that watching television is a choice rather than a conspiracy. Modern folks use entertainment in the same way ancient people used religion and Victorian
families used dinner. It is a kind of ritual, a way for us to remind
ourselves what we believe in — and to expose our children to an
established set of values, to reinforce cultural literacy. Television
functions like an everyday nocturnal festival. That's why we move
into the family room each evening or during a Sunday afternoon
football game, because we want to highlight the life choices we have
made. We want to celebrate the world we have collectively fashioned
by opting in to Industrial Age divisions like the one between home
and work.

Consider the family room. University of Pennsylvania architecture professor Witold Rybczynski describes it as the place in the home that is relaxed, where our behavior becomes informal, and where social expectations and inhibitions can be set aside. He recognizes the same thing I see when my kids sit on the sofa. Cross-legged in their fuzzy bathrobes, they are comfortable and completely at ease. I am not entirely sure, however, that I agree with Rybczynski about the family room being sheltered from social conventions. Instead, it may be a place where these conventions are rigidly enforced. After all, informality has become orthodoxy for the modern household. Our afternoon and evening routines correlate to unspoken rules. Society demands that we experience the family room as a refuge from responsibility. We're expected to feel uninhibited on the sofa, distanced from scary economics and a world of coldhearted commerce that exists beyond the boundary marked by perfect picket fences.

The family room is supposed to be a nest where we embrace our unguarded private selves. It's a sacred temple in which we honor and worship the part of our lives that matters most: the nuclear family's bond. So, is it really surprising that twenty-first-century grown-ups struggle to accept and embrace digital media when you consider that tablets, smartphones, and laptops threaten to disrupt our sacrosanct sofa traditions? The image of parents, with their children, whiling away the evening together — eating dinner, playing board games, watching TV — sits comfortably in the La-Z-Boy of our minds. Thus, we adamantly protest anything that might jeopardize it.

But our resistance is misplaced. We've confused comfort with tradition. There's nothing essential about these prime-time rituals. They've just been fashionable for a while. In fact, the family room is a distinctly modern phenomenon, linked to a specific technological era. According to Rybczynski, preindustrial households looked very different from ours. Prior to the nineteenth century, the term "family" would have referred to anyone and everyone who lived in the household. There was no special bond among biological kin. Domestic helpers, visitors, and apprentices were all considered members of the family. In fact, the word "family" comes from the Latin *famulus,* which translates directly into English as "servants."

For anyone and everyone living in a preindustrial household, a large open chamber called the great hall would have been the center of a rowdy and raucous family life. At the end of each evening, all the furniture in the hall would be pushed to the side, making a space for communal sleeping. There were no bedrooms, because privacy had not yet become an essential aspect of domesticity. Nobody would have wanted to be alone. People lived, worked, and slept in a way that was much less divided and compartmentalized than it is now. In fact, all of life's most meaningful moments were once blended together in a much more public way. Ordinary activities, events, and rituals happened in the sort of communal space that the ancient Greeks called an agora.

The most famous agora is the marketplace beneath the Acropolis in Athens. But the word refers to any location where people assemble. Piazzas, social clubs, temples, and cathedrals are all agoras. These were the kinds of places where preindustrial folk gathered. They may have had their own houses, but because their conception of family was so different from ours, they spent much less time there. Home life was not so guarded, individualistic, or isolated. It spilled out onto the streets.

The kind of private time that I aim to experience in my family room — snuggling with my boys, bonding together over a video game or in front of the television — would not have been imaginable. That kind of comfortable routine did not become the norm until after programming like Roosevelt's Fireside Chats transformed radio and television into an intimate hearth. That's when something strange and contradictory happened: electronic entertainment, secluded in private homes, somehow became the primary agora. Everyone listened to the president separately, but nevertheless they experienced a sense of togetherness. TV and radio allowed folks to tune in to something that felt collective but did not require leaving the comfort of a plush sofa.

At the end of a hard day's work, and after a long commute, twentieth-century families became exclusive and close-knit because the TV hearth made it possible for them to be part of something collective without having to be physically present with others. The glowing box replaced both the great hall and the physical agora. It allowed families to experience an old-world sense of camaraderie while remaining sequestered within their modern private dwellings.

In other words, electronic communication technologies never threatened family time; they created it.

The New Agora

Today's communication technologies continue to connect us to the outside world. They may even fulfill our desire for agora experiences better than anything ever has, because they link us to a global community and a seemingly unlimited marketplace. But they also complicate our family time and muddle the practice of child-rearing. The new digital devices do little to reinforce our sense of comfort, privacy, and family well-being. Unlike Roosevelt's broadcast media, which disrupted the previous split between home and work but also offered a synthesized engagement with both inside and outside, digital media just confuses things. It aggravates our sense of anxiety. It presents a fresh screen-time dilemma. In a connected world, our children isolate themselves in order to interact with others. They are always alone but also very much together. And therefore, grown-ups are finding they're forced to reimagine the relationship between agora and hearth.

Let's be clear: today's kids get plenty of agora experiences — so many, in fact, that it seems crazy for people to worry about how digital play impacts communication skills. Online games involve constant and immediate connection with people in faraway places. Kids communicate in ways previous generations never could have imagined. Still, many argue that today's methods of digital communication are not the same as face-to-face interaction. And, of course, they're right. But different does not mean worse. Sometimes it can mean better.

Researchers have known for more than a decade that online multiplayer games can help people develop lasting social relationships and feelings of community. A 2007 study from the University of Jyväskylä in Finland found that most online games actively incentivize collaboration. Players quickly discover that they succeed when working together. The procedural rhetoric of online gaming encourages communication, interaction, and connection. Moreover, the bonds that develop among players are likely to be based on shared values and goals, rather than on appearance, age, socioeconomic class, race, religion, gender — all those culturally constructed signifiers of identity that often shape traditional social bonds but have also historically driven prejudice and discrimination.

It turns out that physical proximity is not necessarily the best criterion for meaningful or healthy connection. My children would rather play *only* online with their friends. Even when I suggest that they invite their classmates to our house, they refuse. My boys insist that it is more fun to sit in separate places, playing on a virtual playground. When I do convince them otherwise, their friends arrive with laptops in hand, and all the kids sit together at the kitchen table staring at their devices. They are immersed in a digital world together, paying barely any attention to their tangible surroundings (until snack time, of course).

In 2017, the Organization for Economic Cooperation and Development found that students who use the internet outside of school, to chat or to access social media, tend to score higher on global assessments of essential twenty-first-century collaborative problem-solving skills. For example, they're "significantly more likely to say that they enjoy working as part of a team." Still, it is common to hear grown-ups complain that activities involving screens are antisocial.

For instance, you've probably seen adults roll their eyes as they describe the way their teenage children sit together on the sofa sending SMS text messages across the room. The implication is that communication mediated through mobile devices is somehow less authentic. Maybe grown-ups believe the distance an electronic signal travels — from regional cell tower, through fiber-optic cable, to a mobile switching center, and then back out to the BFF (best friend forever) on the other side of the family room — is anathema to intimacy. But that's not necessarily true. Smart devices can facilitate strong personal bonds, especially for young people who are still learning to understand the nuances of social interaction. They might prefer the simplicity of mobile communication. Text messages may feel more approachable, more fun, and less likely to end in conflict.

Many parents struggle to recognize the potential benefits of this sort of digital connection because the etiquette of everyday face-to-face contact used to be considered the foundation of good communication skills. Experts taught us about body language and facial expressions. We read about social cues in business guides and self-help books. We learned to avoid physical habits that could make us appear insecure. We practiced subtle intimidation tricks that could give us an advantage when negotiating with a used car salesman.

Our body language was honed to project competence and confidence. We "dressed the part" because we knew that people do, indeed, judge books by their covers.

Parents made sure that kids learned how to present themselves appropriately: no mohawks, limited piercings, modest clothing, combed hair. My mother constantly reminded me about the importance of first impressions. She made it clear that people would always be forming judgments based on my physical appearance and the nuances of my behavior. She reinforced this idea constantly. Even when I wandered through our house in my threadbare flannel pajamas, my mother expected a certain level of civility. Say please and thank you, excuse yourself when you burp, don't use swear words, and speak respectfully to your parents and siblings. I learned lessons about personal grooming because my older brothers tormented me when they caught even the slightest whiff of body odor or bad breath. I practiced a kind of stoic resilience when thoughtful dinner-table debates with my siblings quickly turned into ferocious ad hominem insults and I had to hold back tears.

Within the safety of my childhood home, interactions with my family taught me the behaviors that would eventually shape my agora performances. The household microcosm prepared me for personal and professional communities. I learned the values and principles that would anchor me as I moved out into the wider world. This is the core developmental benefit of home and hearth. Early experiences with our parents and siblings provide us with a social and emotional foundation. We learn habits and manners that will carry us forth while simultaneously keeping us tied to our origins. The family hearth affords us a sense of ethics and morality. Its customs and traditions help us focus, protecting us from chaos and keeping us moored as we move through the tumult of a public marketplace.

When politicians speak of "family values," they are not talking about the worthiness of biological kinship; they are evoking the emblematic power of the traditional hearth. But what remains of the traditional hearth in an era when the split between home and work is almost dissolved? If handheld digital devices separate us from the people with whom we're physically closest, pushing us outward into a connected world, how do we maintain our sense of family values? The answer is complicated. But one thing is immediately clear: we must resist the urge to blame the technologies.

Of course, it's true that today's tools have disrupted our habitual ways of interacting with the symbolic hearth. However, we built the tech for a reason, and it's not going anywhere. So, if we want to get the most out of the benefits of a connected world — while also preserving a sense of grounded presence, focus, and a respect for home and tradition — we need to reimagine the hearth's flame in a way that's fit for the twenty-first century. But first, we need to understand the hearth separate and distinct from sofas, pajamas, and family dinners. We need to see it unattached from the familiar conventions of the twentieth century.

Family's Flame

Shift your mindset around family. Replace togetherness with rootedness. It's not about intimacy, comfort, bonding, or close ties. It's about having a stable launchpad. Like home base in a playground game of freeze tag, family is the stalwart mainstay to which we always return. In fact, as anyone who's gone through psychotherapy can attest, it's like an anchor that can never be lifted. For better or worse, you're always tethered to the hearth.

In preindustrial times, home and hearth literally referred to the same physical thing: a dwelling built around a fire pit. The ancient Greeks used the same word for the fireplace, the warm flame burning within it, and the immortal deity of home and domestic-ity. Her name was Hestia. In Rome, Hestia took on the Latin name Vesta, related to the Indo-European word *vas*. Like a vase or a vessel, there's something inward about the hearth; it signifies an interior — a home that holds, embraces, and contains.

Vesta's famous temple in the Roman forum was built to hold her sacramental fire. Encircled by marble columns, six Vestal Vir-gins tended the goddess's flame, which burned uninterrupted. It symbolized the security, stability, and good fortune of the state. It demonstrated the permanence of Rome's character. Her eternal fire was nothing less than the communal soul of a people, their shared identity — a symbolic precursor to hotheaded modern nationalism. Today, ceremonial flames remain lit all over the globe. You'll find them in religious temples, at national monuments, and often as part of war memorials. At the time of this writing, Wikipedia lists more than a hundred perpetual flames burning in fifty-one countries.

On a smaller scale, however, the flame in Vesta's hearth represents familial roots, the eternal bloodline, the anchor of heredity — what the Romans referred to with the Latin word *gens*. It's from here that we get the modern terms genetics and genome. We borrowed Vesta's concept of ancestral continuity and expressed it through the scien-tific, technological, and economic metaphors of our time. The traits of the goddess are now primarily reflected in our DNA, our biologi-cal code, the schematic plan for our hardwired physiological charac-teristics. The lab is now her temple, the geneticist her priest. A human being is imagined to be constituted like computer hardware and software. We trade and exchange chromosomes with our mates; inherited algorithmic matter moves like data, tying us to the past and paying dividends as our offspring are carried into the future.

The trouble with this mindset is that the old continuities of home — the values, behaviors, ideas, customs, and traditions that previously ignited the familial hearth—are being extinguished. Vesta's power is becoming invisible, catalyzed only at the microscopic and cellular levels. The hustle and bustle of an electronic commons threatens to snuff out Vesta's fire, and we desperately need to find new ways to fan the goddess's flame. This is the difficult job that confronts today's parents. We need to provide an anchor—a symbolic hearth that prepares kids to live a productive, ethical, and fulfilled adult life.

If your home is anything like mine, it's full of objects and artifacts that do just that. They communicate your family's narrative and keep its flame burning. Framed photos line my walls, pictures from vacations and weddings, images that mark milestones, threading together a story of my life. The most prominent ones feature my kids. Many of these are Instagram snapshots that I took while we were traveling. I uploaded them to an internet service that printed them onto stretched canvas. In one, my two sons, holding umbrellas, walk on a rainy Paris street with the Eiffel Tower in the distance. Another was taken as a selfie with my Android phone held at arm's length. It features all three of us, heads pressed close together, with London's Tower Bridge filling the rest of the frame. These images are not just memories of our visits to international tourist attractions; they also communicate a sense of kinship. "Cameras go with family life," writes American intellectual Susan Sontag. "Through photographs, each family constructs a portrait-chronicle of itself—a portable kit of images that bears witness to its connectedness."

My kids and I look at our Instagram memories every night while we eat dinner. They hang on the dining room wall beside pictures of my parents. It is almost as if my mom and dad are gazing down at us while we sit around the antique table that once belonged to my now deceased grandparents. The credenza is full of heirloom porcelain china, visible through its glass doors. Together with the pictures on the wall, the inherited furniture functions almost like a perpetual flame, a symbol of our roots. My familial hearth is located in the dining room. But just like the family dinners we enjoy there, it is trapped in a bygone era. Family photos first became popular in the mid-1800s. Elite Victorians sat perfectly still for shockingly long durations of time. In 1839, it took thirty minutes to expose a daguerreotype — an early form of the photograph that was developed onto thin sheets of silver. These pictures were cherished objects, a precursor to the family photo album, an acknowledgment of ancestral roots. By 1841, exposure length was down to about a minute, making everyday portraiture a reality. But taking pictures was still pretty inconvenient until 1884, when George Eastman invented film as an efficient all-in-one alternative to the professional photographer's cumbersome plates and chemicals. Then, right at the turn of the century, the Eastman Kodak Brownie camera turned photography into a mass-market success.

From the start, Kodak sold the camera as a quintessential technology of family values. A 1908 newspaper advertisement read, "In every home, there's a story for the Kodak to record." A decade later the company suggested that all parents should "keep a Kodak story of the children" (1917). And even in wartime, it stayed on message: "To a homesick boy at the front, a picture of Dad pushing the lawnmower in the old front yard is worth more than the Croix de Guerre" (1918). Like the radio, the television, and the commuter locomotive, photography was a tool that made it possible for people to think about home life in radically new ways. Pictures aligned perfectly with the Industrial Age inclination to rearrange the household away from the great hall and into what Sontag calls a "claustrophobic unit." People displayed precious framed pictures of their relatives, and therefore nuclear families could isolate themselves while still feeling part of a larger clan. "Photography came along to memorialize, to restate symbolically, the imperiled continuity and vanishing extendedness of family life," writes Sontag.

Many people compare smartphone cameras to Kodak's original Brownie, noting how both inventions made photography significantly less expensive and considerably more accessible. The problem with this comparison, however, is that it doesn't take into account the enormous differences in how these two technologies impacted family life.

In 2017, 95 million smartphone photos per day were posted on Instagram. But these were not family pictures, at least not in the same sense as Kodak's. Even when social media posts do feature parents and kids together — portraits of a life lived among kin — they are intended for an audience outside the home. This is clear from a 2015 Pew survey that investigated how parents use Facebook. Only about half (47 percent) are friends with their own children. They are far more likely to be connected and share pictures with their extended families (93 percent), with current friends or friends from the past (88 percent), and with their own elderly parents (53 percent). Social media sharing has nothing to do with fortifying the nuclear family's roots; it's all about projecting a story out into the agora.

More interesting still, today's photographs are streamed, not framed. The Professional Photographers of America (PPA) found that 67 percent of people now keep their photos solely in digital form. Portraits have lost their value as cherished objects, as symbolic artifacts that facilitate the rites and rituals of the nuclear family. Among those surveyed, fewer than half had printed a photo in the past twelve months, and 70 percent no longer have photo albums. The camera phone doesn't fuel Vesta's fire. That's why, in response to these findings, David Trust, CEO of PPA, said, "I think time will prove that we have gambled away our family histories — trusting too much in our ability to protect our memories on our phones, tablets, and other devices." What he seems to forget is that photography was only a tool of the Industrial Age.

In today's world, we need to understand that family values are not about supper, board games, photos, or sitcoms. The hearth is not even about the nuclear family per se. Instead, it's about establishing a firm foundation, anchoring our lives with a new kind of fire pit. If we want our kids to develop a productive and healthy sense of self — to feel settled, to value stillness — even in a fast-paced and turbocharged networked world, we'll need to show them that their lives are tethered to the long thread of history. They need to experience a sense of permanence. They need to recognize that even when the flow of time feels impossibly hectic, their personal journey is connected to something slower than their immediate surroundings.

The family room no longer provides an old-fashioned sense of stability. The objects in our homes become obsolete as quickly as the next shopping season arrives. Kids are rarely exposed to durable symbols, artifacts, or stories. They have nothing solid against which they can consider and compare their own experiences. Parents need to provide it.

Takeaways

Change is scary, but also inevitable. Don't cling to what's customary, because kids need grown-ups to help them make sense of an unfamiliar world.

Nowadays, parents are always complaining that their children spend too much time staring at "addictive screens." According to the grownups, kids never want to do anything else, and therefore they're losing out on the real joy of childhood. But statistics tell a different story. On average, today's kids get roughly the same amount of screen time as their parents did. The only difference is the kind of screen. The previous generation watched cartoons on television. Now, kids spend most of their time on connected mobile devices like smartphones and tablets.

The distinction is important because it reveals the true nature of parental anxiety. Grown-ups are disoriented because, at first glance, today's screen media seem personal and private. When kids are watching YouTube videos or playing video games, it feels like the devices are pulling them away from the family and into a cocoon. But also, in a paradoxical twist, the screens function like portals that transport kids out of the house, beyond the perfect picket fence, and into a vast public dystopian virtual reality. Hence, parents are confused. They don't know whether their kids are too detached or too exposed. All they know for sure is that traditional home life feels out of order; things aren't neat and organized.

This anxiety is understandable. But remember that new technologies will always beget new routines. Your job as a parent is *not* to stop unfamiliar tools from disrupting your nostalgic image of the ideal childhood, nor to preserve the impeccable tidiness of the Victorian era's home/work split. Instead, it's to prepare your kids to live an ethical, meaningful, and fulfilled life in an ever-changing world.

Embrace the new past. Family time is history.

Images and definitions of family are always changing. The one with which we're most familiar — with its dinners, sofas, barbecues, and summer vacations — is a unique feature of the Industrial Age. Likewise, the modern home — with its private bedrooms, sprawling kitchens, and wall-mounted flat-screen TVs — is just a tool that was designed to facilitate the routines and habits of the perfect twentieth-century family.

Still, there is something about home and family that is essential, that transcends the vicissitudes of time. I call it the hearth, a universal element of the human experience that was once represented by the Greek god Hestia and her Roman counterpart Vesta. The hearth is what provides us with a sense of stability. It anchors us to something greater than the individual self. It provides a thread that roots us to a shared past.

If the rooms in our houses are like the pulpits and pews on which we perform Industrial Age rituals that honor the hearth, then the family portraits, heirlooms, and cherished objects we display on our mantels are just emblems and talismans—symbolic artifacts that remind us of family's importance. These are not the things that constitute family values, but rather the tools and totems we use to communicate and experience a sense of groundedness. That means grown-ups need to quit demanding allegiance to old-school idols— the obsolete technologies of family values. Recognize instead that it's not family or home life that needs to be preserved, but rather our connection to the primordial hearth.

In a world where everything is always revolutionary, innovative, and reinvented, it feels like there's little tethering us to the long thread of history. Your kids seem to be connected to everything except the past. They need a new image of home, something that signifies permanence and durability. So, teach them about antiquity. Share family stories. Celebrate your heritage. It doesn't even have to be related to your own ancestral origins; any engagement that emphasizes the value of history is better than the current cultural obsession with freshness and novelty.

In my family, we talk a lot about the ancient Greek world—I've been reading my kids the mythology and teaching them about Socrates, Plato, and Aristotle from the time they were very little. This is the history with which I'm most familiar, so it's an easy choice for me. Other parents might focus on something else. It doesn't matter;

whatever works for you is fine. You can even strengthen the hearth through legacy entertainment. When three generations enjoy *Star Wars* together you may not be building a foundation that reaches back into the annals of history, but you are still setting small tent stakes in the ground.

Many cities have museums and monuments that were designed to tell the historic narrative of place. Of course, older kids will resist visiting, but you can drag them along even if they kick and scream. Remember, your job is not to maintain the copasetic harmony of the industrial family, it's to counterbalance the incessant "progress" of a connected world.

Private preparations for a public marketplace.

With digital devices, children isolate themselves to interact with others. They are always alone but also very much together. Digital play detaches them from their immediate surroundings but connects them to faraway places. The relationship between public and private becomes confused. Where does the hearth end and the agora begin?

At first, this may seem like a minor dilemma. But consider that almost a century's worth of psychoanalytic research has shown that the private relationship between parent and child is the formative basis of a public persona. We learn our earliest lessons in social etiquette and ethics through interactions with our immediate family members. This was especially true during the twentieth century, when we all developed a sandbox sense of self. The home/work split turned the nuclear household into a secure playground where young children could practice social skills. At home, kids were uninhibited, comfortable, and safe enough that they could experiment with agora behaviors without worrying about the consequences of failure.

Nowadays, when parents agonize about the rapidly eroding boundaries between hearth and agora, they're intuitively recognizing that they can no longer identify the right time and place to teach their children the values and principles that anchor individuals as they move out into the wider world. But once grown-ups acknowledge that this is their real concern, they can stop blaming digital technology for introducing new complications. Instead, they can rise to the challenge and make an intentional effort to inject an ethical education into emerging technological contexts.

CHAPTER 6

THE NEW PUBERTY

FOR HIS NINTH birthday, my son asked all his grandparents, uncles, and aunts to give him gift cards to the Apple Store. Then he used the combined till to buy a refurbished iPod touch. He really wanted a phone, but I wouldn't let him get one; something felt wrong about the idea of a small child walking around with a luxurious digital device in his pocket.

Just about every day, he would ask, "Why can't I get a phone?"

I couldn't really answer. I made up some explanation about how expensive and fragile it would be. And then, using my best authoritative voice, I probably told him it was "just not appropriate!"

But that's not the real reason I objected. It was because I was beholden to the Industrial Age distinction between home and work. Unconsciously, I feared that handing my son a connected device would be tantamount to opening the floodgates to the outside world. On some level, I was worried that sin and temptation might come rushing in. The constant stream of alerts and notifications might've contaminated the purity of his childhood experience.

Of course, as soon as I realized how irrational I was being, I changed my mind.

I bought a phone not only for him, but also for his younger brother. Both kids already carried tablets and regularly used personal computers. They'd been doing that for years. They visited websites, chatted with their friends, watched YouTube videos, and played online games. They had the access already. So, drawing the line at smartphones made no sense. It meant they could do everything *except* call me in case of an emergency.

Now, at ten and twelve years old, they both send text messages constantly. They use social media. They stream music. They share photos. In this way, they are average American kids. According to Influence Central's 2016 Digital Trends report, ten is the age when most kids in the United States get their first smartphone. By the age of eight, 45 percent already have their own mobile device — most likely a tablet or a portable gaming console.

When kids have their own digital devices, parents have to teach them the proper time and place to use them. And that's a struggle. Grown-ups are often frustrated to hear themselves saying the same thing over and over, day in and day out: "Turn it off. Put it away. Now's not the right time." But it's probably a good thing whenever parents repeat themselves. It means that we're reinforcing manners and etiquette, bolstering conventions and social norms for a life lived with digital technology. This is an important part of child-rearing. It's just like reminding them to say "please" and "thank you." We need to acquaint our kids with rules that the majority of adults are already in agreement about.

A 2014 Pew study found that roughly three-quarters of adults surveyed approve of smartphone use while walking down the street, riding public transportation, or waiting in line. Forty percent are fine with smartphones at restaurants. But about 90 percent want them turned off during family dinner. And almost everyone objects to using portable screen media during meetings, at movie theaters, or while attending religious worship services. In my family, there are certain additional times when phones are off-limits. For instance, I don't let the boys play video games in the car except on long drives. It's somewhat arbitrary, but I think it's important that they develop an appreciation for boredom; everyone should be able to sit still, with very little stimulation, for twenty to thirty minutes. In addition, there is no screen time allowed before school, but that's mostly for my own selfish reasons: it's hard enough to get them out of the house—lunches packed and shoes laced up—without added distractions. I also have a strict rule against using personal screen media after dinner; that's a time when we all do something together—usually watching television or a movie. Just before bed, it's books-only, no-screen time for all of us, myself included. I think of reading the same way as brushing teeth: a healthy routine that my kids and I are expected to perform every evening (yes, eBooks are okay).

When rules like these are clear and consistent, they're easy to enforce. But that doesn't mean they're easy to follow. My kids are always breaking them, sneaking a few minutes with their phones and hoping I don't notice. I raise my voice, and they say, "Just let me save my progress." Mostly, I try not to let their insubordination bother me too much. A little disobedience is a good thing. Besides, my job is to prepare them for the future, not to expect perfection in the present.

Whenever I talk to groups of parents, somebody asks about "screen addiction." I try to be polite and not roll my eyes. But let me be clear: Children are not addicted to their devices; they're using them whenever they can because they feel embraced by them. Their smartphones and portable gaming consoles function like a nest, the bosom that gives kids a sense of security. As journalist Sierra Filucci says, kids may "*feel* addicted," but that's not the same as "experiencing the symptoms of true addiction" such as "interference with daily life" and "needing more to achieve the same feeling."

Digital media is not a gateway temptation. Overindulgence won't lead kids toward sloth. In fact, their devotion to devices could constitute a critical step toward healthy psychological development.

Their gadgets may be transitional objects.

Transitional Gadgets

Pediatrician and psychoanalyst D. W. Winnicott coined the term "transitional objects" in the mid-twentieth century. He recognized that young children often become attached to a special blanket, a teddy bear, or some other toy. It helps them learn to see themselves as autonomous individuals. The transitional objects operate like a bridge between child and parent.

To understand this idea, think about a newborn baby. He does not realize that Mom is a separate being — she is only an extension of Baby's own need for comfort, sustenance, and safety. But one day, Baby cries and Mom doesn't show up immediately. Suddenly, the true uncertainty of the external world becomes painfully clear: Baby is not in control of his mother. His subjective experience is just a fantasy that will be constantly challenged by objective reality. Life now feels unstable. Baby cannot make meaning out of his existence. His sense of self has been irrevocably altered. Yesterday, Mom was half of who he is, and now there is an enormous chasm between them.

Teddy bear is the answer. Teddy bear feels nice. It feels warm. It feels fuzzy. And unconsciously, it can be experienced as both an extension of the self and something altogether separate. Baby feels like he is in control of teddy bear. He holds that bear — holds it close to his chest — because it provides the comfort he craves as he navigates the difficult transition into conscious independent personhood.

It may sound abstract, but I saw it happen with my own son. He was a typical toddler. He had a fuzzy red monkey and a cheap rayon sarong that he used as a "blankie."

The term "security blanket" was popularized in the 1950s by the thumb-sucking *Peanuts* character Linus van Pelt. It was Charlie Brown and his friends who helped Winnicott's theory become common knowledge. Parents accepted it, but that doesn't mean they understood what it meant. For instance, I didn't have a clear enough grasp of the concept to recognize that something can be comforting even if it is not soft and cuddly. I barely noticed when my son's Nintendo DS portable gaming console became his transitional object. It was made of hard plastic and not conducive to hugging. Still, he would throw temper tantrums if we forgot it during the changeover between my house and his mother's. And even when he wasn't playing, he insisted that it be within arm's reach.

Today, his Android smartphone fills the same role. I suspect that just knowing that he can send text messages twenty-four hours a day helps to create the impression of a connection between two separate households — it bridges the gap exacerbated by divorce. Likewise, casual games give him a sense of control. That is why, when we're on vacation, he never seems to stop playing.

"Hey, buddy," I say, imploring him to look out the hotel window. "You can play *Terraria* at home in your bedroom, but how often do you get to see Utah's snow-capped mountains?" I forget that he is homesick, that the phone feels safe and reliable. I want him to be present on our adventure. But he is a kid; he is still trying to work out what it means to have a sense of self that is not connected to place — one that remains stable even when all of his contextual landmarks are thousands of miles away.

The phone plugs him into a familiar world. It connects him to his cohort. It gives him the impression that his friends are there with him. It also feels deeply personal. On the touchscreen, his private ideas and emotions can take shape; they go from abstract to concrete. His internal dramas become explicit, like action figures on a rug or the menagerie of animals in a therapist's consultation room. The smartphone lets him manipulate symbolic objects in three dimensions. It transitions him between real and imagined experiences, between internal and external narratives. He's not ignoring the mountains; he is working hard to cope with them.

Still, I am annoyed. I planned this trip for weeks, and I am excited to show him a new landscape. I want to expose him to something unfamiliar.

"What are you, addicted to that thing?" I ask.

"I'm sorry, Dad." He looks down, embarrassed and ashamed. Reluctantly, he turns the smartphone off and slips it into his pocket. But he does not focus on what's around him. Instead, he zones out, completely disengaged. He becomes lost in his own thoughts. He is hurt and angry.

Rightfully so.

Just think about what it must be like for kids to hear us refer to their transitional objects with the same language we use to describe cigarettes and drugs.

Now I'm like the giant at the top of the beanstalk. Fee, fi, fo, fum!

My son is afraid of getting eaten. Not only by me, but also by a big, scary, two-headed monster. He is twelve years old and struggling to learn how to show up simultaneously in the physical and the virtual worlds. Both threaten to devour him. Both constantly attune him to the fact that his private sense of self is not necessarily aligned with the way others perceive him. He sometimes gets in fights with his friends. He gets in trouble with his teachers. He pisses off his younger brother and frustrates his father. Each situation is unexpected. He doesn't see it coming. What's going on inside his mind is not the same as what's happening around him. Like all tweens, his internal and external experiences are way out of sync.

That must be devastating. He must feel lost a lot of the time.

I can empathize. Most grown-ups probably can. That's why we're wary of social media. We remember the difficult parts of the prepubescent struggle, and we can see how some elements of the digital landscape might intensify our kids' sense of discomfort. Smartphones and other connected devices seem to create a situation in which tweens and teens cannot escape the anxieties of the brutal social agora even when they get home at the end of the school day. There's no sanctuary; the popularity contest never seems to end. It just moves online, inside the bezel of a device.

Parents are triggered by memories of their own awkward middle-school years. They want to protect their precious children from the hurt feelings they remember. But they've got it wrong. They mistakenly cling to the old delineation between hearth and agora. They try to make a twenty-first-century home into a twentieth-century safe space by limiting access to screens and social media. They don't realize that sometimes, digital devices offer another kind of refuge — one that their kids desperately need.

My son finds his smartphone to be personal and dependable. He feels like it holds him, or at least holds the data that defines who he is. The AI assistant claims to know him, to anticipate his needs. The search bar says it will be there for him, to answer his questions, minimize his uncertainties, and settle his arguments. Is it any wonder that he freaks out when I take his phone away or tell him to turn it off? He's not addicted to his devices; he just doesn't like it when I disrupt his coping mechanisms. What he really needs is for me to accept, support, and mentor him as he learns to use these tools to express and articulate a positive identity narrative.

He is actively developing the capacity to deal with the dissonance between what is happening in his head and what is happening all around him. He needs help feeling positive and confident about the good choices that he makes. It's important because the patterns he establishes now will impact the rest of his life. "The task of reality-acceptance is never completed," Winnicott writes, "...no human being is free from the strain of relating inner and outer reality."

Think about every argument you've ever had with a co-worker, a lover, or a spouse. It is the result of a disconnect between expectations and results. You feel anxiety, frustration, and disappointment whenever real outcomes contradict your imagined plans. Why? Because a plan is about a lot more than just strategic design; it is an internal narrative through which you articulate a fantasy about future potential. All day long, when you are telling yourself stories — practicing the argument you're going to have with an antagonistic colleague, silently recounting events as if you're describing them to your mother, calculating how much money you're going to earn and how you might just be able to afford that luxury vacation — you are also reinforcing an identity narrative. The problem is that eventually real life steps in, and it rarely matches your plans. You discover that the sense of self you just constructed is actually inaccurate. You feel the strain between inner and outer reality.

How do you cope?

According to Winnicott, that depends on how well your early childhood experience with transitional objects went. If they were used appropriately, you developed the necessary skills to live confidently in the adult world. If not, you will always want other people to accept your perspective as their reality. Of course, they won't accept it. They can't. So, you'll suffer.

To avoid discomfort, to be "well adjusted," children need what Winnicott called "good enough mothering." The good enough mother intuitively acknowledges the transitional object. She does not challenge Baby's fantasy. She mirrors, and therefore validates, it. She indulges Baby's ambiguous relationship to the teddy bear. She pretends to talk to it and calls it "Mr. Bear-Bear." Maybe she gives Mr. Bear-Bear kisses goodnight. Perhaps she lets it join the family on the living room sofa. Each time she accepts Mr. Bear-Bear, she is reinforcing habits of mind that will form the foundation of Baby's grown-up capacity for resilient self-expression and confident relatedness. Through Mr. Bear-Bear, the good enough mother helps Baby cultivate a "healthy" sense of self. Certainly, Baby knows Mr. Bear-Bear is not real. But when Mom plays along, she demonstrates that the inner, subjective fantasy has a value even if it is contradicted by the outer, objective reality.

Grown-ups tend to accept that stuffed toys function as transitional objects. But they panic when kids grow attached to electronic objects. Why? I guess they worry that digital devices will suck kids into immersive virtual fantasies that cannot be distinguished from reality. They believe that a tangible fantasy world constructed from physical objects — a tea party of dolls or an epic adventure of action figures on the family-room rug — is better aligned with the fundamentals of healthy childhood development. What they don't realize is that, just like the sandbox, the family dinner, and the photos on the wall, Mr. Bear-Bear is also the product of a particular time and place.

All teddy bears are named after Theodore Roosevelt. During a hunting trip in Mississippi, he refused to shoot a black bear cub that was tied to a tree. Although Roosevelt was an avid hunter who killed thousands of animals during his lifetime, shooting a helpless baby bear did not seem like an enviable sportsman's accomplishment. It conflicted with his sense of self. In response, a *Washington Post* political cartoon entitled "Drawing the Line in Mississippi" pictured the president wearing hunting khakis and a bandanna, rifle in hand, bespectacled, with one side of his hat brim turned up. In this iconic image he is turned away from the cute, cuddly bear that is tied by the neck and looks terrified. That cartoon bear became the inspiration not only for teddy bears, but also for the entire stuffed animal industry.

"Stuffies" are a twentieth-century invention. According to historian Steven Mintz, they reflect "new ideas about childhood and the emergence of a modern consumer economy." They were originally sold as bedtime companions for terrified infants who were trying to fall asleep in the private bedrooms that had recently become part of the family home. In those days, it would have been radically progressive for parents to indulge children's personal fears and anxieties, so buying a teddy bear must have made parents feel enlightened. It was also becoming conventional for adults to embrace the individualistic frontier exceptionalism — a version of the sandbox sense of self — that the twenty-sixth president of the United States embodied.

Mr. Bear-Bear helped initiate Baby into an Industrial Age view of independent personhood. He helped Baby develop his own internal sense of determined authority and persistent individuality. He prepared Baby for adulthood in the twentieth century. Most grown-ups think that the teddy bear is just a quintessential part of the childhood experience, something that must have existed since the beginning of time. But really, it is unique and well suited to a specific social, cultural, and economic paradigm.

What does that say about my son's smartphone? Is it a modern-day Mr. Bear-Bear for connected preadolescents? Will it teach him healthy habits of mind? Will it help him foster strong character skills for a connected world? That depends on how he thinks about it. If it is all about the gadget itself, there is a problem. If he becomes obsessed with upgrades and accessories — with having the shiniest new object — something is out of sync. In that case, the device has become a status symbol. He is using the object to compensate for feelings of inferiority. I'll need to teach him that, in the long run, this kind of fetishization will only intensify his sense of inadequacy. After all, Apple and Samsung have mastered the cycle of planned obsolescence. Nothing stays shiniest or coolest for very long. Tech companies will continue to make sure that we are always just about six months away from a new aspirational product. Advertising will encourage consumers to covet each new iteration. And marketers will exploit the deep emotional bonds we form with our smartphones; they will leverage our psychological dependency for profit.

We are, indeed, dependent. We are attached to our digital devices. But that is not necessarily a bad thing. After all, life is always lived through the tools of the times. Digital tools act like a bridge between individual and common experiences. They help us to mediate our relationship with the world around us. They ease the strain between inner and outer realities. They do this exceptionally well. But it is not because of the brushed-aluminum chassis, the Gorilla Glass, or the multi-mega-pixel-front-facing camera. If my son thinks that better specs will help him fit in or feel like one of the cool kids, he is mistaken. He does not realize that social rank is not the same as social skill.

That is my fault. It is my job, as his father, to make sure that he doesn't confuse the material object with the transitional experiences that it can help facilitate.

Adolescence in the Digital Agora

Think about Facebook, Instagram, Snapchat, and Twitter. They are all platforms, accessed through smartphone apps, that can provide a transitional space where preteens and adolescents get to sample and try on identity narratives. They get to experiment and see how their internal experiences translate into external contexts. Grown-ups worry about the superficiality of online social networks; they dismiss them as narcissistic popularity contests. But when kids are going through the difficult process of "finding themselves," these spaces can be exactly what they need.

Consider how typical tweens transition through adolescence. As they attempt to express themselves as autonomous individuals, they struggle to separate from their parents. Think of it as the time during which they develop their independent agora selves. They experiment with personas that can show up in a connected marketplace, that can perform in the commons, that can fit in socially and culturally.

To step into a world that extends beyond the parental home and hearth, they need to reinvent themselves, cut the cord, sever ties with old ways of being. That's why, in his original book on the subject, G. Stanley Hall called adolescence "a new birth" and compared it to "some ancient period of storm and stress when old moorings were broken and a higher level [of development] attained." Hall imagines the preteen as a primitive human, discovering consciousness and civilization for the first time, fragmenting from the panacea of nature and wilderness, disconnecting from the navel of primordial tradition.

If only puberty were really so epic!

Modern tweens and teens just become rebellious and sometimes self-destructive. They distance themselves from anything reminiscent of "kid stuff," including their parents. But it's impossible to leave everything behind. After all, we each construct our identities on a foundation built from early hearth experiences. Our executive function develops, through imitation and pretense, in response to our caretakers' habits and routines. Our sense of self is deeply rooted in familial interpretations of cultural values. Our parents and the other adults in our lives constitute the whole world's authority until, as tweens, we begin to recognize that grown-ups are actually fallible. Mom and Dad have imperfections. Grandma and Grandpa's views are outdated. Teachers can sometimes be insecure and spiteful.

Adolescents and prepubescent kids can often become self-righteous and indignant as they recognize grown-ups' errors and contradictions. They point out adults' inadequacies in order to articulate their own independence. For parents, it stinks, because our kids know us really well, and nobody enjoys being on the receiving end of an accurate assessment of ongoing failure. For the kids, however, it is even worse. They need to develop a unique sense of self that simultaneously rejects and accepts the overbearing expectations of their flawed role models.

Luckily, as child psychologist Alan Sugarman explains, smartphones can help. They have the potential to provide kids with access to the "naively idealistic values and symbols of their cohort" in a virtual space that is "separate and differentiated from their now imperfect parents." In other words, think of social networking as a teens-only hybrid: combining the sandbox and the dinner table. If used appropriately, kids get to rehearse living well together in a private agora that has its very own social conventions, expectations, and forms of etiquette. They get to practice adulthood.

Of course, social media without mentorship can quickly get out of hand. We've all read stories about cyberbullying. And even adults sometimes demonstrate obsessive superficial behaviors when trying to look good online. "There was a time when I allowed myself to be more than what could fit onto a 2-by-4-inch screen," Clara Dollar wrote in a submission to the popular *New York Times* column "Modern Love," "when I wasn't so self-conscious about how I was seen." Ms. Dollar describes how difficult it can be to transition between the selves we create online — our personality brands — and the versions of ourselves that show up in face-to-face encounters. "The caricature of me that I had created and meticulously cultivated," she wrote, "got her start online as my social media persona, but over time (and I suppose for the sake of consistency), she bled off the screen and overtook my real-life personality, too." A senior at NYU when she wrote this, Ms. Dollar was still in the throes of adolescence, and it seems like she was trying to fend off the same two-headed dragon that threatens to devour my twelve-year-old son.

How can parents help their children navigate the tension that Ms. Dollar is describing? How can they assist as their kids develop a stable sense of self for a blended online/offline existence? One way is to start joint media engagement early and continue it often. Parents should incorporate digital play into early family experiences and then integrate online social media as their kids grow older. Grown-ups need to make digital rituals a part of family life with the same regularity and urgency of the teddy bear, the bedtime story, and the family dinner.

Through video games, text messages, chat streams, and photo timelines, we can prepare our kids for a new social agora.

My Avatar, Myself

To help your children develop a healthy sense of self for a connected world, think back to Bruno Bettelheim's theory about the way the enchantments of storytelling lead to catharsis (Chapter Four). First, consider the way his thinking translates to video games. Then, expand your understanding to include social media.

Experiences in the digital world all include something that gamers call an "avatar." An avatar is to a video game as a protagonist is to a bedtime story — compare Jack, of beanstalk fame, to Link, of Nintendo's *Zelda* franchise. The difference is that we can only *relate* to the heroes in fairy tales; we imagine ourselves in their place. But we *control* the avatars in a video game; we govern their movements and actions.

The word "avatar" is originally Hindi. It literally means something like "manifest." Understand it in the sense that things manifest or come into being in certain ways. The original Sanskrit root is *avatara,* which means "crossing over" or "descent." In the Hindu religion, the avatar is the body into which gods are reincarnated. So, Buddha is one of Vishnu's avatars — the body the deity uses to come into being in the material (or earthly) world. Buddha enables Vishnu to descend, or cross over, from the heavens. In digital console games such as *Mario Kart*, players choose among avatars like Donkey Kong, Yoshi, Luigi, Peach, and so on. Like a board game's piece, the digital avatar is the body we use to descend or cross over into an immersive game world. It is how we manifest; it's the self we control in the game space.

The avatar makes it so that every video-game experience involves more than one *I*. There is the *I* that holds the controller. And there is the virtual *I* that travels around the game space. The *I* that holds the controller is aware of the avatar. He recognizes it as something separate from himself. He can easily jump out of the game world and return to the life world to grab a snack, talk to his father, or come to the dinner table quickly.

Think about how that separation between the player and the avatar can be applicable to our life-world experience. At some point during our childhoods, we learn to imagine the idea of ourselves separate from the *I* that reflects on our experiences. We make a distinction between body and mind — between our life-world avatar and the gamer in our heads.

Around 1936, a French psychoanalyst named Jacques Lacan identified the "mirror stage." It is a developmental phase at which kids are suddenly able to see their reflections in the mirror and recognize themselves. That may seem like a simple everyday event, but it's about more than just checking out your appearance. Seeing the reflection forces a child to acknowledge the disconnect between how she experiences herself and how the outside world sees her. Nobody looks the way they imagine.

Like Winnicott, Lacan is talking about the strain between internal and external experience. He knows that once a child realizes that she has both a conception of herself and a version of herself that is projected for (and experienced by) others, life changes completely. She becomes aware of herself as both subject and object. The subject is the part that she thinks of as *I*. The object is how she's viewed by others. When she becomes aware of this subject/object distinction, she begins to make intentional decisions about how to control her life-world avatar. She learns to paint a caricature to display to the world. She builds the real-life equivalent of a social-media profile.

But don't take Lacan too literally; the mirror stage is meant to be a symbolic description of a universal psychological phenomenon. Even if we never gaze into a mirror, if we never see our own reflections, we'd still develop this capacity for self-awareness. This is the foundation of human consciousness. And we're all confronted with it when we are toddlers (around twelve to thirty-six months). Then, we spend the rest of childhood practicing operating our avatars. It's part of every routine and ritual in our young lives. It's happening in those trips to synagogue, during all that sandbox play, and when we take our elbows off the table during dinnertime. In each of these moments, we're learning how to steer through the game world of real life. We're learning how the environment responds to our actions. We're learning how we need to modify our choices depending on the context. In fact, we can even understand executive function and self-regulation as the critical skills needed to operate the game controller of consciousness and steer the avatar body. When you don't master the basic operations early on, you're certain to flounder when you get to the boss level.

So, where does puberty fit into this analogy? It's a level during which the game play gets exceptionally hard — not because of the obstacles or antagonists, but because just when we thought we had mastered the game, everything about our avatar changes. Adolescence sends us into physiological chaos; the pubescent body becomes like a respawned game piece that defies the way our fingers manipulate the controller. The avatar morphs in unpredictable ways. It veers toward power-ups that we used to ignore.

To manage these changes, kids need transitional spaces in which they can practice. They need the life-world equivalent of casual games: low-stakes opportunities for playful experimentation. They need environments where they can become accustomed to the way a new avatar navigates the world. They need sandboxes where they can try out secret moves and special powers. The twentieth century's most famous coming-of-age motifs — pink Cadillacs and cruising hot rods, sock-hop school dances, shopping mall food courts, Slurpees on the curb of a 7-Eleven parking lot — are all transitional spaces linked to specific tool sets. Automobiles, electric guitars and tube amplifiers, retail location and design, candy and processed junk food — each time the industrial economy innovated and upgraded, an entire era of adolescents rebranded and reinvented themselves along with it. Is it any wonder that today's teenagers also need their own technologically relevant versions of transitional spaces? Nope.

Whether we like it or not, today's tweens and teens now use smartphones and social media as their transitional space. And it is a waste of energy to worry that it might be the wrong choice. After all, it is not possible for them to abandon these virtual spaces in favor of the outdated equivalents that feel more wholesome and familiar to grown-ups. Part of the adolescent process involves resisting parents' ways of being, rejecting the old status quo. Moreover, as researcher danah boyd has observed, "They would far rather meet up in person, but the hectic and heavily scheduled nature of their day-to-day lives, their lack of physical mobility, and the fears of their parents have made such face-to-face interaction increasingly impossible." Therefore, we should stop fighting the future and recognize that what our kids really need is assistance figuring out the best ways to steer their avatars through these experiences. How can we help them do it in ways that are kind, constructive, and safe? The answer is joint media engagement.

If you played video games with your kids when they were little, you're already halfway there. Every dinnertime conversation you had about gaming modeled a thoughtful, considerate approach. You prepped your kids, from the start, to reflect on the avatar experience. More important, you provided them with an image of maturity: a picture of Mom or Dad, on the sofa, controlling a virtual self.

Now, it's time to do the same thing with social media.

A Connected Sense of Self

Immediately after they make new friends, my kids always ask me if they can download new social apps. I'm never quite sure how to feel about it. I know that they are just trying to connect with other people, to feel closer to their peers. But I can also see that they're jockeying for status. Today's social apps are the equivalent of the cool kids' table in the cafeteria. And everyone wants to be part of the in-crowd.

Whenever I speak to groups of parents, they ask me questions about specific apps. "What about Snapchat? Is it safe? How 'bout Instagram?"

They're concerned. They're trying to assess the potential dangers. They want to strike the perfect equilibrium between protection and permission. Grown-ups were all tweens once, so we know that access is the prerequisite to acceptance, and that oversheltered kids can quickly become social outcasts; it's a delicate balance. And faced with an unfamiliar landscape, parents don't know where to draw the line. They think it all comes down to which downloads they allow and which they forbid. But they're wrong.

No matter the app in question, the answer is always the same. From a safety perspective, there's nothing substantially different from one platform to another. The real issue is not which app, nor what behaviors a particular app enables. Instead, it's that your kids are now getting into the world of teen popularity, gossip, cliques, nerds, and dorks. Are they prepared for the emotional stress and turmoil? You need to make sure they have the confidence and the ethical backbone required to navigate an avatar through a high-impact social agora. Then, you need to monitor their interactions in an ongoing way. You need to help them learn from their mistakes and persevere through the inevitable deluge of hurt feelings, broken hearts, and severed friendships. Social media may look unfamiliar to you, but the truth is, we've all been through this transition ourselves. It may have manifested differently in our technological era, but we still know exactly which kinds of things we need to worry about.

Unfortunately, when kids start to engage with social media, their parents almost always respond with a knee-jerk reaction. They try to restrict opportunities for participation. They try to limit their kids' access to certain apps. It never works. Prepubescent children are adept at circumventing parental obstacles. They ignore adults' warnings and log on to whatever they want anyway. Sure, some apps have automatically imposed age limits, but tweens find a way around that quickly. According to my twelve-year-old's online profile, he was born in 1983. Just as I snuck into R-rated movies and bent the truth when my mom asked if my sleepovers would be chaperoned, kids will always find ways around the rules.

Eventually, most grown-ups just surrender. They accept that social media is part of growing up in a connected world. But then they make an even bigger mistake. They leave their children to wander alone online. They think of the social-media agora as a far-off place where kids should be able to roam free, out of view and unburdened by their parents. They treat their children's digital life as if it were like a locked diary or a shoebox of love letters. These adults mean well; they are just trying to respect their kids' privacy. But their approach doesn't make much sense. You wouldn't let a hormonally charged preteenager date before having the "sex talk," so why let them explore the new social agora without making sure they understand how their avatars work?

Perhaps grown-ups neglect their children's online lives because the devices themselves seem so personal. Our kids hold their smart-phones in the palm of a hand. They slip them into a pocket. They tuck them under a pillow or let them charge on the bedside table. Digital devices are never far away, even during sleep. They are almost like an extension of our bodies. And maybe adults accurately recognize that the transition through puberty and adolescence requires a separation, a physical detachment, privacy. Parents try to give their kids some space. But when it comes to digital devices, that's a mistake. These are not parts of your kids' body. And social media is not private. It is a twenty-four-hour-a-day public party. So, parents should constantly check in. Or, better yet: join in.

Start now. Begin using social media with your kids. Let them get an account even if you think they're not old enough. Don't wait for them to ask. You are more than just a gatekeeper. Your job is to pre-pare them. Parents need to introduce their children to digital social spaces early and with clear intentions. We do this intuitively when it comes to books, movies, and sometimes even video games. When my kids were toddlers, I read them *Mr. Pine's Purple House.* As preschoolers, I introduced them to the *Star Wars* movies. And we played *New Super Mario Brothers* as soon as they were physically capable of working the controllers. I wasn't just sharing the things I loved, I was also actively shaping their personalities. I was introducing them to an aesthetic sensibility. I was exposing them to a set of values, tastes, and preferences that are expressed through specific tool sets.

Almost all parents go out of their way to expose their kids to certain experiences and to teach them the corresponding etiquette and behaviors. My brothers, for example, are both big football fans, and they had their children dressed in little green Philadelphia Eagles jerseys watching Sunday afternoon games and screaming "E-A-G-L-E-S" before they even understood spelling. The kids didn't just learn which team to root for, they also learned all the rituals and rites that go with being a football fan. I can't describe what they learned because I'm not a football fan. I don't understand the ritual. I don't get the procedural rhetoric. I'm not literate when it comes to professional sports. Therefore, I can't even begin to interact with my nieces and nephews when they start to talk about the Super Bowl. Neither can my kids. I never taught them how to steer their avatars through this particular mini-game. They're at a disadvantage on game day. From my perspective, that's okay; spectator sports are fun for some people, but it's not an essential literacy needed for living a productive, ethical, and fulfilled life.

Social media, however, seems to be critically important in a connected world. Therefore, all grown-ups should consider it their responsibility to prepare their kids for it. Make sure they're not at a disadvantage when entering the digital agora. Expose them to online behavior that aligns with your values. Do it sooner rather than later. Do it when they are young and still enjoy interacting with adults. Connect them to safe communities that model mature etiquette. It's easier than you think. Get your relatives to play along. Uncles, aunts, cousins, and grandparents make for great online buddies. You can tag each other in snapshots from holiday dinners.

You can all also talk to all the parents in your kids' social circle and get everyone connected before puberty kicks in and the grown-ups get kicked out. For this, sports teams and church groups can be a great resource. Everyone can share videos and stories of weekend milestones. Kids will see the kinds of comments you make on each other's posts. You'll create models, in their minds, of mature social media engagement. They'll see appropriate ways to manage online conflicts. They'll be prepared to do it themselves when the adults finally do log off.

The bottom line is that there's no more reason to be worried about social media than there is to be worried about anyplace your children play — that is, unless you don't feel like they're adequately prepared. If so, it's time to realize that the only way to get them ready is to hold their hands and lead them forward. When we teach our kids to cross the street, we walk with them for years before ever letting them do it alone. Nobody just tells them once, "Take safety precautions, look both ways. Now you're on your own, see what happens!" If we did, they'd almost certainly get hurt, run over, maybe even killed. Yet, when it comes to online life, that's precisely what we do. We don't guide our children; we instruct them. We don't lead them; we restrict their access.

There was a time when people had to change their parenting strategies to adjust to a world of automobiles and street crossings. They figured it out. Dr. Benjamin Spock helped. *The Common Sense Book of Baby and Child Care* was the twentieth century's bestseller. At fifty million copies sold, it was bested only by the Bible. The opening pages read, "Trust yourself. You know more than you think you do."

Dr. Spock claimed to have answers that would cut through all the noise. "Everywhere you turn there are experts telling you what to do," he wrote. He recognized the pressure that parents must have felt, midcentury, as tradition fell out of fashion. Grandma's advice was no longer good enough — it was just an old-wives' tale, a folk remedy. The TV hearth now beamed "experts" into family rooms, and these "specialists" were the new arbiters of universal, research-based, scientific parenting advice. It must have felt intimidating.

Luckily, Dr. Spock was there to put parents at ease. He assured grown-ups that "bringing up your child won't be a complicated job if you trust your own instincts." But it was sort of tricky. After all, wasn't Dr. Spock an expert? His research may have suggested that a mother's instinct was best, but it was grounded in what historian Paula Fass called the "new confidence" that mothers found "from statistics." Dr. Spock claimed to empower individuals, but he was covertly endorsing a standardized and commercialized parental sense of self. Mother probably felt like she knew best, but it was not necessarily because she had what Dr. Spock called "instinct." Instead, she was surrounded by coaches.

We are all constantly exposed to images showing us what the good parent looks like. Dr. Spock is correct that nobody needs a PhD to know what is in their family's best interest. But that is only because the answers are already there; the media broadcasts best practices all day long. Television sitcoms show us the perfect family dinner. TV commercials feature fathers playing catch with their sons. Magazine ads show mothers pushing toddlers on swings. Department store displays tell us what to wear while walking with a stroller. The packaging on toys reminds us how happy siblings look when they play together. And billboards encourage us to run on the beach, laughing and splashing, during family vacations.

When I was growing up, my father knew nothing about G.

Stanley Hall, Melanie Klein, Carl Jung, Bruno Bettelheim, Sigmund Freud, D. W. Winnicott, or Jacques Lacan. But he did know
that it was good parenting to coach my Little League baseball team.
The messaging he was exposed to offered a few different parenting
avatars that he could choose to manifest through. At the time,
American media organized the parent-child relationship into a variety of different demographic buckets. It was clear to grown-ups that
rural families went on fishing trips. Blue-collar kids worked on car
engines with their dads. And the urban elite wore khaki shorts and
polo shirts while coaching Little League. My parents envisioned
their children becoming members of the college-educated upper
middle class. Therefore, we spent Sundays doing what elite families
are supposed to do — conforming to a particular sense of self. We
learned about "culture" at the Philadelphia Museum of Art. And we
spent Saturdays learning "competitive teamwork" on the ballfield.

Baseball is one of the ways I bonded with my dad. He would take
me to the park and help me improve my hitting or pitching. Sometimes he would hold my hand while we crossed the street to buy a
pack of bubblegum trading cards from the neighborhood store. He
taught me to read the player statistics on the back of the cards,
encouraging and reinforcing an economic mindset that tries to predict outcomes using metrics. I don't even like sports, but I have fond
memories of those outings. I can almost still feel his rough skin
against mine. Those giant dark and hairy hands held my little fingers completely — safe, like the smell of his Old Spice aftershave.

At dinner, our family talked about Phillies' baseball, Flyers'
hockey, or Eagles' football. My mother pinned the schedules to the
refrigerator with a magnet so we always knew when the next game
day would be. We used familiar metaphors: to hit a home run meant
to be successful in any endeavor, just as striking out meant to fail. It
was easy for my folks to integrate sports into everyday family life. It

felt natural because there were so many clear pop-culture images of family life in relationship to the ballfield. The media talked about "soccer moms" driving kids around in minivans. The obsessive sports dad — living vicariously through his children's achievements — was a trope that showed up on TV and in the movies. Everywhere you looked, idealized images of perfect twentieth-century families were displayed.

Twenty-first-century parents, however, have no idea what a parent is supposed to look like in a world where electronic media and digital devices are everywhere. What is a gamer parent? Should Dad be just another player, trying equally hard to defeat Bowser and Dr. Robotnik? Or is he a coach? Does he mentor the way my father did on the baseball field, making sure he integrates the important life lessons that can be learned from the game? What is a social-media Mom? Is she a mentor or a BFF? Does she join in the fun, or chaperone it? Can she click the heart icon? Can she "like" her children's Instagram posts? Or, should she just lurk in the background as a quiet observer? Nobody knows for sure. We continue to be bombarded with unhelpful images of an outdated household model. We're encouraged to maintain family values in ways that are no longer tenable.

But the goal is not to integrate new tech into an old paradigm; it's to reconstruct the family so that it prepares children to live in a world with new tools.

Takeaways

Keep your hands off the new security blankets.

There's a lot of hype around digital media addiction. But at this point, it's mostly just moral panic. The real science isn't very conclusive. For example, you've probably heard about the way social media platforms hack the brain's dopamine reward system. This is called "persuasive tech," and it draws its inspiration from early-twentieth-century psychologist B. F. Skinner's research on behavioral conditioning.

App developers and video-game designers do everything they can to make their products desirable and to keep us coming back for more. And from a neuroscientific perspective, the reason we return again and again is because we receive lots of little random "dopamine hits." Like dogs, who will roll over, sit, and beg because of the possibility that their master might feed them another beef liver treat, we all keep checking social media because the platforms are programmed to deliver random dopamine rewards.

Dopamine is the chemical neurotransmitter that correlates with your sense of pleasure, lust, desire, arousal. It's what makes you enjoy sex, drugs, and rock and roll. But that doesn't mean it's all temptation and seduction; dopamine is also involved in executive function, regulated attention, physical movement, and ambition. Research even suggests that our kids become motivated to get good grades or achieve athletic success because they crave the dopamine release associated with these activities. Would you complain if your kids were "addicted" to behaviors that you consider to be positive? Probably not.

When it comes to screen media, the term "addiction" doesn't describe an unhealthy chemical dependency, it's just a moral pejorative. The truth is that children are not addicted to their devices; they're using them whenever they can because gadgets are the new transitional objects. They help to expedite a critical part of individual psychological development. Like teddy bears and security blankets (tools that presumably facilitate dopamine release with each snuggle), digital devices help preteens and tweens bridge the cognitive gap between their internal experience and the external reality.

With smartphones, they're able to manage the tension between a private and a public sense of self.

Our job as parents is to support kids' individuation processes. But when we refer to our kids' devices using the same language we use to describe cigarette, alcohol, and drug abuse, we're doing them a terrible disservice. We're not helping them transition into a connected adulthood. Instead, we're seeding unnecessary anxiety. Now they're confronted with conflicting messages about what it means to conform to the expectations of the external world—hearth and agora are out of alignment. And children will suffer through the neurotic struggle to mediate the tension between these two realms of experience.

Be careful how you talk about your kids' devices. Remember that in a connected world, an individual's sense of self is caught up in their relationship to an online avatar.

Help kids master manners for a connected world.

When children have their own digital devices, parents need to teach them the proper times and places to use them. Just think about all the effort grown-ups put into helping kids become acquainted with the rules and manners of the physical world. We are so committed to teaching our kids to say "please" and "thank you" that we expect it to become automatic. When they're little, we provide constant reminders: "What do you say?" and "What's the magic word?" But unfortunately, we don't do the same when it comes to digital devices.

Parents seem far more likely to complain about their kids' inappropriate use of gadgets than they are to teach them better behaviors. Why? Because grown-ups feel helpless when confronted with digital devices. But the truth is, if your kids don't know when to stop, it's your fault. You haven't made the etiquette of a connected world clear to them.

The good news is that it's not too late to teach them manners for a connected world. Right now, decide what feels appropriate to you and draw a line in the sand. In my house, there are no devices allowed at the dinner table or while eating in restaurants. I tell my kids to turn off their phones if we're watching a movie together and in the mornings before school. And for at least an hour before bedtime, it's books only, no screens.

Of course, just because I have clear rules doesn't mean my kids always follow them. I'll be honest, it's a constant struggle. But that's okay, my children sometimes forget to say please and thank you, too. As their dad, my job is *not* to have perfectly behaved children, but rather to raise them into well-behaved adults.

Yes, it's unfortunate that parenting involves a lot of nagging, but that's just the nature of the job. And while it's certainly no fun to be the disciplinarian, we need to be persistent. Eventually, the pestering parental influence becomes the internal voice of a child's conscience.

Let your kids follow you online.

Digital tools function as a bridge between individual and common experiences. As communication technologies, their entire purpose is to help manage our practical relationship with the social and cultural world around us. For pubescent kids, they also help to ease the strain between inner and outer realities.

Teens are glued to their smartphones because social media constitutes their transitional space. It's a place where they can practice operating new adolescent avatars. And it's perfect for a connected world because all culture—even teen pop culture—is mediated through the tools of the times. Unfortunately, grown-ups are so committed to the old images of teen life that they resist the transitional spaces of the new childhood. That's a problem, because what kids really need is for their parents to stop fighting the future and start helping them understand how to steer their avatars in kind, constructive, and safe ways.

If you played video games with your kids when they were little, you've already done them a great service. In subtle ways, you've helped them develop a stable sense of self for a blended online/offline existence. Every dinnertime conversation you had about gaming modeled a thoughtful, considerate approach. You prepped your kids, from the start, to reflect on the avatar experience. More important, you provided them with an image of maturity: a picture of Mom or Dad, on the sofa, controlling a virtual self.

If you never played video games with your kids, that's okay, too. Just remember that children need role models. So, don't just leave them to their own devices. Start using social media with them. Make an intentional effort to demonstrate online behavior that aligns with your values. Show them what it means to be a grown-up in a connected world. Give them something to emulate.

PART THREE

SCHOOL

CHAPTER 7

THE NEW SCHOOL BELL

FROM THEIR VERY first days in school, children are conditioned to think in ways that are compatible with the tools and technologies around them. It happens in subtle ways. For example, my sons were in first or maybe second grade when they began to tell time. They learned to read a clock with an hour hand, a minute hand, and a second hand. They did worksheets, filling in the blanks, writing the way we speak.

Quarter to four.

Half past three.

Eight-oh-seven.

Telling time is a kind of tech literacy. And when I was a kid, I learned to do it, too. Teachers passed out illustrations of those plastic radios that folks kept bedside in the days before smartphones. Purple mimeographed pages showed rectangular digits. Students were asked to translate the language of time from one kind of clock to another. We drew the short hand on the nine, the long hand on the seven, completing a picture of a round clock face.

Back then, digital clocks were still a novelty. Horologists had been experimenting with "jump-hour" mechanisms since the late nineteenth century, but the technology didn't become commonplace until the Hamilton Watch Company released the Pulsar digital wristwatch in 1972. Its smooth polished metallic casing and red light–emitting diodes evoked a sense of optimistic space-age futurism. But the promise of progress is always balanced by a measure of Frankensteinian technophobia. Parents and teachers worried about digital clocks the same way that today's grown-ups worry about smartphones and video games. They passionately espoused the superiority of old tools, panicked about what might happen if kids never learned how to read a ticking clock.

My mother might be upset that, despite all the worksheets and practice, my boys still count from twelve by fives to decode the minute hand. But they also think of time in a more sophisticated way than I did at their age. Both of my kids keep track of multiple time zones on their smartphones and laptops. I'd like to think that the hour in faraway places is important to them because I'm often traveling and they want to know when to video chat with Dad. But the truth is, it has very little to do with my schedule. Instead, it's because they recognize that if they want to play in a global sandbox, they need to pay attention to when their friends in other countries are sleeping or awake. When will kids in Bosnia log on to *Minecraft*? When can they call Greece with Skype? What time will folks in the UK connect to *Discord*? I barely understood the concept of time zones when I was their age. But in the twenty-first century, children's understanding of time is different.

Physicists and philosophers know that there's no intrinsically accurate way to think about the flow of time; humanity's experience with it shifts as we adopt new technologies. In each era, grown-ups teach children a unique set of temporal conventions. Not only do kids develop the knowledge and skills needed to operate specific time-measuring tools, but also they learn to pace their actions, to see their lives in stages, to assess their own successes and failures so that their sense of self remains compatible with current time-telling practices. Most of this learning happens in school. We teach kids to consider how long it takes to accomplish a task. We celebrate good time management. We proctor tests with a stopwatch. In fact, all the most familiar classroom procedures reinforce a specific conception of time. And everyday interactions with the clock anchor students' experiences to the current economic model.

Think back to your own school days: bells, attendance sheets, and tardy slips taught you to think about time in a way that was aligned with the standards of the workplace. You learned that labor should be valued by the hour — cards punched to measure time at work. You mastered deadlines and punctuality. You tracked progress in semesters or quarters. The way we think about hours, minutes, and seconds is linked to specific economic, political, and historic events. And clocks — which hang on the wall of most classrooms, and influence almost everything that happens during the school day — shape our theories of learning, our standards of child development, and our definitions of identity.

Yet, when most people consider how to prepare kids for life in a connected world, they rarely talk about how clocks are changing. They don't acknowledge that our version of timekeeping is the result of a series of technological advances that happened over the past few centuries. That's unfortunate, because once you understand how clockwork perception came to be, it's much easier to see how teachers need to change their classrooms.

A Monastery Model of Education

Humans have been tracking time for millennia, even building devices to do it. Sundials, hourglasses, and water clocks are all antiquated technologies that measure duration. They show time pass-ing; they articulate its flow. But they do not keep track of synchronized time. Humans did not agree to coordinate the hours in the day until the nineteenth century. It's a development that arrived along with mechanical clocks. And it is only possible because of a much older technology called the *escapement*. The escapement is simple. All it does is push a gear forward in tiny increments. Think of the pendu-lum on a grandfather clock; each time it swings from side to side, it moves the gearwheel by just one cog. The spacing between teeth, combined with the length of the gear train, allows an escapement to move a clock's hands by precisely measured intervals, and therefore, to tell time.

The earliest escapements were created by monks living in Euro-pean monasteries around the thirteenth century. Cloistered within high stone walls, these devout worshippers kept an unyielding sched-ule of prayer and ritual. They built the first mechanical clocks to manage the rigidity of an abbey's religious agenda, to keep things on schedule. In those days, being orderly was considered pious, and clockwork mechanics guaranteed a previously unattainable level of regimentation. But the timepieces in medieval monasteries didn't look like the ones with which we are familiar. They had no minute hands. The monks wanted to measure only seven intervals during the day: the canonical hours. These were distinct periods of prayer, decreed by the Vatican, that determined when and how much time one should spend praying in relation to working or sleeping. Abbots, priors, and friars all organized their lives around these activities, and they used bells or chimes to communicate precisely when to shift attention. It is from these monks that we get the modern school bell — telling students to change classes, to go to lunch, to play outside, to head home. Forget what you've heard: your children are not enrolled in the "factory model" of education, but rather the "monastery model."

Today, the bell is one of the most ubiquitous education technologies. It compartmentalizes school days all over the world. Teachers think of it as an interruption to their lessons. Students think of it as an indication that it is time to escape. I have a different perspective. When teaching in the classroom at Temple University, I think of bells as an opportunity. I bring Tibetan *tingsha* bells to campus with me. Two small heavy round cymbals are bound with a brown leather strap. When I strike them together, they resonate and sing peacefully like a gong.

Harmonious. Sweet. Calm.

Tingsha bells were originally designed for Buddhist prayer rituals, so they have a bit more dignity than your average abrasive school bell. I ring them at the start of each class, when the students have already taken their seats but are still not quite settled. The bells work for my classroom the same way they worked in monasteries. The sound tells my students that it is time to shift their attention. It lets them know that we are moving into a sacred, almost prayerlike, metacognitive space. I want the students to leave their social lives behind and summon their innate capacity for deep, focused critical thinking. It takes only a couple of weeks before they understand my expectations. In fact, there is something sort of Pavlovian about it. An entire roomful of eighteen- and nineteen-year-olds quickly becomes conditioned to respond, almost involuntarily, to an aural signal. They just react; it's automatic. The ringing makes them lower their voices and turn toward me. They make eye contact. They're ready to engage.

I didn't come up with the idea of training students to respond to prayer bells by myself. I stole the practice from a professor who taught a course on trauma and psychology when I was in graduate school. And he stole it — whether he knows it or not — from medieval monks. In fact, by the fourteenth or fifteenth centuries, everybody had stolen it. All urban life in Europe, even outside mon-astery walls, was regulated by church bell technology. Every city built its own bell tower. It wasn't a clock tower, because the face — the visual representation of cyclical twenty-four-hour time — had not been established yet. The idea of "reading" a clock is not quite as traditional as you'd think. The first mechanical clocks only served to tell a bell ringer that it was time to do his duty. Everyone else just responded to the time-ordered sounds of Quasimodo's pealing chimes. As Lewis Mumford famously explained, "one ate, not upon feeling hungry, but when prompted by the clock; one slept, not when one was tired, but when the clock sanctioned it."

Can you imagine living in that era? There might be one bell to tell you the market was opening, another to tell you it was time to pay taxes. One meant that the church service was beginning, another that the communal hearth was available. And somehow, you would have known the difference between all these bells' distinct sounds. I guess you would have been able to decode them with your ears. You would have learned what each sound represented. You would have known how you were expected to respond to the different ringtones. Such a skill set was a necessity; one's ability to participate in the established social order depended on it. But there were eventually just too many bells for the average person to track. People recog-nized the need to standardize the hours in the day. Time became like currency: just as a coin unites a disparate collection of bartered products and services with a single symbolic signifier, so naming the day's hours standardizes duration and creates a unified community schedule. Instead of a different sound for each activity, there would now be a distinct number of chimes for each hour. Activities would be assigned to hours, not the other way around.

Folks settled on twenty-four hours. Twelve hours times two.

Why? They probably borrowed it from the astronomers, who had been segmenting the cosmos according to the twelve signs of the zodiac for centuries. Either that, or it came from the ancient Egyptians, who may have measured hours with water clocks—liquid dripping through tiny holes poked in the bottom of ceramic bowls. But the planet does not move in hours. The day is not really divided into minutes and seconds. Humans made the decision to do it that way—to experience our lives according to the zodiac twelve instead of, maybe, the canonical seven. We could have done it with any number, any unit. We'd just need to train future generations to abide by our decision.

That's precisely what was happening when my children's school careers began. They sat in a circle on the rug each morning and talked about the day's schedule. What happens at 10 a.m.? When's recess? When's lunch? When's math? When's choice time? They were learning to comply with a twenty-four-hour clockwork perception of time. Like monks, they were adopting a practice of dividing the day into periods. Like my undergraduate students, they were being trained to shift their attention from one activity to the next. After discussing the day's schedule, they'd always look at the calendar. Their teacher taught them how to measure a year. She'd speak enthusiastically about holidays and seasons. And my kids learned to divide their lives into school days, semesters, spring breaks, and summer vacations. Everyday routines equipped them to think in harmony with the tools of the times, and by now, they've gotten plenty of practice understanding their lives according to the pacing of escapement mechanics.

But that medieval version of clockwork perception is becoming obsolete. And therefore, as digital technology changes the way we experience time, the conventions of the classroom will need to transform along with it.

The New Timekeeping

Microsoft Outlook and Google Calendar have already altered the way I think about my daily agenda. All day long, notifications compete for my attention. Text messages, tweets, and Instagram posts ring my smartphone like church bells. Also, I rarely ever tune in to scheduled entertainment anymore; streaming video services like Netflix and Hulu now deliver TV on demand. I'm not tethered to the clock like a monk whose day was organized into compartmentalized devotional periods. Timekeeping has changed, but the monastery model of education has stayed the same. Learning remains tied to the escapement. The school day still consists of a collection of clockwork routines. These customs feel like fundamental aspects of school itself, but they were designed to help kids think in ways that align with a specific set of technological and economic norms. Those norms are changing, and classroom conventions will need to be redesigned for a new era.

Consider class periods. They are descended from the canonical hours that organized devotional practice within the abbey. With each bell, you shift your attention to a single subject. You become like a monk. History class is from 8:15 to 9:25. Math class is from 9:30 to 10:45. It seems to make perfect sense, especially to grown-ups who themselves were once trained to abide by the rules of the monastery model of education. But if you really think about it, the idea that every task should fit into a predetermined period of measured duration is absurd — especially in a digital, nonlinear, connected world. Sure, the ability to focus is important. And school is precisely the place where kids should learn how to allocate their attention. But does attention really need to be linked to the clock?

Remember: *focus* is the Latin word for "hearth." It denotes a familial gathering place, a sense of continuity. Or, in the case of a camera's lens, it is the point at which an image becomes clear. It has nothing to do with time. Measured durations of focus may have made sense for a world in which monastic clock literacy was the lens we used to regulate everything, to bring clarity to our daily routines. But in the twenty-first century, interactive engagement happens on a whim, and notifications constantly call for our response. Therefore, our children need to learn to live productive, ethical, and fulfilled lives—even when their attention is dispersed. They need to master "drip engagement."

The term drip engagement describes the process of turning one's attention to small things as they arise. Imagine ideas as if they were falling from a leaky faucet rather than a pail of water. Think of academic content as if it were delivered like raindrops rather than a deluge. Currently the monastery model of education floods our students with information for fixed durations of time. My younger son has 35-to-40-minute periods in elementary school, my older one 60 to 75 minutes in junior high. University students are typically expected to engage for somewhere between 90 and 180 minutes. The assumption is that as people spend more time in school, they adjust to sitting still and focusing for lengthier periods. It's like kneeling for penance, a sacrament—the longer you can bear it, the better you are. Soon you'll be prepared to sit quietly at a desk or in a cubicle all day long. It's one of the first things kids learn during their school careers. They adjust to what it means to be "on the clock."

Even in their earliest years, we're already preparing young kids for jobs. But work is changing. The popularity of messaging platforms like Slack and Microsoft Teams suggests that drip engagement will be what the workplace of the future demands. Instead of the old nine-to-five office model—with the long meetings and measured desk time that the current classroom routines prepare us for—employees will be able to contribute from anywhere at any hour. Many already do; you have probably received and replied to work-related messages while reading this chapter. In 2016, a Gallup report found that 43 percent of workers in the United States complete at least some of their job responsibilities from home. And CNN reported that in 2017, 3.9 million U.S. workers telecommuted more than half the time. These numbers will only increase. And folks with an acumen for dispersed focus will soon have a competitive professional advantage. Therefore, schools need to adopt a similar distributed approach. Just as the monastery model prepared us for the episodic agendas of the industrial era, the drip routines of the new classroom will function as practice for the conventions of a connected workplace.

I borrowed the drip imagery from online marketers, who use the term "drip campaign" to describe the way an automated advertising process can guide a customer from web browsing all the way through to a final sale. Think about when you search online for something, put it in your shopping cart, but don't click the Buy button. You're likely to receive an email in a few days suggesting that you reconsider the purchase. Soon, advertorial content will show up in your mobile news stream, educating you about the product's best attributes. Did you search for robot vacuum cleaners recently? If you did, I'd bet you're regularly seeing articles that review the top five. You are now a potential customer, and the retailer, with the help of search engines and social platforms, guides you toward checkout by dropping dispersed hints into your online life slowly and consistently over the course of days or maybe weeks. It may not have been intentional, but with a single search term, you embarked on a buyer's journey, and advertisements now show up right when you need them—to hold your hand and mentor you along the way. Because of ecommerce, browser cookies, predictive algorithms, and an inundation of digital information products, we've all become accustomed to these kinds of drip campaigns.

Social media has also made drip engagement a regular part of our lives. And it has the potential to change the way kids learn. Unfortunately, grown-ups often dismiss it as something frivolous. They mistakenly equate the shortness of an utterance with a lack of attention. They think that the 280-character tweet represents a superficial distraction. But any tween will tell you that nothing is finished after just one post: a social group remains engaged with the same thread for days, sometimes weeks, on end. Their attention is disseminated, not limited. Snapchat recognizes this; they've embraced users' taste for drip engagement and added a "Snapstreak" emoji. It's a badge that celebrates consecutive snaps sent among the same group of users. Appropriately, the Snapstreak emoji is a small orange-and-yellow flame — almost like a talisman of the Roman goddess Vesta and the focused continuity her fire represents. Snapchat began as a platform rooted in impermanence. It was originally a way for lovers to trade selfies, scandalous temporary photos that were erased immediately after viewing. It celebrated the single moment. But now, one's overall status on the platform depends on the length of a streak, a demonstration of longevity, driplike continuity.

Imagine what school will look like when teachers embrace the drip model of time, attention, and continuity that digital technology has already introduced into our lives. They will think of a tweet more like a sentence — as one small part of a deep contextual engagement with a complex idea. They will design learning activities that leverage ongoing disseminated focus. They will teach students to see the time between each utterance as a space for exploring new concepts, trying on different perspectives, doing research, and incorporating new data.

The challenge will be to change the way we think about attention.

Focus, Attention, and Concentration

Currently, we associate focus with measured periods of attention, without realizing that the clockwork era is the original culprit responsible for dividing up our concentration. Church bells were the first thing that interrupted our thinking, asking monks to shift their focus even if their thoughts remained unfinished.

Drip engagement demands slow, sustained, ongoing focus turned toward a dispersed set of sequential stimuli. Alternatively, a single episode encourages compartmentalization and interruption — continuity is defined temporally, as a collection of adjacent moments. We once needed to teach kids how to divide up their time into packaged instances so that they were prepared for industrial-era jobs. Class periods worked because they drew from the same logic as the commuter's split between home and work: division as piety, everything set in its proper place. But historically and culturally, the monastery model of episodic attention has not always been the preferred choice.

Compare interrupted clockwork thinking with the deep intellectual engagement that Plato presents in the dialogues of Socrates. From ancient Greece, we get accounts of all-day-long philosophical discussions with a singular focus. Drip engagement is the norm. *Symposium*, for example, tells the story of an all-night party in which friends take turns making arguments about the nature of love. They stop to eat, dance, laugh, and drink along the way. But they never lose focus. Likewise, many indigenous people participate in nonepisodic models of focus. They practice place- rather than time-based engagements with ideas. For example, beat poet Gary Snyder once wrote an essay about his experience driving around the western desert of Australia in a pickup with an Aboriginal Pintubi elder. The old man speaks so fast — telling so many rapid-fire stories about the hills and the mountains — that Snyder can barely keep up with the onslaught of information. Eventually, he realizes that the problem is not the elder's pacing, but rather the truck's engine. "These were tales to be told through *walking*," Snyder writes. The vehicle forced their conversation into the logic of the commute. But the Pintubi communicate their wisdom, knowledge, and learning differently. They do it through cycles of journey songs, stories about special places and "teaching spots." They use space, rather than episodes of time, to organize education. Elders walk the landscape with the youth, communicating relevant knowledge as they pass each natural landmark. Certainly, they don't need to talk the whole time. They may even stop along the way — perhaps picking berries, collecting supplies, doing business, or talking to friends and acquaintances. This is a kind of drip engagement: focus is disseminated, and concepts are presented and connected in response to the landscape — when the earth delivers physical notifications.

Note that, despite all the fearmongering about digital technology keeping kids indoors, the drip logic of online life may be better aligned with the rhythms of the natural world. Add GPS-enabled devices delivering location-based notifications, and EdTech suddenly has the potential to promote a more grounded engagement with place, one that's reminiscent of the Pintubi's. Of course, it works only if grown-ups reconsider their understanding of what it means to "be present." Because our concept of focus derives from monastic life, we still consider episodic attention to be sacred, holy, and pure. When we do it well, and concentrate our focus on the right activities, we feel good about ourselves. The popular backlash against multitasking is part of a leftover medieval fairy tale that resides deep down in our psyches, telling us that we should all try to act like elite monks; supposedly, they were morally superior people. Now, we try to teach our children to focus the way they did.

But that's not what today's students really need. We should be teaching them to embrace drip engagement—helping them culti-vate focusing skills for a new economic and technological context.

Practicing Drip Engagement

Drip engagement is one way that students can participate in what educators currently call asynchronous learning. That term describes activities that don't require participants to be present at a specific time or place. Most of the familiar "blended learning" models, like the flipped classroom—where instruction is delivered at home by video, while practice happens at school with hands-on assistance from the teacher—embrace an asynchronous model of instruction. Folks call it blended learning because it mixes online and offline activities. It also merges synchronous and asynchronous modes of attention: students still have traditional class periods, but these are supplemented with a digital component that allows them to com-plete a portion of the work at their own pace.

In theory, blended learning sounds great. It seems to be exactly what today's students need to be prepared for a future that demands both face-to-face and digital interactions. But unfortunately, the well-intentioned teachers who are currently trying to incorporate this model into their classrooms often end up with something that is not actually a hybrid learning experience at all. Instead, it's two dif-ferent paradigms stacked on top of each other. Students are still forced to engage in all the routines of the monastery model, and then they also have to do asynchronous work at home. This may be part of the reason why, according to author Malcolm Harris, today's kids spend about 20 percent more time in class than their parents did and triple the amount of time studying. It may be common to hear that the current cohort of students are lazy, entitled, and always distracted by smartphones, but the truth is that they're work-ing twice, if not three times, as hard as previous generations. That's because, in effect, they're engaged in dual educations — they're double majoring in the procedural rhetoric of two different economic eras.

A more appropriate model of schooling for contemporary times would avoid being a poor compendium of different pedagogical fads. Instead, it would be designed to encourage the new norms of focus and attention. There would be very little lecture and demonstration — a lot less of the medieval practices that we often consider "traditional" class time. For example, it would abandon the model of teachers solving algebraic equations on a slate chalkboard while a roomful of kids scrawl notes onto spiral-bound paper. This is not because the sage on the stage is an ineffective teaching strategy; in fact, it can work very well if the sage is adept at her craft. The problem is that the procedural rhetoric of this tried-and-true teaching style is now superfluous. We no longer need to prioritize children's ability to sit still and concentrate for long episodes of measured time. They don't need to practice listening to expert authority figures in the ways they once did. Instructions are now delivered electronically, sometimes even algorithmically. Information is now decentralized and retrieved on demand. Our social communications are asynchronous at least half the time. And, as I've already explained, the new workplace requires dispersed focus. Therefore, learning routines should be structured in ways that mimic the skill sets needed to live a fulfilled and productive adult life in a connected world.

I saw a partial version of the new education model in 2017, when I visited schools in Basque country — the region that spans the border between France and Spain. The Basque people are among the oldest indigenous inhabitants of Western Europe. They've been there for about 7,000 years, and they speak a unique language that is unrelated to Indo-European. They also have a strong sense of cultural identity that's been preserved even as new technological and economic contexts transform the world around them. I visited their schools because I wanted to see how they prepare children for a connected future while simultaneously maintaining an anchor to a historic cultural identity. What I found was fascinating. In primary and secondary schools, everything is conducted in Euskara, the old Basque language. Even the social banter, gossip, and giggling among peers is carried out in the traditional tongue. But the academic engagement is far from old-fashioned.

In giant school buildings that were constructed in the midtwentieth century, I saw hallways that had been refashioned into modern breakout spaces. They looked almost exactly like what I'd find at a hip Silicon Valley start-up or in any of WeWork's international locations. On the floor, big letters spelled out: "Co-Working Space." And a variety of seating types — beanbags, conference tables, nooks, and countertops — all facilitated different kinds of intellectual and social engagement. This is where most of the kids seemed to be spending their time. A pair of seven-year-old boys, wearing bright blue headphones, were playing a math game together on a shared iPad. Four older girls were huddled over a 3-D printer, watching it pipe out melted plastic filament. Some kids were reading alone. Others were hanging out and talking.

I found a more mature version of the same spirit among the young adults at the Mondragon and Deusto universities. In an Entrepreneurial Leadership and Innovation program, folks were organized into "companies" and "teams" rather than "classes" or "sections" — these student cooperatives mimicked the democratic culture of professional Mondragon corporations. Young people sat around conference tables. They seemed enthusiastic and committed as they exchanged ideas and resources with one another. The curriculum requires working with peers to self-manage a business from the ideation stage through to final execution. It's what venture capitalists call an incubator. Students learn about marketing, sales, negotiation, customer service, financial management, and more — but only as each need arises. I kept wondering when the tour would take me to a classroom, but it never did. I understood why when I finally met members of the faculty. They were sitting at a table separate from the students because their job is to guide and mentor, to assist along the way, but not necessarily to direct the course of study. They meet with the teams regularly, and they are always available to the students, but their role as teachers might best be described as curators of drip engagement.

Yardsticks and Milestones

Picture a typical kindergarten classroom. These days, it is still reminiscent of the gardenlike space that Froebel promoted over a century ago. Finger paintings hang overhead from a clothesline that spans the length of the room. Building blocks are in one corner, a guinea pig cage in another. Bright-colored letters and numbers are posted on the walls. Construction paper and craft supplies are organized into little plastic bins. And books are everywhere.

The teacher — the same one who taught my kids to tell time — comes into class one morning and complains that the rug on the floor is filthy and stained.

Adults may not realize that for kids who are five and six years old, rugs are a big deal. Remember that children spend most of their time on the floor. Their school day is spent among desks, playgrounds, blocks, tables, sandboxes, and beanbags. But they come together to sit in a circle on the floor at set times throughout the day. The rug is home base, the center of their world. So, when the teacher complains about it, the kids pay attention.

She sits down, cross-legged, scowling at the floor, shaking her head in disappointment. Then, she pulls the mobile phone from her pocket and pretends to dial.

"Get a green one!" one kid screams.

"Polka dots!" shouts another.

"No, red. I like red."

"How come he gets to pick? That's not fair. I wanna pick! I want blue."

She holds her index finger in front of her lips and motions for the kids to quiet down. They submit quickly. She's an expert at classroom management. They know her expectations; they've been trained.

Once the kids are calm, she speaks into the phone, "There are just a lot of stains, a bunch of spills." She points at the rug as if the person on the other end of the line can see her fingers. "I'm afraid cleaning doesn't cut it anymore. We need a new one."

Suddenly, her eyebrows scrunch and the kids can tell that she is puzzled by the reply. Maybe she's confused. Or worse, worried. She shrugs, looks at the students, and whispers, "He wants to know what size — how big? What do I tell him?"

Blank stares. Puzzled five- and six-year-old faces.

Kids trying to figure out how to communicate width and length over the phone.

What unit of measurement should they use? Sneakers? Pencils? Crayons? Blocks? What symbolic metric — what analog to distance — could be consistent between their classroom and a rug shop?

They need to think only for a few moments before it clicks, like magic.

They get it. From this masterful lesson, they've discovered the need for standardized units of measurement. The teacher hands them yardsticks and rulers, and they are initiated into a certain way of being and thinking. They start measuring everything. They're excited. They just learned a new philosophical outlook, a thought tool with which to organize and perceive the physical world around them. Now the stage is set for multiplication, division, fractions, geometry, physics, chemistry, engineering, and more. After all, rugs aren't the only thing we measure. We measure everything, including time. Through the routines of the classroom, students even learn to measure their sense of self, evaluating their successes and failures using clocklike intervals.

It happens in subtle ways. For example, when my kids were little, I always baked cupcakes that they could take to school on their birthdays. Over time, I learned that more frosting was better; candy on top was the best. It made my kids smile ecstatically as they passed out the treats to their classmates. It never occurred to me that these confections represented a way of perceiving the world.

Believe it or not, celebrating birthdays is a kind of tech literacy. And when I was their age, I learned to do it, too. But not my grandmother; she had to adapt. For her, birthdays were as unfamiliar as the radio, the television, and the airplane. In fact, she never even knew when her real birthday was; for her entire life, she just guessed her age. Growing up in Polish Lithuania back before centralized government bureaucracy had made its way to rural villages, her parents had no access to a nearby office from which to get a birth certificate. They did not make the trek to town — by foot — until all their kids were born. And this means that my grandmother and her sisters all had the same legal date of birth.

I thought that was the craziest thing when I was a kid. It just did not compute. Socialized, since kindergarten, into an industrial-era conception of time, I found it unimaginable that someone could not know their actual birthday. It had never occurred to me that just a few generations earlier, people thought about the process of aging in drastically different ways. The average life — the way we experience it — was a brand-new concept in the nineteenth century. Remember

163

that, for most of human history, the death of a child was an everyday occurrence. And when mortality arrives just as suddenly for kids as it does for adults, age is less relevant. Why? Because there is no standard life span. My grandmother couldn't take it for granted, the way we do now, that barring some unforeseen tragedy she would survive for almost a century. It wasn't because she lived in a poor village in the middle of nowhere. In fact, nobody expected to live for seventy or eighty or ninety years before modern medicine made it plausible and commonplace. Sure, old age happened sometimes. But in general, folks accepted that they were just as likely to pass away at fourteen as at forty-nine. And therefore, people couldn't possibly think of childhood as a time when you prepare for adulthood. Grown-up years needed to be guaranteed before humans could perceive them as the primary part of life.

Can you imagine a world in which age has so little authority? Realize that all of history's child prodigies and tweenage kings are the product of this mindset. We're usually told that the young people of the past did more because their life spans were shorter; but that's not precisely true. It is really because adulthood wasn't so significant. The very idea of puberty and adolescence as transitional periods on the way to a well-adjusted adult life is a peculiar part of the present era. All the developmental milestones—the standard increments and stages with which we measure our time on the planet—are products of the nineteenth and twentieth centuries. But just like the clock's twenty-four hours and sixty minutes, the universe doesn't necessarily agree. These increments and stages are not written into the cells of our bodies. They are just useful categories with which to measure duration and progression.

Nowadays, it may make sense to organize our reality around grade levels, birthdays, sweet sixteens, and midlife crises. But the big milestones of our lifetimes are ultimately just elements of clock literacy. Ages and stages did not exist until there was a reason for our experiences to be regulated by the mechanical escapement. The reason for this arrived by steam engine in the 1820s. Railroad time-tables forced us to set our bell towers so that they were synchronized with clocks in faraway places. We suddenly had time zones, minute hands, and a new sense of simultaneity. Individuals had their own pocket watches and alarm clocks. And children needed to learn how to live with immediacy, to operate in a world that measured dura-tion in seconds, to understand that life ticked away in progressive measured stages. They needed to see the world from the perspective of the predominant technology. But that technology is changing.

Now, our task is to make sure kids can think beyond the limits of Industrial Age clockwork perception. We are actively outsourcing chronological thinking to intelligent machines. Therefore, success, happiness, and fulfillment will soon depend on one's ability to think outside a linear timetable. Schools must redesign their routines accordingly.

Takeaways

Time's up!

Our children's lives are currently quantified, their progress orga-nized into developmental milestones. Birthdays punctuate the sched-ules of our existence. And our allegiance to a clockwork view of the universe manifests as a school-day commitment to standardization.

The habits and routines of the classroom reinforce our loyalty to a specific technological paradigm. We teach kids to conform to an epi-sodic reality in which duration is measured by seconds. Minute hands, time zones, and a twentieth-century sense of simultaneity shape our theories of learning and our definitions of identity.

This outlook made sense at one time. Ages and stages were

perfect for a world of monastery clock towers and railroad timetables. But now the toolset is changing. In fact, it's already changed. So, our current task is to make sure we prepare the next generation to think beyond the limits of clockwork perception.

Your children's success, happiness, and fulfillment will be dependent on their ability to operate outside a chronological timetable. You will need to abandon your current dedication to grade levels, on-schedule achievements, and episodic attention. The time for that way of thinking has come and gone. New routines that promote a nonlinear view of growth and a distributed command of the present will soon emerge. Try to be open-minded.

Rearrange classrooms to reflect the new timekeeping.

Grown-ups are constantly teaching kids to see their lives in stages, to organize their existence according to the clockwork logic of an Industrial Age technological paradigm. For example, our commitments to clearly defined grade levels and rigid developmental milestones prepare kids to assess their own successes and failures so that their sense of self remains compatible with current time-telling practices. We teach kids to consider how long it takes to accomplish a task. We celebrate good time management. We proctor tests with a stopwatch. We ring the school bell at the end of each class.

The monastery model of education consists of a daily collection of episodic class periods through which even the youngest children are being prepared for old-school jobs. They're learning what it means to prioritize punctuality and to be "on the clock." But meanwhile, the economic value of time is shifting. The success of Uber, Airbnb, Etsy, and Udemy are all indicators that the gig economy's task rabbits are rapidly replacing the punch-card professionals. A 2016 report from the McKinsey Global Institute estimated that 20 to 30 percent of the working-age population in the United States and

Europe currently engage in some sort of "independent work." That number is projected to grow considerably over the next decade.

Already, online calendars have altered the way we think about our schedules. Smartphone notifications are the new church bells. And even in familiar white-collar jobs, the popularity of messaging platforms like Slack and Microsoft Teams suggests that the workplace of the future will replace the cubicles and conference rooms of the old nine-to-five office model with a more dispersed image of "the workday."

In response to these changes, teachers will need to replace the monastery model with drip routines that require students to embody the conventions of a connected workplace: Adopt online social platforms. Divide classes into a collection of blended and nonlinear utterances so that kids learn, by example, how distributed pieces of information can be thoughtfully assembled into a coherent and comprehensive engagement with a complex idea. Design learning activities that require ongoing but disseminated focus.

Preparation for the future is not about the skills needed to operate new technologies, but rather about familiarizing students with new ways of thinking.

Teach kids that information and knowledge are constructed socially.

One of the biggest challenges schools currently face is preparing kids to be kind and thoughtful participants in a changing social structure. Episodic class periods and sage-on-the-stage pedagogical practices always prepared kids for a top-down world. Because they were required to sit still, face forward, and listen to lectures for a fixed duration of time, children learned to submit to the expertise of the person in charge. An intricate system of rewards and penalties taught them that success was predicated on their ability to identify a centralized authority and then to abide by his stipulations. Sports teams had their coaches and team captains. Cliques had mean girls and lemmings.

The procedural rhetoric of the classroom helped kids become accustomed to the organizational conventions of the Industrial Age meritocracy. They were primed for a world of corporate CEOs, rabbis, ministers, mayors, foremen, and bosses. They watched how classroom aides turned to teachers for validation, how teachers were required to treat condescending principals as experts, how principals acquiesced to administrators.

The power dynamics of authority were obvious. And underneath, an implicitly hierarchical understanding of intelligence was simultaneously taking hold. Kids learned to imagine that information and knowledge are transmitted through pyramid schemes — disseminated downward and outward from a single point of authority. They learned to see socioeconomic status and professional achievement as indicators of superior character and wisdom. Intelligence became something you hoard, like wealth. Ideas were owned like property. And perhaps, at one time, this model was appropriate. But in a world of Google searches, Reddit forums, blog posts, and social news streams, the old steadfast devotion to an intellectual pecking order becomes a liability.

Today's learning routines need to be structured in horizontal ways that mimic the skill sets required to live a fulfilled and productive adult life in a connected world. Classrooms should be redesigned to resemble co-working spaces. A cohort of peers should be assessed collectively, their capacity to openly exchange knowledge and skills prioritized above individual achievement. Teachers should imagine themselves as Sherpas, who are available to guide students through self-directed project-based learning activities.

The new educators are not experts, but rather curators of driplike and participatory intellectual engagements.

CHAPTER 8

THE NEW LANGUAGE ARTS

WHAT IS IT about fingers? Finger painting was invented by Ruth Faison Shaw at the beginning of the twentieth century. Of course, prehistoric people rubbed pigment onto cave walls with their fingers more than forty thousand years ago, but Shaw was the first to formally introduce finger paint into education.

"It all began, in the most natural way in the world," Shaw explained in her 1947 book, *Finger-Painting and How I Do It,* "with a little boy at the school who smeared the bathroom wall with iodine." Shaw believed that "'smearing' with the hands is a primary impulse," and in 1931 she patented a set of paints that kids could use to "smear to their heart's content."

She promoted finger painting as if it were a practice of abandoned creativity. "No one can or should tell another how to paint or how to 'make a picture,'" she wrote. "Creative work must come from the imagination and personal experience." She saw finger painting as an opportunity to indulge children's impulses and free them from restraint: "Begin with one color. 'As much finger paint...as you would [put] ice cream on your spoon if your mother wasn't watching you. And you may take more if you want it.'" There is a theme of permissive indulgence throughout her work.

There is also an implicit reference to Freudian psychology. When we imagine boys rubbing iodine against a tiled wall, it reminds us of ancient cave drawings and reinforces Freud's archaeological approach to psychoanalysis — digging for truth among the primitive parts of our minds. Moreover, finger painting's origin story takes place in the bathroom, almost as if Shaw wanted her readers to think about Freud's anal stage, in which children are either letting go or holding in bowel movements. Did she know that from a psychoanalytic perspective, our potty-training experiences shape our adult personalities, cementing lifelong habits and neuroses around repressed conformity and/or unrestricted creativity? It certainly seems so. She focused on loose, fluid, unregimented individual authorship in a way that's unique to the twentieth century — another example of the sandbox sense of self.

"See what *your* hand will do. Your hand is characteristic of you. You have certain ways of using your fingers, the shape and imprint of each finger are yours and yours alone," she wrote. "Your imagination, which directs your hands, will lead you to produce something individual and representative of you." Note the connection Shaw draws between hands and creativity. It goes back thousands of years. Aristotle considered the psyche, or soul, to be "analogous to the hand," which he called "the tool of tools." Already, in ancient Greece, the connection between consciousness, hands, and technology was what distinguished the human animal from the rest of nature. That notion has barely changed. Our hands, and their relationship to creative toolmaking, still hold primary status in our imaginations.

In 2007 Steve Jobs said, "We are all born with the ultimate pointing device — our fingers — and iPhone uses them to create the most revolutionary user interface since the mouse." He was announcing Apple's first smartphone. And just as the clock's hands were replaced by digits, the touchscreen shifted navigation from our palms to our fingertips. Since then, we've all heard stories about small children who try to interact with books or magazines as if they were iPads: swiping across pages and wondering why still photographs won't move. People worry that the "intuitive" multitouch technology might be "reprogramming" our kids. Of course, in a sense, they're right; that's what tools do, they become invisible bodily auxiliaries that mediate our perceptions. But there's no need for worry. It's not a bad thing. It's just a human thing.

Why do we complain every time one technology disrupts our kids' capacity to operate another? Because sometimes it's hard not to be anxious. Especially when it comes to our bodies, we struggle to distinguish between what constitutes "health" and what constitutes obsolete technological proficiency. We've become wedded to certain developmental milestones that are tied to a specific tool set. The schools of the future will need to fix this — adapt standards to take into account the demands that new technologies make on our bodies. Educators can start by letting Shaw's beliefs about finger painting transcend oversize pages of newsprint paper. Allow her ideas to inform the acts of swiping, tapping, and clicking. There are literally thousands of ways that the touchscreen and the keyboard can promote a sandbox sense of self, enabling unfettered expression and raw creativity.

It is a teacher's job to encourage students, showing them how to use the tools of the times in thoughtful and empowering ways. How can coding lead to poetry? How can Snapchat become dialectic? First, we will need to assimilate touchscreens and keyboards fully into the learning experience. We should be as mindful about incorporating digital platforms as we have been about paper and pen. We will need to imagine new kinds of milestones that focus on how children integrate digital behaviors, physically, into their bodies. It's time to tend to the swipe as we once did to penmanship.

What starts with the touch of a fingertip—against a page, a screen, a keyboard—can and should become a fulfilling, meaningful, productive, and contextualized expression of the self.

Keyboarding versus Penmanship

My son's fingers move across the keyboard at an astounding pace. He doesn't touch-type the way I learned, with index fingers resting on the J and F keys. But he doesn't hunt and peck either.

His technique developed organically, out of necessity and without training. First and foremost, it is a gaming position. The right hand moves quickly back and forth between the keyboard and the mouse. His generation has outright rejected the laptop touchpad; I don't know one kid who uses it. My son has a cordless mouse designed for gamers—with it, he manipulates the camera's point of view. Meanwhile, his left hand navigates, attacks, digs, builds, strikes.

His pinky moves between control, shift, and tab almost involuntarily. Then, without pause, he switches to the chat stream using just a keystroke. He types a sentence, sometimes an acronym, perhaps just a few words. Before I can finish reading it over his shoulder, he has switched back again. There is an ease with which his fingers move around, inputting commands with an entirely different kind of efficiency than the one with which I'm familiar. He navigates his keyboard like IT professionals and the engineers I see writing code whenever I visit software companies. I feel good about that, knowing that it will help prepare him for professional success. It must mean something to his future employers that the keyboard is already deeply embedded in his muscle memory. He seems at home when he operates it. Watching from behind the sofa, I see that his hand

and his fingers flex and stretch into shapes specific to the games he loves. They glide in a way mine don't. They claw into unfamiliar positions, like a guitarist's hand fingering the frets. But it is not elegant. His fingertips are often greasy. His posture is poor. His forearms maneuver haphazardly, like octopus tentacles. Sometimes it looks fluid, but mostly it is a violent staccato: banging, tapping, clicking, pounding. It's never controlled.

I tell him about the piano teacher who made me practice scales with pennies on the backs of my hands — palms parallel to the keys, fingers perfectly curved, ninety-degree angles at the elbow. He looks at me like I'm crazy. I also describe the teacher who walked around the computer lab in my high school. She would constantly tap us between the shoulder blades with a twelve-inch wooden ruler, reminding us to sit up straight.

"Posture, Mr. Shapiro. Posture, Jordan!"

I learned to type on boxy Apple IIe computers with beige keyboards and five-inch slots for Mavis Beacon's floppy disks. The teacher was the school's bursar, but as the only one who went to secretarial classes as a young woman, she was asked to teach typing. We had no choice but to deal with the vestiges of a time when girls were supposed to look charming for the benefit of their employers: shoulders back, hair in a bun, hem at a respectable length, no sudden movements — control of the body equals control of the mind. It is always hard to teach in ways that differ from the ways one learned. And our typing teacher seemed to be sentimentally attached to the same propriety and order that inspired regimented medieval monasteries to build clocks. It is the mindset of compliance that cemented the rituals of the perfect dinner into the twentieth-century family home, too. And it is where we get those handwriting worksheets — the reason some schools still teach cursive despite knowing that it has become completely obsolete.

Forget all those studies about the benefits that come from writing in script. Yes, I've read them. Plus, I grew up with an occupational therapist for a mom, so I constantly heard how important it is to start my letters from the top. But when you know the history, it becomes very difficult to take any of the pro-handwriting dogma seriously. After all, those cursive letters that I had to draw onto aqua-lined paper worksheets were loaded with baggage from the start. "Health" and "moral" benefits were always a part of penmanship's snake-oil sales pitch.

Today's handwriting style is directly derived from the work of a guy named Austin Norman Palmer. At one point, he controlled a penmanship empire. He operated business colleges, offered correspondence courses, and sold textbooks. By the middle of the twentieth century, the Palmer Method was used in almost every school. It was an innovation, involving simpler letter shapes than those people were used to at the time. Before Palmer, Spencerian was the standard. It was an elegant alphabet, artfully designed by Platt Rogers Spencer. Picture the logos of Coca-Cola and the Ford Motor Company; they are both written in Spencerian script. They also involve complex and difficult-to-execute ornamentation: curlicues, sweeping curves, rounded edges. Palmer could see that those decorative details were becoming superfluous in a world driven by technologies of efficiency. The typewriter was gaining market share, and if his product was going to stay relevant, the new cursive needed to be fast, fluid, and simple. So, Palmer stripped handwriting down to its basics, creating a script that was much easier to draw than Spencer's.

Palmer was living at a time very much like our own. It was the last decade of the 1800s, and people saw huge technological and industrial changes happening all around them. They were worried about how their children would fit into a new kind of economy that they didn't quite understand yet. But Palmer was prescient. He sold his product as "The Palmer Method of Business Writing" because he knew Spencer had done one thing right: appealing to people's sense of insecurity. In those days, parental guilt and shame revolved around religious and moral convictions, so Spencer posited that good handwriting, executed with physical discipline, was indicative of virtue. Think about Bart Simpson's famous school punishment — copying a sentence onto the chalkboard during the show's opening credits. It is derivative of a Victorian-era belief that good penmanship meant good values. "Victorians were to form their letters as they formed themselves," writes historian Tamara Platkins Thornton, "through moral self-elevation and physical self-control." Folks imagined that if bad kids copied sentences neatly, over and over again, they would be reformed — from a pure soul, to a pure hand, and onto the page. But Palmer knew that story wouldn't work anymore. He could see that the world was changing, and that handwriting's branding would have to change along with it. He not only made the letters less frilly than Spencer's, but also adapted the moral messaging in a similar way. He promoted penmanship as a symbol of professional veracity. Handwriting became all about strength and power. Advocates pointed to the "muscular" benefits. Why? Because religious expertise was rapidly being replaced by scientific expertise, and therefore morality was being replaced by health and well-being. Nowadays, if you know a child who has been referred to a therapist to address possible problems with the fine-motor skills associated with bad penmanship, you've experienced the impact of Palmer's life's work.

Classroom handwriting drills first became commonplace in the early twentieth century, emphasizing a kind of precision and uniformity that matched those of modern manufacturing processes. Because of big economic and technological changes, all virtuous people were now expected to write in the same industrious way — neatly, quickly, and legibly. These values then got mapped onto a clockwork image of child development so that now, by eighteen months, a "healthy" child should be scribbling on paper. By one to two years, imitating horizontal and vertical lines. By three or four, drawing circles without models. By five, copying crosses, squares, and triangles. By six, children should be able to write their names. And by seven they should no longer confuse similar letters like *b* and *d*. These are the developmental milestones on the way to literacy that are currently accepted by the medical and educational establishments. But few people recognize the degree to which this twentieth-century view of children's bodies, perceptions, and abilities was determined by both a specific tool set and a distinct definition of the self. As the typewriter became popular and letter shapes became standardized, the ability to draw uniform script became much less important. Instead, people focused on making sure individual progress happened on schedule, a kind of muscular compliance with grade levels, birthdays, and adherence to the new clockwork sense of self.

Around the same time, something else happened: handwriting became personal. Children started collecting autographs. Detectives used penmanship as forensic evidence. Psychiatrists analyzed it as if it were an expression of character. And it's the legacy of these trends that makes today's critics of the keyboard complain that the machine separates the scribe from his or her authorship. "When we write by hand, we connect to ourselves," wrote Julia Cameron, author of the bestselling book *The Artist's Way: A Spiritual Path to High Creativity*. She is notable for inspiring millions of people to wake up every day and write "Morning Pages," filling three pieces of paper with words about whatever comes to mind. She insists that this stream-of-consciousness writing must be done by hand. In 2012 (still going strong twenty years after the original book was published), she posted on her online blog: "We may get speed and distance when we type, but we get a truer connection—to ourselves and our deepest thoughts—when we actually put pen to page." My son's teachers seem to share Cameron's sentiment. Although most curriculum standards have moved away from penmanship and toward keyboarding skills, they still insist that the first step in writing should involve paper and pen. They push him to work in notebooks, believing that it will make him less inhibited and more creative. For them, handwriting is like finger painting: an expression of individual personality, a demonstration of one's compliance with the sandbox sense of self. But this modern idea that there's something personal and creative about writing by hand is, quite frankly, a little absurd. Especially when you consider that it has no correlative in previous eras.

Historically, writing by hand has always been just a skill, a craft, a trade, a vocation. It was like cabinetmaking, agriculture, and metallurgy. Writing was certainly not a career for the lowest-ranked members of society, but it also wasn't for the intellectual elite. Monarchs were considered too pure for it. After all, Jesus never wrote anything down; that was the work of his humble servants and disciples. Mohammed could neither read nor write; he dictated the verses of the Qur'an (which translates as "recitation") to scribes. Most wealthy citizens of ancient Greece didn't write. Their academies were all about the spoken word. In fact, we get the word "school" from the ancient Greek σχολή (skoli), which means "leisure," "play," or "rest." The upper classes of ancient Athens spent their time in symposium, which literally means eating, drinking, and talking with friends. For them, speaking offered the truest freedom of expression (through debate-style drip engagements with philosophical ideas). Hence, oral rhetoric was the superior craft. Writing was a lowly chore to be done by the middle classes; there was nothing creative or admirable about it. Until the modern era, it just meant the labor of copying—either copying down what your master or employer says or copying from existing texts.

By medieval times, most writing happened in monasteries. Monks copied texts whenever the clock bell interrupted their prayers. But while wielding a pen may have made a monk pious, it did not make him unique. The focus was exclusively on the product; the work didn't signify personal esteem. Any sense of creative individuality would've been forbidden. The goal was obedience and accuracy so perfect that the scribe himself became invisible. In this way, the medieval Christians were a lot like the Hebrews, who called themselves "the people of the book." Judaic calligraphers are called *soferim*. And to this day, each one serves a long apprenticeship before being allowed to produce a holy document, by hand, on animal skin parchment. Only these master scribes are permitted to write a Torah (the Hebrew version of the Old Testament). It is not because the letters are difficult to draw, but rather because the ancient law decrees what constitutes a pure document. Only a seasoned professional has been trained to adequately obey the many complicated laws about things like the preparation of the parchment, the spaces between the letters, how many times you can erase, and much, much more. But the scribe doesn't matter, only the book does. According to the rabbis, the Torah you'd find in any synagogue, anywhere in the world, is an identical copy of the original—handed down from Moses, through the generations to Ezra, who assembled it on scrolls in the middle of the fifth century BCE. But Moses didn't write the words; he was just a scrivener who took dictation from the Lord.

All ministers and religious leaders throughout the Middle Ages were taught to read, but few would have been trained in the craft of writing. Surprisingly, the idea that literacy requires both doesn't really go mainstream until the invention of the printing press. Think about that for a moment: handwriting became a common skill *after* Gutenberg, at the start of the Industrial Age. Ironically, cursive style is linked to typesetting. It's a product of technology that arrived when average people started to read, when they suddenly had access to mechanically printed material. That's when text became a primary part of commerce—when receipts, contracts, and invoices all entered the everyday economy. Since it would have been inefficient to set up the presses to print a single page, folks developed distinct formal writing styles for each kind of business document, and thus "scripts" were born. Think of them like handwritten fonts. There were scripts appropriate for legal work, accounting, government files, just about anything you can imagine. There were thousands of them. Some were so complex, with decorative features, you might not recognize the letters if you saw them today. Even then, most scripts were illegible to the uninitiated; only those who worked in a specific vocation were trained to read and write them. But the ability to use these scripts guaranteed gainful employment in a burgeoning capitalist marketplace. So, people naturally took pride in their mastery of penmanship. It had nothing to do with personal expression. It was all about socioeconomic status.

Ultimately, Spencerian Script, the Palmer Method of Business Writing, and all the worksheets I did as a kid were tantamount to today's computer literacy classes—simple up-skilling programs designed to circumvent an economic participation gap brought on by a new technological paradigm. Still, I bet Austin Norman Palmer would be pleased to know that his sales pitch worked so well that people continue to believe the health claims he made. Nearly a century after his death, today's handwriting advocates tell variations of the same old story.

Writing Instruments

Recent research suggests that when very small children draw letters by hand — as opposed to typing on a keyboard — the action cements stronger understanding. But I wonder what would happen if the same study compared finger paint and pencils? If smearing won, would we advocate for eliminating writing instruments from primary school classrooms? Turn everyone back into a cave artist? Of course not. The purpose of school is to teach students how to express themselves using the tools that currently shape their world.

Other studies suggest that note-taking by hand forces students to re-frame information and thereby increase their overall retention. Apparently, handwriting is better than keyboarding because today's kids type fast enough to transcribe lectures word for word, which can make them numb to their meaning. With laptops open, they race to record everything the teacher says. Alternatively, when pressing a ballpoint pen onto the pages of a spiral notebook, they actively translate ideas into something akin to succinct bullet points. They process each concept and rearticulate it in their own words, ending up with deeper comprehension. At least that's what the data seem to suggest. But I doubt that the differences between these outcomes are *caused* by the note-taking tools themselves. Instead, it may have to do with the way students have been taught to think about using each technology. They've been conditioned to interact with pen and ink since preschool. They've watched teachers scrawl main points onto giant whiteboards with dry-erase markers. But how often have they seen the digital equivalent modeled? Maybe we just need to teach keyboardists better note-taking skills. After all, it seems crazy not to take advantage of today's platforms; there are so many things this technology can do that pen and ink can't.

Consider a few basic examples: Digital notes offer students an infinite-size blank folio stretching in all directions—there's no need to turn the pages of a marbled composition book. Learners have the ability to tag and hyperlink words across documents and multimedia sources—an introduction to the complexities of modern information management. Digital notes also make it possible to create a common cloud-based canvas on which instructors and classmates can work collaboratively, sharing notes, doodles, resources, and ideas. One teacher called digital note-taking "a window into students' brains," because it allowed her to log in to their notebooks, assess comprehension, and deliver real-time feedback. The new note-taking is so much more than a digital replica of a pad and paper.

Microsoft's OneNote adds a collection of "Learning Tools," including features like their "Immersive Reader." It's a smart text-to-speech engine that not only reads notes back to students, but also uses artificial intelligence to identify and display color-coded parts of speech, grammar, and syllables. It works with any piece of text—typed, scanned, photographed, or handwritten. The feature was originally designed for kids who needed assistive technology to help them overcome learning disabilities like dyslexia, dysgraphia, and visual perceptual/visual motor deficit, but it has become a shining example of good universal design. The Immersive Reader destigmatizes those who struggle to make sense of their notes, while simultaneously enhancing everyone else's experience, too. One study, done by RTI International, declared that Learning Tools "levels the playing field." They saw how it helped an entire cohort of fourth graders improve their reading and writing skills. All it took was a creative teacher who actively and intentionally integrated digital note-taking into the lesson plan—a teacher who understood that the memo book is obsolete. The new note-taking is not about using virtual scratch pads to record memories in shorthand. It's a digital sandbox where students can play with ideas, reconsider content, organize concepts, and share epiphanies.

We've come a long way from folders, dividers, and loose-leaf paper tucked into the Velcro-topped three-ring Trapper Keepers that were all the rage when I was a kid. Nevertheless, many parents and teachers remain apprehensive about incorporating personal devices into the classroom, especially when it comes to the humanities. At my university, hardly a semester goes by without the faculty listserv being flooded with complaints about students using laptops or tablets to take notes. Many of my colleagues in the College of Liberal Arts want to ban devices from the classroom altogether. They deliver their grievances bedecked with lament and nostalgia for simpler times. Each email is peppered with links to pro-handwriting studies like the ones I've summarized above. Does the research they quote prove that screens are an affront to paper in the classroom? That connected devices are a source of distraction that leads to poor academic performance? Or is this merely a case of simple confirmation bias? Likely, it's the latter. Most research demonstrates that banning devices only leads to positive outcomes among the lowest-achieving students. It has virtually no impact on the high achievers, which indicates that the real issue has to do with whether kids have been taught effective study skills prior to class. My guess is that fourth graders who use OneNote's Learning Tools, with the support of good teachers, grow into college kids who can manage digital distractions effectively. What's more, they've practiced learning within context. They've come to understand the benefits and challenges associated with the technologies around them. And this is what will really make them high achievers in the long run.

Intellectual abilities, academic aptitudes, and even twenty-first-century "character" skills — like grit, perseverance, resilience — are advantageous only to the degree that they can be leveraged through the tools that currently shape our world. But most grown-ups struggle to recognize this, because they remain wedded to an outdated understanding of what constitutes good instrumental self-expression. They are unaware of the history of handwriting; they forget that almost all human communication is technological. They're still loyal to the nostalgic idea that the human hand is linked to a divine soul, that true creativity needs to be pure, natural, and untainted by modernity. They buy into yet another variation on the Frankensteinian technophobia narrative — worrying that digital machines will destroy our humanity, take the nuance out of imagination and understanding, kill creativity, and make everything rote and repetitive. Does it have something to do with the nature of computers? Do these folks recognize that digital technology is limited by its capacity to obey commands? Are they concerned that too much exposure to the procedural rhetoric of algorithms will turn kids into recipe-following zombies? That may be one explanation they'd offer, but I don't think it's so simple. After all, Socrates worried about the same things; this tension is way older than keyboards. Fear and apprehension have always accompanied creative technology.

The word "technology" is derived from the Greek root *technê* (τέχνη), which means "craft" and is often considered in relationship to *epistêmê* (ἐπιστήμη), which means "knowledge." When you think about the familiar dichotomy between practice and theory, you're drawing on the same separation between these two categories that was established by Aristotle in the fourth century BCE. But before Aristotle, this distinction between doing and thinking barely existed. Plato often uses the two words — *technê* and *epistêmê* — interchangeably. Why? Because knowledge needs to be articulated in order to manifest, to be useful. Thoughts, no matter how brilliant, are all ephemeral. They will drift away as easily as they arrived unless captured and expressed through some technological means of communication. Expression requires craftsmanship, and craftsmanship requires *technê,* or tools. Rhetoric is the tool of the orator. Writing is the tool of an author; it not only requires people to use an instrument — quill and ink, mechanical pencil, dictation software — but also constitutes an apparatus in itself. Literacy *is* technology. That fact becomes clear when you consider the origins of writing.

The oldest examples of writing come from ancient Sumer, in what's now called Southern Iraq. We know it because museums are full of millions of little clay tablets that functioned as scratch pads on which students practiced. They copied the same text over and over again. It was a typical school exercise at the time. Teachers would etch cuneiform symbols onto one side of a tablet, and students copied them onto the other. Cuneiform looks like wedge-shaped fingernail markings pressed into handheld clay slabs about the size of a smartphone. We say it is the first written language, but that's not precise. Prior to cuneiform, humans had used pictographs — a standardized set of simple drawings with which to communicate common objects. Think of something like a logo or a trademark, abstract images of a familiar thing: a stick figure means "man," an oval beside a triangle means "fish." That's what writing was like at first. Then, almost like computer software iterating from alpha to beta versions, cuneiform added signs. Suddenly, for the first time in human history, an arbitrary collection of squiggles could have any meaning that a community ascribed to it. The written symbol no longer needed to look like the thing it represented. It needed only to function as an analog.

That's a pretty amazing innovation, because first it becomes possible to articulate abstract ideas in writing — concepts you can't envision, like "happiness" or "power." And then it enables the creation of an alphabet. But this kind of writing also presents new challenges. With it, communities need to teach people not only how to draw the signs but also what they represent; they need to learn how to use the apparatus. Symbols are ultimately tools; and if the symbol for "grain" doesn't look like grain, a student can't be expected to understand how to use it intuitively. Thus, the Sumerians developed the first literacy curriculum. It was a kind of technological proficiency program that was accomplished by combining phonics and semantics, grouping words by both sound and category. It was a primitive version of exactly what we do today. No wonder so many grown-ups struggle to imagine the school of the future. Our concept of literacy education is almost 5,000 years old. "Tablet house" is what the Sumerians called school. But they didn't think of it the way we do. For them, school was much more like vocational training, a trade education. Cuneiform wasn't for everybody; writing was just a technology that facilitated specific bureaucratic objectives, so only those who would use it needed to learn it. Tablet houses were all about teaching certain students to use a particular set of tools.

Nowadays, written communications are a part of just about every profession. Of course, we no longer press a reed into a clay tablet. We also don't rub pumice into stretched animal skins to prepare parchment the way the ancient Greeks did. I wouldn't even know where to start if I had to mix iron gall ink as medieval monks did. Those parts of literacy training are now obsolete. But there are plenty of new technical factors that today's kids need to learn. So, perhaps we'd do well to emulate the ancient Sumerians and think of our schools as "computer houses." That way, we'd always consider the important questions: Have we adequately prepared our children to live a productive, ethical, and fulfilled life within the technological context in which they find themselves? Can they leverage the tools of the present era to fabricate a world that draws instrumentally on the values, wisdom, and ingenuity that has historically served humanity so well?

The Future of Self-Expression

My son was in third or fourth grade when he was first introduced to persuasive writing. His language arts teacher was not an overly zealous advocate for new technologies, but still, she seemed to recognize that they could help kids learn. She presented the classic rules of rhetoric by assigning him PowerPoint presentations to build.

The subject matter was his choice: *Star Wars* Jedi. He assembled an impressive collection of slide decks that described the experience of living a hero's life under the strong arm of the Galactic Empire. He developed research and analytic skills as he browsed through fan sites full of facts and figures, translated the info into bar graphs and pie charts, and then edited and organized all the material so that it flowed logically. Just as with a five-paragraph essay, he needed a thesis, three pieces of supporting evidence, and finally, a conclusion. He was learning about argumentation. And he was simultaneously honing his ability to read media from a critical perspective; it's only by constructing their own arguments that kids will learn to distinguish between sources, to separate real from fake, to recognize how and why other people craft messages the way they do.

At this point in my son's academic career, he had already seen me give presentations to large audiences, and so he was excited to emulate Dad. He would play "public speaker" and share his expertise with his classmates. I watched him focus on these projects for extended stretches of time, and I was impressed by his enthusiasm. Motivation is key, and his teacher knew it; that's why she let him pick the subject. She also recognized that the skills involved in argumentation can easily be separated from those needed to craft a sentence. She avoided the old-fashioned essay because she suspected that if rhetoric was tied too tightly to prose, one skill would become an obstacle to mastering the other. Instead, she compartmentalized the two competencies, and in the process added a third: PowerPoint skills. My son learned to create all kinds of complex animations and transitions with the software. He now operates the Microsoft Office Suite with ease.

At other times, she had him practice creative writing. Again, he picked the subject matter. The goal of these assignments was for him to get comfortable expressing himself in prose. Before instructing him in the technical aspects of writing, she just wanted him to become accustomed to using words. It's always through practice and repetition that one acquires fluency. He typed epic silly adventures about pirates and soldiers into his laptop. But there was very little description. Mostly, he just spelled out explosive sound effects, heroes and villains battling, their grunts and exclamations converted to dialogue.

"Ugh!"

POW!

"Go get him . . ."

"AAAAHHHHHHHHHHHHHHHHHH!"

BOOM!

"Phew."

"Run. Run. Go!"

He was transcribing imaginative play into type. He made the characters on the page behave the same way as the action figures that always seemed to be spread out on our living room rug. And I think that's precisely what his teacher wanted. She was using a pedagogical approach that educators call process writing.

Popularized during the 1970s progressive school movement, process writing is so named because it focuses on the process rather than the product. It asks *How* does writing happen? As opposed to *What* does it look like when it's done right? It is a nondirectional method in which the teacher acts like a facilitator or a guide rather than an authority or an expert. In the beginning, she gives as few prompts as possible. She just lets the kids go — lets them practice free writing. They shouldn't worry about making mistakes, correcting their work, or second-guessing their ideas. Not because grammar, spelling, and syntax don't matter. It's just that they don't belong in this phase of the process.

Supposedly, the method is derived from a study of how most writers ply their craft. First, they make room for the Muses. In just about every one of the hundreds of variations on process writing pedagogy, students start with some sort of "prewriting" or brainstorming work. This can involve telling stories, drawing comic books, or acting out skits. LEGO Education even makes special StoryStarter sets with bricks and pieces designed to encourage kids to invent their own tales. And I've met a few teachers who encourage their students to use *Minecraft* for this brainstorming work. Kids act out events in the virtual block world and then describe them to their peers. Afterward, they'll convert oral storytelling into prose — trying to write the way they'd talk.

Next, students move on to proofreading and editing. I doubt that anybody ever objected to using new tech for revising. We all realized very quickly that navigating a virtual document with a movable cursor, a backspace button, and copy/paste functionality was far superior to the alternative. I remember watching in awe as my father worked late into the evening on an early IBM Wheelwriter. It was a fancy typewriter with a small liquid crystal display that showed about three lines of low-resolution text in neon green letters. The machine had a bulky red chassis and a tiny memory. It could store only a few hundred words, which users could review before printing. Today it seems primitive. But back then, even a small child could see that word processing was the future. Unfortunately, nobody understood yet that business machines had a place in an elementary school classroom. My friends and I still had to copy out each draft of our stories by hand, extra neatly, getting a final version ready to "publish."

That's when the art teachers got involved. Not only did we illustrate our stories, but we also bound and sewed handmade books with colorful laminated covers and shiny tape reinforcing the spine. Bookmaking was a popular classroom undertaking in the 1980s because it complemented the process-writing curriculum. It was a creative endeavor that added fine arts and "handwork," like sewing, threading, and lacing—the same activities Montessori schools use to build kids' fine-motor skills, concentration, and self-confidence. You don't see much bookbinding anymore, now that art budgets are shrinking. But still, when I visit primary schools—especially in the United States and Europe—the hallways tend to be plastered with illustrated student stories. That too is a kind of publishing, putting work on display.

In today's tech-savvy schools, a computer specialist often helps where art teachers once did: students finish their process-writing projects by sharing creative work with family and friends via a flashy website or an online blog. These projects might include narrative or persuasive writing accompanied by digital illustrations, photographs, or animated GIFs. Sometimes the kids even write HTML code themselves, or at the very least they customize the stock themes on popular content management systems like WordPress, Tumblr, or Ghost. Big software companies, like Adobe and Microsoft, have designed utilities like Spark and Sway that make the process of creating short, animated, documentary-style videos simple enough that even the youngest kids can combine images, text, and voice-over to tell stories or share information. These are the new book reports; nobody should ever have another anxiety dream about standing at the front of the class and reading from index cards.

Process writing has been a standard pedagogical method used throughout the United States for decades. Grown-ups like it because it emphasizes the same values found in the sandbox: an appreciation of an uninhibited, separate, individual self where imagination and exploration meet practice and perseverance. Authorship becomes about creating not only sentences and paragraphs but also lifestyles, belief systems, and experiences. It is no accident that my son's writing reminded me of his action figures; the work was designed to cultivate the same skills as sociodramatic play. It was meant to help him discover a strong inner self and to develop a confident voice that can publicly articulate his distinct value in structured ways.

Fortunately, there are already some educators who understand that they can achieve comparable process writing outcomes while incorporating new tools. Moreover, they recognize that if they're teaching only with the old tools, they're being irresponsible. Today's kids need to learn to communicate using a combination of traditional and digital apparatus, because the process of self-expression cannot be separated from the instruments used to facilitate it. Remember Marshall McLuhan? The medium is indistinct from the message. Therefore, without teachers who intentionally integrate current technology into the learning experience, kids will never be able to cultivate the kind of fluency needed to make their creative expressions relevant in a connected world.

Constructing Fluency

If there's one educator who understood the importance of incorporating digital technology into the learning experience — even before most grown-ups had ever touched a personal computer — it was Seymour Papert. Around the same time that process writing was first becoming popular, Papert was working with colleagues at the Massachusetts Institute of Technology to develop a computer programming language called Logo. Logo was designed especially for children, and in its most memorable versions, a robotic contraption resembling a turtle rolls around on the floor.

Picture a transparent dome — glass or plastic — forming the carapace that covers motors, sensors, and circuit boards. The turtle drags a pen behind it and draws lines in response to simple computer code. Eventually, the physical turtle was detached from its ribbon cable and replaced with a virtual clone; the animal's silhouetted shell became part of the graphic interface. Now, a cute turtle-shaped cursor moves around the screen, leaving lines in its wake.

Kids type commands. Forward 30 (fd30) tells the turtle to take 30 steps. Right 90 (rt90) tells it to turn 90 degrees. Back 5 (bk5) sends it back five steps. Pen Up (pu) prepares it to move without drawing. As kids experiment with different ways of manipulating the turtle's movements, they learn to think about how angles and distances combine to create shapes. Imagine how easy it would be to draw an equilateral triangle with Logo. Make the turtle move forward, spin around, turn 60 degrees, move forward again, and repeat. Papert called this "turtle geometry," and it's a perfect example of how he believed digital technology should be used for learning. "When people talk about computers in education they do not all have the same image in mind," Papert wrote. "Some think of using the computer to program the kids; others think of using the kid to program the computer." In other words, he didn't want educators using computers to distribute information like robot teachers, nor did he imagine that learning to code was a kind of job training for a new economy. Instead, he saw the computer as an "object-to-think-with," sort of like Froebel's gifts.

Papert is probably the most influential thinker in the history of computer education, but I doubt he imagined himself as a computer educator. His background was in philosophy and mathematics.

Before arriving at MIT he was in Geneva, working with legendary psychologist Jean Piaget on questions of epistemology. Together, they were trying to understand how kids learn to think mathematically.

Piaget is famous for a very influential learning theory called *constructivism*. Put simply, constructivism describes the idea that kids are active participants in their own learning. They're not blank canvases on which grown-ups imprint information. They're not repositories for academic content. They're not like animals that can be trained through a simple system of bells, rewards, signals, and punishments. Instead, they are always interacting with their environments, testing ideas and hypotheses, constructing knowledge, and building social meaning systems. Think back to Chapter Two, where I described kids on the playground pretending to be space cowboys while also learning self-regulation and cultivating executive function through a process called *accommodation*. That's all part of Piaget's constructivism.

Seymour Papert drew his inspiration from Piaget's theory, but he expanded it into a theory of his own he called his *constructionism*. "I take from Jean Piaget a model of children as builders of their own intellectual structures," he wrote. But from there, he steered his turtle in a unique direction. To understand Papert's constructionism, think about all the things kids can learn completely on their own. "Children learn to speak, learn the intuitive geometry needed to get around in space, and learn enough of logic and rhetorics to get around parents — all this without being 'taught,'" Papert wrote in his book *Mindstorms: Children, Computers, and Powerful Ideas*. But what about all the things kids can't learn spontaneously? Why does some learning necessitate a more deliberate teacher-student relationship? Piaget assumed that it had to do with formality and complexity; certain ideas are just too difficult for kids to learn impulsively.

But Papert disagreed. "All builders need materials to build with," he insisted, pointing out that culture supplies adequate building materials for some types of knowledge but not for others. "The fact that so many important things (knives and forks, mothers and fathers, shoes and socks) come in pairs is a 'material' for the construction of an intuitive sense of number," he explained. The difficulty involved in learning some things is a result of what he called "the relative poverty of the culture." By this he means that we don't provide kids with enough building materials to construct certain kinds of ideas. But Papert was an optimist. He saw computers as a way to supply more; a programmable robotic turtle can provide the blocks needed to construct an understanding of many complex mathematical concepts.

One thing to notice about Papert's thinking is that the computer is secondary. Knowledge comes first. Sure, kids learn how to write code, but only so they can talk to the turtle. "In order to use a computer language you do not need to know how the computer works," he wrote, "no more than you need to know how a human brain works in order to give a person instructions. In both cases you need only know how to describe what you want in an appropriate language." In other words, Logo was not really about computer science. Technological fluency only facilitated mathematical literacy. The real learning happened as a result of tinkering and making. It was projects that mattered to Papert. He envisioned an education system in which all kids were making things all the time. Why? Because, as Mitch Resnick, director of the MIT Media Lab's Lifelong Kindergarten Group, explains, "As children construct things in the world, they construct new ideas in their heads, which motivates them to construct new things in the world, and on and on, in a never-ending spiral."

Resnick worked with Papert for many years. Together, they adapted Logo so it could be combined with LEGO bricks. Today's

LEGO Mindstorms products are the result of that work. They created the quintessential erector set, combining tangible and digital play into something way more complex and exciting than just a robotic turtle. Using LEGO Mindstorms, kids have built machines that solve the Rubik's Cube, play guitar, cook pancakes, and more. And in the process, they've figured out quite a bit about robotics, engineering, math, and physics. But what's most important is that kids found ways to use the tools of the times to express themselves creatively. To emphasize this, Resnick once told me that he sees coding as an extension of writing. "The ability to code allows you to 'write' new types of things — interactive stories, games, animations, and simulations," he said. "When people learn to write, they can share their ideas with the rest of the world. So too with coding."

Compare Papert and Resnick's way of thinking with the economic and politically motivated push to equip tomorrow's labor force with adequate computer skills for the new industrial revolution. It's all about job skills. And it's the wrong way to think about digital technology in education. Schools should not aim to teach kids how to code; they should make sure kids understand enough about the language of computing to be in control of the machines that now dominate our lives. Forget vocationalism; the majority of coding jobs will soon be automated anyway. But children will still need to understand the way computers work if they want to make informed and thoughtful choices about how to best contribute to a connected world.

Today's educators need to combine *technê* and *epistêmê* when designing pedagogy. They need to recognize that computational thinking is indistinguishable from computational expression. And that shouldn't be too hard to accept; after all, we already approach older expressive technologies in this way. "Even though most people don't grow up to become professional journalists or novelists, it's important for everyone to learn to write. So too with coding — and for similar reasons," explains Resnick. "Becoming fluent, whether with writing or coding, helps you to *develop your thinking, develop your voice,* and *develop your identity.*"

Clearly, he sees the computer as an instrument with which folks can develop a sandbox sense of self. That's why, along with a team of colleagues at MIT, he developed a platform called Scratch. It's a visual coding language that allows kids to create interactive stories, games, and animations by simply dragging and dropping commands into sequence — like Logo for the iPad generation. It's easy and intuitive to use. And although Resnick and his co-creators don't explicitly compare it to process writing, there are many similarities. For instance, every Scratch project begins as an exercise in open-ended imaginative tinkering. Although the coding language provides a limited collection of building blocks with which to develop a project — just as English provides a fixed set of words, grammar, and syntax — the possibilities for how they can be assembled are endless. As Marina Umaschi Bers explains, Scratch works like a playground, not a playpen. "Although playpens are safer, playgrounds provide infinite possibilities for growth and learning."

After brainstorming with Scratch there's a revision process, which consists of what computer programmers call debugging. Users need to isolate and identify any errors in the code, then iterate a sequence of commands in an attempt to fix it. We all undertake a similar process whenever solving a problem or completing a project. When writing a traditional paper, for example, students spend the revision process looking for "bugs" in their argument, trying to identify why their main point is not clear to the reader. Debugging may be one of the most important skills anyone can master. And coding projects provide some of the best opportunities for kids to practice it. Why? Because the computer always provides immediate feedback — the program either runs properly or it doesn't, there's no ambiguity. Imagine how much easier life would be if all our problems revealed their bugs so quickly.

Of course, the final step in process writing is publishing, and Scratch also makes it easy for kids to share their creations. At the time of this writing, Scratch had a community of more than 25 million registered users. Kids post their projects, provide feedback on one another's work, and learn together. This part is especially important to Resnick; he recognizes that a strong community of expressive and thoughtful playmates is the precursor to "a creative society," his term to describe a world where connected individuals can easily imagine ways to follow their interests, explore their ideas, and develop their voices. A creative society is made up of citizens who feel fulfilled because they can adapt to new instruments of self-expression. They can convey a sense of self, articulating their identities and making sure their productive output remains relevant, even in new technological and economic contexts.

Digital play should always encourage kids to perceive the technologies of a connected world as instruments they can command — not boxes that distribute content to be consumed or rigid systems that confine the shape of their communications. Children need to learn that the computer is a tool for creative self-expression, an opportunity to articulate a narrative of the self.

From Writing to Reading

In the summer between my older son's kindergarten and first-grade years, his teacher sent me a text message with photos of a few *Star Wars* picture books. She was excited that she had found stories that would stimulate my son. She knew that with these books, his reading would fall into place quickly.

At the time, I remember constantly talking to other parents who were worried that their children couldn't read yet. Of course, they blamed video games, iPads, and touchscreens. They wanted my opinion, since they thought of me as an expert. But I just repeated the same thing my son's teacher told me: it's all about keeping letters in front of kids, making them go through the motions. "Eventually, it just clicks," she would say, "at different times for different people. Don't worry. You'll see."

She was right. Now my son is twelve years old yet reads at a college level. But it didn't "just click." The truth is, his teacher did a lot more than wait. Picking specific books that he liked made it not only fun but also relevant. Which matters, because when it comes to reading, comprehension and context are just as important as sounding out the letters. Reading is not only a matter of technical skill. Kids also need to understand what they're reading about. Reading involves deciphering a code on the fly while filling in a bunch of meaningful details that text just can't express. Mark Seidenberg explains that we omit these details "because they are predictable from other things we know — about the topic, about the context in which a sentence occurs, about spoken language." Learning to read without any context would be like trying to put together a jigsaw puzzle without knowing anything about what the final picture was supposed to look like. You need hints. Likewise, young readers need to be exposed to the words before they try to sound them out.

The sounds, represented by letters, are what experts call *phonics*. The meanings, represented by words, are what they call *semantics*. No matter what the advertisements tell you, just getting kids "hooked on phonics" isn't enough to make reading easy. It is also critical that parents, teachers, and caregivers talk to babies, toddlers, and preschoolers all the time. And they should talk about a variety of topics. That's how children develop vocabulary; that's how they learn what words mean. Think about Seymour Papert's constructionism: kids need chances to experiment with intellectual building materials — to play with words, to make sure they understand them, to try various responses, to figure out how words work together to form ideas. Child development specialists call for "serve-and-response" interactions, instances when communication is going back and forth between grown-ups and children. For a long time, family dinner was the best opportunity for grown-ups to talk to their kids, and this is one of the reasons why experts love the evening meal so much; it has nothing to do with eating. The evidence is clear: young children who get more serve-and-response vocabulary-building opportunities end up better prepared to learn reading in kindergarten and first grade.

Of course, the teacher still needs to constantly set the stage. She needs to reinforce the mechanics of reading. Which direction should the eyes track across the page? What is a sentence? What is a word? What are those funny punctuation marks? She also needs to make sure the sounds of the words and the child's ability to understand their meaning is ready at hand. She picks a classroom theme for more than decoration. By focusing the lessons in every discipline on a common knowledge base, she creates opportunities for repetition. The names of the planets in the solar system will show up in more than science period. The students get used to hearing those words throughout the day, associating them with images and stories and meanings. And then, when it is time to read, sounding out M-A-R-S feels comfortable and familiar. The word makes sense in context, and it's right on the tips of their tongues.

Likewise, when my son plays *Minecraft,* the vocabulary of the block world is right on the tip of his tongue. Redstone, creeper, nether, enderman, mod, pickaxe, server, skin: these words are constantly scrolling through the chat stream. Therefore, when he was first learning to read and write, *Minecraft* was a blessing. Playing the game online made it easy for him to match semantics and phonics, and he was motivated to do it fast, because then the game was more fun. Reading and writing made the fantasy more real. Had we lucked into a perfect playground for practicing literacy skills? At this point, it's hard to know. There is very little good research about how screen-based interactions impact reading and writing. We do know that, as great as *Sesame Street* is, it doesn't build vocabulary as effectively as talking to a live person. But that is because there is no serve-and-response on television. Digital media is much more interactive. How do the differences between the virtual back and forth and the physical back and forth impact learning? We really don't know yet.

Here's what we do know: most of the everyday reading that my son and his friends will do as grown-ups will be screen based. And despite what the technophobes seem to think, screens are not in an antagonistic relationship with the written word. In fact, the opposite is true. Thanks to smartphones, today's society is more text dependent than it has ever been. More people read more words more often. Still, it's not books that they're reading. And some people think that because web-based interactions with text are so superficial, they herald the end of thoughtful literature. But folks think that only because they romanticize the past. They imagine a time when everyone read Plato and wrote thoughtful prose. That time never existed, not only because most people didn't read and write, but also because even those who did, enjoyed their fair share of pulp. For example, in Kyoto, around 1000 BCE, Murasaki's *Tale of Genji* — often recognized as the first great novel — was just a forbidden superficial soap opera about the Japanese royal court. It's only in retrospect that we recognize its brilliance. Likewise, Cervantes's *Don Quixote* was originally nothing more than a spoof on the trifling romance stories that folks were reading in the early seventeenth century. According to

Harvard literature professor Martin Puchner, *Man of La Mancha* was created as a cautionary tale: "If you read too much of the wrong kind of literature, Cervantes was warning, you will get hurt." But nobody got hurt. A few hundred years have passed, and now more people are literate than ever before. They also have better access to reading materials, both the "right" and the "wrong" kinds. In this regard, digital technology is a gift.

However, we do need to reorganize the school day so that it teaches children how to have more meaningful and discriminate engagements with words on screens. Already, it is not enough to teach kids to read only paper books; they also need to know how to transfer good reading strategies from the page to the screen. Right now, that's not being taught. Instead, folks in the developed world are debating whether or not digital reading is good for kids. Nobody is having that discussion in places with emerging economies — what we sometimes call the global south or the second and third worlds — because in these places, where the underprivileged have historically had little or no exposure to books, smartphones are like a godsend. Suddenly, the contents of the world's biggest and best libraries are available to people who have never had access before. In other words, the debate about digital reading is exclusively a first-world problem.

In the United States, digital naysayers constantly point to studies that show paper is better, while early adopters promote the research that supports digital reading. Both groups seem extremely susceptible to confirmation bias. After all, there are no adequate randomized trials on the differences between screens and paper. That would involve giving a test group of privileged kids as much lifetime exposure to screens as they currently have to paper. I mean that in terms of quantity, quality, and variety. Certainly, at this point, lots of kids start swiping an iPad at a very young age. But that's not the same thing. Think about how, from birth on, most grown-ups are not only providing their kids with positive reinforcement about books, but also showing them how to interact with words and crayons. Bedtime, daycare, preschool, and kindergarten all include ongoing ritualized interactions that celebrate text on paper. But there's a poverty of culture when it comes to words and ideas on screens.

The schools of the future will need to incorporate ritualized interactions with screen-based text. That is the only way that digital content will be transformed from superficial to meaningful. Why? Consider the way early childhood lessons in reading are already prepping our kids to engage with literature. We build their skills slowly, compounding one proficiency on top of another. For example, every time a kindergarten teacher asks the class questions about a picture book, it's about more than just reading comprehension. The students are learning that it is important to analyze text. They are also learning a lesson about technology. They are being taught that what is printed on paper is worthy of interpretation. But when you combine that lesson with the rules that limit computer time and exile smartphones from the schoolhouse, a problematic hierarchy of text is being created. Students learn that screen-based words are less serious than paper-based words. And that's troubling, because there's an urgent societal need for kids to learn new media literacy starting at a very young age.

Tweens and teens, for instance, need to know how to analyze the memes, videos, and narratives that they will inevitably encounter (and create) on the internet and in video games. Otherwise, their lack of familiarity and understanding will have political, economic, and personal consequences as they transition into adulthood. One cannot question the reliability of a digitally delivered political advertisement without being taught how the medium impacts the message. One cannot make informed purchasing decisions without first learning how to recognize a sales pitch facilitated by a predictive algorithm. And, perhaps most important, one cannot achieve a sense of personal fulfillment without being taught how to construct an identity narrative that can be fluently articulated using the predominant technologies of the time. All three of these ways of interacting with media need to be ritualized in the classroom of the future. That means teachers need to stop dismissing online content as if it's less meaningful than content traditionally printed on paper.

Remember what a lot of old-school literature actually is: artifacts created with obsolete communication technologies — missives, journals, manifestos, and more. It follows, then, that the future's quintessential pieces of literature are probably being published online as we speak. Don't believe me? Just ask yourself if you would want to look at Mark Twain's social media profile if he'd had one. Of course you would. Imagine the hilarious comments he'd make, the ironic status updates he'd share. Like so many great authors, Twain teaches us how to meaningfully engage with the world. And we, as teachers, share his wisdom with our students.

Think about Mark Twain's social-media presence next time you read one of those studies that say teenagers are unhappy, lonely, or depressed when they spend any amount of time online. Realize that the technology is not inherently soul-sucking or narcissistic. Instead, the problem is that grown-ups haven't yet figured out how to provide kids with adequate examples of living the good life online. Books have traditionally done that. First, we teach kids, through process writing, that a text represents an intensely honest personal narrative — it's an uninhibited, albeit edited, record of what went on inside an author's head. Great novels, even with unreliable narrators, are still cognitive maps of great writers' thinking. And these authors are people to emulate, people who know something about life that the rest of us may not.

Who are their online counterparts? They don't exist. Or at least they haven't been noticed yet. There is nobody for kids to emulate — no equivalent of Socrates, St. Augustine, Shakespeare, Flaubert, Kafka, or Mark Twain. No wonder kids don't know how to be happy in a digital world. We've let them loose, without guidance, in uncharted territory. We haven't taught them how to make sense of their online lives. They have no modeling or mentorship besides immature YouTubers. And therefore, they have little sense of etiquette, ethics, or expectations for existing in a virtual space.

The schools of the future need to embrace new forms of language arts instruction — new categories, new genres, new cultures, new kinds of assignments — because until we start to see digital engagements with screen-based text as a primary part of creative self-expression, until we integrate the digital humanities into the school curriculum, our kids will never be able to lead fulfilled lives in a connected world.

Takeaways

Teachers need to incorporate playful and imaginative projects that include digital components into their classrooms. That is how we will encourage kids to perceive the technologies of a connected world as tools for creative self-expression.

The knowledge, ideas, and values that we pass on to our children are useful only if they can be articulated using the tools of the time. All self-expression is instrumental; it requires tools. Rhetoric is the tool of the orator. Writing is the tool of an author. Even language itself can be understood as a kind of technology. An innovation that presumably disrupted the prehistoric grunt, words are just aural symbols that we use to construct and communicate complex ideas.

The ancient Sumerians taught their children to press reeds into clay tablets and therefore called their schools "tablet houses."

Perhaps we should call ours "computer houses." The goal of education is to prepare children to live productive, ethical, and fulfilled lives within the current technological context. But because of our long commitment to process writing, the technological aspect of self-expression has been shortchanged. We've come to take written language for granted, and we've forgotten that creativity is not only about discovering a strong inner self, but also about developing a confident voice that can publicly articulate an individual's distinct value using the tools of the times. Self-expression cannot be separated from the instruments used to facilitate it.

If grown-ups use only old tools in the classroom, they're being irresponsible. It's clear that today's kids need to learn how to use both traditional and digital technologies. And without teachers who intentionally integrate current tools into the learning experience, kids will never achieve the fluency needed to make their inner voices relevant in a connected world.

When all children practice learning in context, they will come to understand the benefits and challenges associated with the technologies around them. And this is what will really make them high achievers in the long run.

We are currently confused about the difference between what constitutes "health" and what constitutes obsolete technological proficiency. Why? Because many of our most familiar developmental milestones remain tied to specific tool sets. The schools of the future will need to adapt their standards to consider the demands that new technologies make on our kids' bodies. Swiping, tapping, and clicking are now the physical prerequisites to human autonomy.

At what age are kids ready to manipulate virtual objects in three dimensions? To connect nonlinear narrative elements? Not only to sort objects into colors and shapes, but also to recognize categorization as a step in the process of data analysis? We need to fully assimilate touchscreens, keyboards, and computers into the learning experience without getting stuck in the quicksand of nostalgic lament. It's good that we identify what's lost as we transition between one set of tools and the next, but it's also important to move beyond mourning and grievance. We desperately need to figure out ways to incorporate old values into new technological contexts.

In the same way that teachers have historically modeled good note-taking skills each time they scrawled a lecture's main points onto a chalkboard or a dry-erase surface, they must do the same with new tools. PowerPoint presentations alone are not enough. Add spreadsheets to the collection of mathematic manipulatives and even primary school kids can begin to build data sets. Draw flowcharts on the fly to demonstrate how to articulate an argument with algorithmic thinking. Build 3-D models with touchscreens. Create virtual dioramas using *Minecraft*. Show students how they can use a digital sandbox to play with ideas, reconsider content, organize concepts, and share epiphanies.

Grown-ups need to stop dismissing online content as if it's less meaningful than content traditionally printed on paper. Until we integrate the digital humanities into the school curriculum, our kids will never be able to lead fulfilled lives in a connected world.

Thanks to digital technology, today's society is more text dependent than ever before. More people read more words more often. But we've yet to adequately reorganize the school experience so that kids learn how to have meaningful engagements with words on screens.

For generations, we've bombarded children with ritualized interactions that celebrate text on paper. Every bedtime story, preschool alphabet song, and kindergarten book discussion teaches kids that words printed on paper are worthy of thoughtful interpretation. Yet there's a poverty of culture when it comes to screens. We are actively teaching our children that screen-based text and images are superficial and frivolous. And as a result, people's lack of digital media literacy contributes to political unrest around the world.

If grown-ups want to prepare children to analyze the memes, videos, and ideas they encounter on the internet and in video games, they will need to encourage more digital play, more creative online activities, more computer-based projects. This is the best way to address the issue of fake news. Through hands-on experience with digital rhetoric (beginning as early as possible), kids will learn to intuitively understand how the media artifacts around them are assembled. Teach kids how to construct an identity narrative that can be fluently articulated using the predominant technologies. Adapt the wisdom of finger painting and process writing pedagogy to the new tool set. Through a curriculum of digital argumentation, kids will learn to recognize how media can be coercive.

They will also become happier, more fulfilled citizens of a digital society. Despite what fearmongering research tries to suggest, technology is not inherently soul-sucking or narcissistic. The real problem is that we haven't provided our kids with images of a fulfilled online life. We haven't yet offered them the digital equivalent of great literature. Hence, our children don't know how to be happy in connected society, because we haven't taught them how to make sense of their online lives.

CHAPTER 9

THE NEW LEARNING OBJECTIVES

THE MINOANS WERE one of the ancient world's most innovative civilizations. Located on the island of Crete during the Bronze Age (circa 2000–1500 BCE), they are believed to have been one of Europe's oldest societies. They were governed, in a centralized way, from the palace at Knossos, a city that had paved roads, a sewer system, and the original phonetic alphabet. Some sources say the Minoans may have come up with the idea of constructing the kinds of straight walls and roofs that still frame our homes. Before that, folks lived in caves, mammoth-bone lean-tos, animal fur tents, and beehive-shaped mud-brick huts.

I like to imagine two citizens of Knossos, sitting beneath an olive tree outside the palace. They're admiring the stunning view of the Aegean Sea in the distance. One turns to the other and says, "I'm worried."

"Why?"

"Just look around," says the first as he takes a swig of wine from a ceramic vessel.

His friend admires the brightly painted goblet, thinking of the mariners who recently introduced the potter's wheel. The earliest thrown-clay jugs came from the Sumerian city of Ur, but the Minoans traded far and wide, and they always returned home with shiny new gadgets.

"How can we continue to adapt to this rate of change?" the ancient man wonders. "For hundreds of thousands of years, people have been hunters and gatherers, living in caves and huts. And now, in such a short period of time, we've not only invented walls, but also trade, a navy, centralized government, the alphabet —"

"People won't be able to keep up!" his friend interrupts.

"Yes, I know. And I can't imagine what's still to come. How will we ever prepare the children?"

Like many of us, they probably thought they were living at a time when the rate of technological progress was outpacing humanity's biological capacity to adapt.

But they were wrong.

And so are we.

A Rigid Commitment to Flexibility

Look back at history. Try to see how revolutionary the past once was. Consider what it must have felt like when the first buildings were constructed. Imagine how many different types of dwellings and shelters existed in Knossos before the Minoans finally settled on the labyrinthine three-story compound that archeologists finally unearthed. To people living at the time, each iteration must have felt as magnificent as the original iPhone seemed to us. Which suggests that in a few hundred years, when our progeny look back at the history of computing, they too will recognize only the biggest changes — those that managed to stand the test of time.

Someday, punch-card tabulators dug up from the ruins of IBM's headquarters in Armonk, New York, will appear to be random and inconsequential. Nobody will think about how those machines are descended from the nineteenth century's mechanical time clocks, how they comprised a critical stepping-stone on the way to quantum computing. The archeologists of the future may not even recognize how electric relays replaced punch cards, how vacuum tubes became diodes. They won't see the significance of keyboard input and the cathode-ray monitor. They won't remember teletype, the Pulsar digital wristwatch, or Hewlett-Packard's first handheld calculator, the HP-35, designed to fit in a shirt's breast pocket.

Forget incremental change; the entire history of the digital era will one day look like a single achievement. Artificial intelligence and bioengineering won't be part of the fourth industrial revolution. Instead, these things will show up in history's narrative as the purpose toward which the first three were always building — and eventually, they will all look only like tiny steps toward whatever comes after the postmodern age. Change seems superfast while you're living in it, but in retrospect it always appears to take hundreds, if not thousands, of years.

The shifts and transformations we're currently living through are certainly significant, and they have huge ramifications for today's schoolchildren. But don't believe that technological change is outpacing humanity's ability to adapt. That story robs education of its potential and gives the tools way more autonomy and credit than they deserve. The truth is that they deserve none: we built them, they're not building us. Moreover, they already constitute a kind of adaptation. They represent our ongoing wish to address the shortcomings of the technological, economic, and social paradigms of the past. Innovative tools are always how we, as a species, satiate our desire to find new (and hopefully better) ways to approach time, place, communication, trade, storytelling, identity.

The overly cautious narrative that warns about the pace of

progress is nonsense. And counterintuitively, it serves to bolster the tech industry's growth. It encourages blind adoption. It prepares us to surrender to a specific technological destiny. Consider Moore's Law, a popular theory named after Gordon E. Moore, who cofounded the Intel Corporation. He noticed in 1965 that engineers were "cramming more components onto integrated circuits" at a rate that seemed to double exponentially year after year. But Moore didn't call his idea a law, at least not in the original paper he wrote for *Electronics* magazine. That's because it is not a law in the accepted scientific sense of the word — not a law of nature or a physical law of the universe. Instead, it's just one man's projection of how an industry might grow as the costs of manufacturing drop. Still, Silicon Valley loves branding Moore's hypothesis as a law and referring to it often. Why? Because it creates the impression that computer processing power will sweep through our lives like the Fates and the Furies. It reinforces a mythology in which tools are portrayed like gods — a story that serves the tech industry well, because when consumers believe it, they don't ask how humans want to use the tools, they ask how the tools want to use the humans.

Notice how the same dangerous framework underlies the current debate about school reform. All over the globe, I've taken part in conversations about how schools should adapt to the perceived inevitability of rapid technological change. Conference moderators often ask me how we can future-proof our children. Of course, they don't say it that way. Instead, they ask what are the most important "twenty-first century skills." For at least thirty years, researchers, foundations, governments, and nonprofits have all been producing reports that identify the key proficiencies for a new century. Each list is slightly different, improving on the previous one. And they all seem to share a common refrain: flexibility, adaptability, and creativity are essential competencies for the future. But we're almost 20 percent of the way through a new century! How can we still be saying our job is only to equip children with flexibility skills that prepare them to creatively adapt to an economy that we grown-ups can't yet imagine? That's not a solution — that's just grown-ups evading responsibility, avoiding the problem and outsourcing the hard work to future generations. Of course "adaptability" is important, but it can't be the answer. When someone asks what skills our kids need in order to adapt, it makes no sense to reply that they need to be adaptable. That's a tautology, self-referential and meaningless.

Furthermore, flexibility, adaptability, and creativity are not uniquely twenty-first-century skills. The future has always been uncertain. Even in 500 BCE, living in a seemingly slower-paced world, Heraclitus of Ephesus recognized that "nothing is permanent except change." Unpredictability is not unique to our time. Nor is the current rate of progress exceptional. Flexibility, adaptability, and creativity have always been what it takes to future-proof our children. These are also the very reasons we send them to school in the first place. We know that the past is full of wisdom, ingenuity, and ideas that need to be transmitted from one generation to the next. We also know that values, skills, and concepts will need to be creatively reimagined and adjusted so that they remain meaningful and applicable even in ever-changing contexts.

Vannevar Bush put it nicely in his famous 1945 essay, "As We May Think" — a work that's often cited as the conceptual inspiration for the Hypertext Transfer Protocol (HTTP) that drives the World Wide Web. As the first U.S. presidential science advisor, Bush initiated the Manhattan Project and lobbied Congress to establish the National Science Foundation. He knew, even decades before the internet existed, that information technologies are useful only to the extent that they ensure that "knowledge evolves and endures throughout the life of a race rather than that of an individual." Even though he never saw his vision of the future realized, Bush somehow understood exactly what twenty-first-century grown-ups often forget: the internet is a memory tool. It's an instance of humans adapting to their biological shortcomings.

Just imagine how hard things must have been for our prehistoric ancestors: hunters and gatherers who relied on the mind's limited capacity to access and organize knowledge, to retain and articulate information, to retrieve and regurgitate collective narratives. One needed to know which plants to eat and which to avoid, which trails were safe and which were dangerous, which neighboring tribes were friendly and which were enemies. One needed the mythology, the knowledge, and the stories to survive. But even when equipped with the best mnemonic devices humans could contrive, the brain has its limitations. We tend to forget things. That is why the people of Sumer and Knossos figured out how to write stuff down. They were designing the first tools to address our species' biological propensity for absentmindedness. They preserved an accessible record of the things they knew so that their offspring could apply foundational knowledge and wisdom to a world that was always changing. They prepared their kids to be adaptable, flexible, creative. These are not twenty-first-century skills. They are the reason we started writing things down in the first place.

Data, Information, and Knowledge

An archeologist once occupied the office next to mine at Temple University. She kept a real Sumerian cuneiform tablet on her desk next to her computer. She used it in class, to show folks what the markings looked like. She'd pass the ancient artifact around the room, letting students hold it. They would rub their fingertips along the surface of the pale-brown hardened clay. She would explain that the object in their hands was a receipt, an account of some small trade made between merchants in one of the earliest urban economies.

Writing began as currency, IOU tokens with pictures of things to be traded: grain, sheep, fish, bread. Coins were the initial pictographic signs. And the earliest human documents are all checklists, precursors to the modern spreadsheet, with notches and symbols that account for the contents of cellars and storehouses. Knossos and Sumer generated thousands of these receipts, coupons, and inventory reports. They wrote everything down. They were the first bureaucracies, dependent on comprehensive centralized accounting, reliant on tools and technologies designed for memory and recall.

Historians generally make a distinction between ancient inventories and the first pieces of literature—between receipts and stories. But in a connected world, I'm not sure that distinction makes much sense anymore. We need to teach our children how to live with networked tools that were built for interacting with data and information in a more fluid, transactional, hyperlinked, and nonlinear way. They need to understand that the dichotomy between the quantitative sciences and the qualitative humanities is built on a false premise. These disciplines are far more similar than they are different. Both are ways of taking human experience into account. Both record the knowledge on which people depend. Math, physics, biology, and chemistry serve the same fundamental purpose as history, poetry, mythology, and literature. Each is a language that humans use to articulate the experiences we've had and to designate the possibilities we can imagine. Certainly, various disciplines describe different things in different ways—and throughout this book, I've discussed the degree to which the medium shapes the message. But for now, let's put differences aside and focus on what all knowledge systems have in common. They aim toward the same ends: taking inventory, communicating data, articulating experience, sharing information, trading knowledge.

To understand what I mean, just think about how knowledge is constructed. It all starts with data. And once data is observed, defined, categorized, represented, and then retrieved, it becomes information. After that, it may or may not transition into knowledge. Consider the random light from the setting sun. It reflects and refracts: blue wavelengths scatter away as the red ones are filtered through the thickest part of the atmosphere. You know this because humans were inspired to make some sense out of the changing colors that filled the sky. We recognized patterns. We labeled the phenomenon in ways that made it easy to describe. Raw sensory stimuli were represented with the word "sunset." It became the end of Helios's daily journey across Uranus's vast sky. It became a painting by Monet with the dome of Venice's San Giorgio Maggiore monastery silhouetted in the distance. It became a Walt Whitman poem singing "the endless finales of all things." It became photons absorbed by gas, waves of light bent through a molecular prism.

Which characterization matters most? That depends on the frameworks people learn in school and how they apply them. In history class, my son reads Homer, discovering that the ancient Greeks believed Helios "shines from his horse-drawn car." In art class, he becomes familiar with impressionist brushstrokes. In his English literature class, he recognizes how *Leaves of Grass* challenged the Victorians by introducing sensory pleasure into the romantic era. In chemistry, he's taught to distinguish among liquids, solids, and gases. And his physics teacher explains that photons behave as both waves and particles. Each discipline is a code, a way of taking account of the colors in the sky, a language that my son learns to speak and decipher. Then, equipped with various frameworks, he can easily exchange ideas with others. He can trade observations. Information becomes currency.

Whenever humans collectively agree on a shared way of encoding and decoding our accounts of the world, information is transformed into knowledge. "Knowledge is information that a person possesses in a form in which he or she can make immediate use," says Keith Devlin, an internationally celebrated mathematician who now works as executive director of Stanford University's Human Sciences and Technologies Advanced Research Institute. "In the twenty-first century, no citizen will be able to function properly without a basic understanding of information, and an appreciation of what is required to turn information into knowledge." I like the way Keith says things. He knows how to pinpoint exactly what people are intuiting when they identify adaptability, flexibility, and creativity as the key skills needed for a connected world. They're really talking about the ability to modify the languages, codes, and information systems of the past so they remain relevant, so they keep their status and utility as knowledge, even in changing contexts. That's the real solution to the twenty-first-century skills problem: school needs to prepare kids to put old knowledge into new information management systems.

Unfortunately, most of our current educational conventions do the opposite. It's like we're putting iPads into a filing cabinet. We're preparing children with an understanding of data, information, and knowledge that's already obsolete. Perhaps it's because we're still infatuated with the information innovations of the past.

Card Catalogs

When Melvil Dewey introduced his decimal system in the late nineteenth century, it disrupted the way libraries operated. Before Dewey, they organized books akin to the way I keep them on the small table beside my big armchair. They're stacked high according to the order in which they arrived. The spines face outward, and when I'm ready to read, I just pull a volume from the pile. Pre-Dewey libraries were only slightly more sophisticated. Upon acquisition a book would be assigned a number and then placed in the next empty slot on the shelf. To find what you were looking for, you browsed through a catalog organized by subject. The catalog listed the location of each hardcover — for example, *The Castle* by Franz Kafka might be book number 4023, stored in the far section of a long room. There was no relationship between the book's topic and its placement. Two titles by Kafka might have been stored on opposite sides of the same building.

It may sound crazy to us now, but it makes sense. If texts are meant to be a record of knowledge, why not organize them chronologically? After all, this accentuates a document's place in the historic timeline. It prioritizes age over subject matter; knowledge builds on its own foundation. But it's inefficient. Each time the collection outgrows its shelves, you need to move everything from one space to another, and that involves assigning a new number to every book. Dewey's system was a revolution. It flipped things around. He divided the library into topics and assigned each book a code that corresponded to a thematic category. Readers could browse the stacks the same way they'd browse the catalog. They learned that when it comes to ideas, subject matter and individual authorship are more important than historical chronology.

I learned how to use libraries in primary school. Dewey's system was a kind of tech literacy, and we had a class dedicated to it. We'd line up to trek down the hallway, arriving at the big room full of books on the second floor. There we were taught how to find what we wanted, how to decode a string of letters, dots, and numbers. After the librarian finished her weekly lecture, I'd head toward the large oak cabinet beside her desk. The card catalog was organized by subject, author, and title — three cross-referenced cards per book.

To reach the drawers, I had to stand on a round Cramer footstool designed so its wheels would roll smoothly until it was stepped on. A person's weight caused the outside rim to sink into the carpet and stabilize the platform. I remember feeling the rubberized nonslip tread against the bottoms of my high-top sneakers as I'd open one of the twenty or thirty little rectangular drawers. Inside was an impossibly long collection of notched cards that flipped, at an angle, back and forth. At the time, it reminded me of the Rolodex my father had on his desk at work. He turned the blue knob on the side to fan through indexed contact cards about the size of ancient clay tablets.

There was a time when everything was indexed on paper or card stock. That's why, in study skills class, I was taught to write down one fact per card as I read through entries in the *World Book Encyclopedia*. The teacher explained that I could easily arrange these note cards into a school report. She told us to organize them first into piles — to put rubber bands around related facts. Then we were supposed to pin them on a corkboard in the order that made the most sense. But I never quite understood what she meant. The assignment seemed silly. None of my primary school research involved enough information to make a complex filing system seem necessary. Index cards just created more work, so I never used them. I didn't understand that my teacher was trying to help me become acquainted with the information management systems that were, at the time, an inescapable element of grown-up professional life.

Index cards, and the repository filing systems they facilitate, predate Melvil Dewey by more than a century. They were invented around 1760 by Carl Linnaeus, the Swedish scientist who gave us modern taxonomy. The classifications we use for plants, animals, and minerals are connected to the information technologies that belonged to the era in which they were conceived. Linnaeus devised a way to organize the natural world so that it adhered to his set of organizational tools — or maybe he designed a set of tools so that they adhered to his vision of the natural world. Either way, index cards are underrated. The ability to easily maneuver through an information database — to expand a collection of knowledge by adding a file without disrupting the overall order — deserves to be celebrated as an astoundingly influential achievement.

Recognize the degree to which Linnaeus's humble innovation shaped our habits of mind. Now, anyone who completes a card catalog education is likely to develop a repository sense of self. The procedural rhetoric of our most familiar routines and traditions guarantees it. We learn that we can rearrange, expand, and shuffle the contents of our minds, but we never stop filling up our intellectual storehouses. Our memories, experiences, and ideas simply compound like the interest in our checking accounts. That's why the great Brazilian educator Paulo Freire called it the banking model, in which "the educator's role is to regulate the way the world 'enters into' the students." All the conventions of school, with the measured outcomes that fit neatly into file cabinets, teach us to see ourselves from a repository perspective. The neat division of knowledge into subject-matter categories, with names that fit on tabbed dividers, belongs to this technological way of thinking. Likewise, end-of-semester grades, course credits, and the way we account for individual student achievement are all products of Linnaeus's filing system.

All student scores were once recorded on index cards sized to fit perfectly into Kardex-brand cabinets. That's where the term "report card" comes from. The history of school is tethered to an information-management system and imbued with the organizational spirit of industrial bureaucracy. Centralized accounting, accomplished by the logic of Linnaeus's index cards, is also the real reason why we have standardized tests. Everyone hates them: teachers, administrators, parents, students. I've never met anyone who is in favor of standardized tests — and I've talked to the CEOs of companies that profit from writing and grading them. Testing is a $2 billion industry, but even its beneficiaries recognize the Kafkaesque absurdity. All grown-ups complain about "overtesting" and "teaching to the test." Exams make students hate their studies and teachers hate their teaching. Tests are poor and often inaccurate assessments of learning. But learning has nothing to do with why we test. We test because exams produce the kind of data that fills the filing cabinets on which bureaucracies depend. Critics can decry the faulty metrics all day long. They can complain about the rubrics standardized tests use to measure intelligence and/or cognitive development. It will make no difference; everyone already knows.

Educators like to resist testing by distinguishing between formative and summative assessments. Formative assessments are done on an ongoing basis throughout the learning process, whereas summative assessments happen at the end. The formative kind are great for learning because they provide a lot of feedback. And when a student can easily recognize where he's succeeding and where he's failing, it's easy for him to adapt his approach — another example of practical, iterative debugging. Alternatively, summative assessments, such as the final exams that constitute a disproportionate share of one's overall grade, don't provide students with any opportunities to iterate their performance. The grade comes down like a judge's gavel and often determines the track on which a student's life can continue. Formative assessments, combined with regular feedback, are the foundation of all good teaching. Summative assessments are the necessary instruments of thriving bureaucracies.

My son's kindergarten teacher did a ton of formative assessment. She was pretty much always checking precisely what my son was learning and how he was performing. Sometimes she did it using quizzes and written questionnaires, but most times she evaluated him by intuition; she just had a feeling — but one based on heaps of data, evidence, and information. She saw his *Star Wars* PowerPoints, his time-telling worksheets, the way he measured the rug, and the silly stories full of battles, explosions, and sound effects. Working with about sixteen other kids, she could always tell if a student was misunderstanding the material. A serious marathon runner, she used her hours of afterschool training to meditate on each day's academic events and kept copious notes of her musings — narratives, anecdotes, and personal journal entries full of questions and ideas about how to adjust her teaching on a day-to-day basis. In this way, she made sure everyone was always caught up. But how could she efficiently demonstrate this to the school principal? How would the principal show it to the superintendent? How would the superintendent present it to the mayor? How would the mayor show it to the governor? How would the governor show the federal Department of Education that all the students in a commonwealth or province were learning at an adequate pace? There's only one solution: you need receipts, tokens of accountability — the kind of data and documentation that fits into a file cabinet, a paper trail proving how every child gets the schooling she deserves. For a government, education is not only a prerequisite to equal opportunity; it's also the way a nation trains a workforce to keep an economy thriving. The state's survival depends on its instruments of bureaucratic accountability. And so far, standardized tests have been the best-known way to report educational outcomes to a centralized agency.

Luckily, that's changing. Soon, video games and other digital activities will bridge the gap between formative assessment and centralized accounting. These activities will produce so much data about its players' competencies that standardized testing will seem archaic. Reams of digital information will make the assessments of the past seem naively reductionist. And once the final trace of

Linneaus's index cards has been eradicated from educational accounting, new pedagogical traditions will transcend the limitations of tiny drawers on tall oak cabinets.

I can see that it's already happening every day on my way to class. I walk by a construction site on Temple University's campus. We're building a new library where most of the books will be housed in a giant underground warehouse. Only 10 percent of the collection will be displayed on traditional shelves. For the rest, students and faculty will use touchscreens and computer terminals to browse the catalog, and then a robotic BookBot crane will fetch their choices from huge steel and aluminum racks 48 feet tall and 119 feet long.

I've overheard my colleagues complain that the new system will eliminate the old romantic pleasure of browsing the stacks. "We find so many of the best sources by accident," they say wistfully. And it's true — at least until virtual-reality headsets become commonplace — that we may lose certain instances of serendipitous discovery. But before we cling to the familiar conveniences of one technological era, we should probably consider what's to gain in another. Remember: perusable shelves are not an eternal or essential characteristic of the library experience. They were only the norm for about a century. Plus, the discoveries you made were never as random as they seemed, because the categories, sections, and subjects were officially defined by a firm called Dewey Services. Specific books only neighbored others when an expert had already decreed that their subject matter was correlative. But soon that will change. Librarians, professors, and even students will be able to curate their own virtual stacks.

Sure, the BookBot system is a shift away from what's familiar, but it offers a much better solution for our times. Why? I can think of at least four reasons. First, because it takes up far less space, enabling the university to make more tomes available to readers. Second, it guarantees that the books will be stored properly in a humidity- and temperature-controlled environment. Third, lazy researchers — who are burnt out from hours of note-taking and too tired to walk back up a flight of stairs — will no longer return items to the wrong place.

But what's most significant about robotic retrieval is that it allows for much more elaborate cross-referencing. When browsing is not confined by the physical laws of space, tangible books can be hyper-linked with the same ease as web pages. On digital shelves, a single copy of the same volume can be filed as psychology, philosophy, education, and cultural studies — all of them at once. It makes no difference to the BookBot; cross-referencing won't slow it down. Hence, a new kind of discovery is likely to emerge, one akin to the web-surfing rabbit hole I often fall into. And from the students' per-spective, this transition away from indexed repositories and toward intricate information exchange represents a new way to think about organizing knowledge.

Eventually, it will even herald a new way to imagine the self.

File Cabinets of the Future

Regardless of how libraries organize their collections, one thing is certain: strictly speaking, the books on the shelves contain no infor-mation. "They contain pages," writes Keith Devlin. "Similarly, those pages carry various markings, but no information."

At first, it may seem like he's quibbling about semantic details, but I assure you, he's not. This distinction is an important part of something called situation theory, which says that the letters, words, and pictures in books are only representations of information. Unless a "cognitive agent" has the adequate means with which to decode them, letters and numbers are just meaningless squiggles. Literacy and numeracy work like Buck Rogers's decoder rings; they're tools designed to let people access the information represented by marks on a page. Likewise, all the other traditional academic subjects can be understood as protocols and processes for deciphering meaning from representative data. They're just like the frameworks we use to understand sunset, the indexes with which we categorize species, and the report cards we use to describe our kids' intellectual achievements. And like all tool sets, they have limitations and biases. Each discipline intentionally filters out parts of the human experience, adding constraints. That's not a bad thing; it's a necessary thing. In the same way that a video game uses rules to create meaning, information exists only because of representations of data that are squeezed into certain kinds of boxes.

School teaches students how to extract information from those boxes. Not only do kids learn to read and write, but they also learn other kinds of processes and protocols for dealing with particular data sets. For example, in history class we teach kids how to interpret the events of the past so that they provide some information about how to understand the present. In framing a historic narrative, we're intentionally constraining data in specific ways. Often, we're trying to tell a nationalistic story. Think back to your high school world history class and imagine how differently the textbook would be written if the Nazis hadn't been defeated and you were living in a country controlled by the Third Reich. Your history lesson would have had an entirely different set of constraints.

Likewise, consider what's happening in this book when I describe sandbox play as the beginning of the age of the individual, dinner as the ritualized celebration of industrialization, television as a new hearth, clockwork mechanics as the foundation of twentieth-century developmental health, penmanship as up-skilling for a burgeoning capitalist economy, and card catalogs as a representation of an obsolete epistemological attitude. I'm situating the familiar technologies of the past in a hopeful story about a digital future — a future that requires folks to understand information in a drastically new way. If the old education cultivated habits of mind for a card-catalog world, then the new education needs to build habits of mind for a world of nonlinear hyperlinks. Luckily, situation theory can help.

"Situation theory is a mathematically inspired attempt to understand the role of context in human activities," Keith told me. He started working at Stanford University's Center for the Study of Language and Information shortly after Jon Barwise and John Perry developed the theory in the early 1980s. "Everyone was talking about the information economy," he said, "and we realized that there wasn't yet an adequate scientific theory to explain what information actually was — people were building these machines and this software that could process an abstract thing called information, but no one could really define it." Situation theory provided a framework. It showed that a stream of informational stimuli gets assembled into a meaningful story only when placed in a context. Contexts are situations that play a particular role. And the information we're able to draw from data is always dependent on the way the context situation constrains it.

But that description is still a little abstract. One way to make it more concrete is to think about the difference between digital and analog technologies. Today, we use the word "analog" to describe anything that is not digital. It refers to the opposite of computer technology. But that doesn't do justice to the original meaning of the word. Analog comes from the Greek *analogos* (αναλόγως). *Ana* (ανα) means "again." Listen to the ancient prefix informing modern English words like "anew" and "another." *Logos* (λόγος) means order, reason, systems, or language. It is where we get the word "logic" and the suffix "-ology" that names many of our current academic disciplines: psychology, theology, biology, sociology. Put the two terms together and *analogos* describes something that has comparable structure, something that repeats the arrangement of another thing. Hence, the metaphors and similes we often use in everyday conversation are called "analogies." Likewise, when a song is recorded using old-school methods like magnetic tape or vinyl records, we call it an "analog recording." Why? Because the electric charges, or the cut grooves, reproduce the sound waves of the music originally played. Think back to those graphs your high school physics teacher showed you. The curvy lines represented the shape of a wave. When magnetic pulses blast through your hi-fi system, the speaker-cone vibrations mimic the exact pitch and frequency of the original sound wave.

Have you noticed that today's digital audio apps sometimes include wave-form visualizations? They consist of little squiggly lines, or a series of rectangular towers that look like a city's silhouetted skyline. If you're using SoundCloud, for instance, white bars scroll along the bottom of the display, turning orange as time passes. That image is counterfeit, just a graphic designed to enhance your user experience. What you see is only a rough estimate of peaks and dips in volume. There is no device, like a record player's needle or the head of a 1980s cassette deck, that can read SoundCloud's wave form and play the music back again. That's because it is digital, not analog. Whenever music is digital — read by a laser from a compact disc, or streamed on the web through a platform like Spotify — the code does not represent sound itself. Instead, it provides compressed instructions that are processed algorithmically, telling your device what to play and how to play it. It is all just encoded bits. Ones and zeroes. Digits.

A digit is any number less than ten, any number I can count on my fingers. The Latin word *digitalis* means "having to do with fingers." It is a term that was related to music, specifically piano, long before it had anything to do with numbers. I think about the word every afternoon when my nine-year-old bangs away on the same old Estey wooden upright piano I practiced on when I was his age. He is currently learning to play the theme from the *Super Mario Brothers* video games. It involves mastering complex timings and syncopated rhythms. He strikes a key and there are about thirty mechanical parts engaged. They are made of wood, steel, copper, felt. His finger touches B-flat and drives a counterweighted hammer to hit its strings. The tone is crisp, the volume controlled by the force of his touch. It works perfectly. Piano technology has barely changed over the past few hundred years because it doesn't need to; the instrument is a masterpiece of mechanical engineering. It has no electric impulses, no signals, no code, and no numbers. But the piano is still technically *digitalis*. All keyboard instruments are literally "digital," because you play them with your fingers.

The letters you tap on your laptop and desktop computers are descended from the piano's keyboard. First, the typewriter, of course — but before that, the piano. An 1867 issue of *Scientific American* actually described an early "Type Writing Machine" as the "literary piano." It was fitting, because some of the very first prototypes were built from repurposed piano keys. Those familiar round ebony Remington buttons — the ones with the chrome border that you see on antique typewriters — didn't show up until a few years later. They were designed by Christopher Latham Sholes to mimic the circular polished surface of a telegraph knob. It was part of his marketing strategy. Typewriting's early adopters were the operators who transcribed electronic signals from Morse code into type. That is also how the QWERTY layout came to be a standard and ubiquitous part of our children's lives, sliding up on their smartphone screens whenever they thumb-type a WhatsApp message. Originally, the letters were positioned to help telegraph operators transcribe beeps and clicks into type more swiftly.

Oddly, however, Morse code's beeps and clicks tell us more about why mathematicians called very early computer technology "digital" than any finger-operated keyboard does. There were no keyboards on the first computers. Punched film and magnetic tape were the preferred methods for inputting instructions. Computers were called "digital" because they relied on Boolean algebra, a system of logic based on philosopher Gottfried Wilhelm Leibniz's study of the *I Ching* (the ancient Chinese *Book of Changes*). The duality of *yin* and *yang* is the real inspiration for the code that now articulates complicated mathematical expressions with just two binary options: on/off, one/zero, yes/no, true/false. Just like Samuel Morse's dashes and dots, everything on your kids' smartphone screen is constructed symbolically from the combination of two choices, two numbers, two *digits*.

But a string of digits is only useful if you have a tool that can extract meaning from the bits — something like an iPhone, a browser window, a virtual-reality headset, or a 3-D printer. Of course, analog technologies also required secondary devices that could translate stimuli into meaning. You needed a record player or a cassette deck to play a vinyl phonograph or a magnetic tape. And to make music, my son depends on ebony and ivory piano keys to strike a hammer against tuned strings. But neither of these old-school technologies requires a process of data conversion. So, a mathematical theory of information isn't really necessary to understand how they work. In an analog world, it's fine to imagine that records contain music and that books and index cards hold ideas. But now we use bits — ones and zeroes — to transmit coded instructions to machines that convert them into all kinds of things: sounds, pictures, maps, games, even 3-D printed objects. Essentially, those machines are providing context, delivering representations of data into meaningful situations. They take digits and convert them into information that we can utilize as knowledge.

When we understand information from the perspective of situation theory, it's easier to transmit, exchange, and cross-reference ideas. It also prepares us to teach students to see themselves like web browsers and 3-D printers. They are cognitive agents who decode representations of data into meaningful projects. They add the constraints of character, put things in personal boxes, and create situated contexts based on their values and opinions. Kids should no longer imagine themselves as isolated repositories filled to the brim with academic content. Instead, let them know that they are nodes of connection — points at which the transmission of human wisdom can intersect across time and space.

The New Math

When I first met Keith Devlin, he was in the early stages of developing a video game called *Wuzzit Trouble,* which was the long-term consequence of the work he did with situation theory some thirty years ago.

Picture a clockwork apparatus that turns by specific increments, virtual gears that you nudge forward and back. To solve each puzzle, a player figures out exactly how many teeth a cog must turn to end up in a specific spot. It's all about understanding intervals and becoming familiar with integer partitions. When large numbers are understood as the sum of their smaller counterparts, you're dealing in "number theory." That's the name of the branch of mathematics that has replaced arithmetic. It goes all the way back to ancient Sumer and Knossos. Few if any of the foundational human concepts have changed, but the methods we use to situate and articulate them, the ways we give them meaning in context, are always adapting. You don't grab a clay tablet full of number tables anymore. You don't use an abacus. Now you can just download *Wuzzit Trouble* to your smartphone.

It's a fun game; I've used it to pass the time on many otherwise unbearable long-haul flights. I also try to get my kids to play it as often as they're willing, because there's evidence that it will help them improve their math scores. One study showed that after just two hours of game play — conducted in ten-minute increments at the end of class—students' math problem-solving skills increased considerably. How? According to Keith, it's because it works like a piano. No, not because the game is digital—although, like all touchscreen games, you do play it with your fingers. But that's not what Keith has in mind. He compares the game to a piano because, in the same way a child can fiddle at the ivories and learn something about music, a child can fiddle with *Wuzzit Trouble* and learn something about math. Keith calls it a mathematical instrument because he thinks of it not as a game that teaches math but rather as a gamelike representation of an actual mathematical process. Just as one "plays" music on a piano, one can also "play" math on *Wuzzit Trouble*. A piano gives you immediate feedback about resonance and dissonance. You can experience the boundaries of harmony, counterpoint, and rhythm. Likewise, *Wuzzit Trouble* gives you immediate feedback about how numbers relate to one another. Through trial and error, a player strengthens her number sense.

The term "number sense" might be unfamiliar, especially if you're not a math teacher. But anyone who deals with kids should probably know what it means. Number sense is one of the most important things your children will need to learn in a twenty-first-century math class. And it looks different from what you remember studying during your student days. Ever wonder why there are so many social-media memes complaining about "the new math"? It's not because math itself has changed. It is because kids now come home with assignments that look strange—problems that don't have clear right and wrong answers. The grown-ups in their lives don't understand the worksheets. "Why can't my child do the same kind of math that has served me so well?" they ask. It's because math education is already adapting to a connected world.

With new contexts come new ways for cognitive agents to decode old data into new information. And often, in the process, the old applications become irrelevant. Already many grown-ups, for example, who currently hold advanced degrees in mathematics, can't be sure that their skills will remain valuable as technological, cultural, and economic changes continue to take hold. In fact, Keith would be the first to tell you that most of the math skills he learned as an undergraduate math major are now obsolete. Math teachers traditionally taught people how to solve equations, how to tabulate answers. We memorized the best ways to process numbers, and our minds became stainless-steel tool cabinets full of algorithmic wrenches, screwdrivers, and hammers. But we don't need to own those tools anymore; we can borrow them. "All the formulas and procedures that for many centuries have constituted the heart of a university mathematics degree have now been automated and are freely available on sites such as Wolfram Alpha," Keith explains. We don't talk about it much, but math jobs were among the first to be replaced by automated digital tools. There was a time when research labs and engineering firms all relied on roomfuls of people who could solve equations by putting a pencil to paper. That time has passed.

Of course, that doesn't mean math education is going away. Since ancient times, math has been among the most relevant knowledge systems humans can use to describe their world. And it will likely remain so. But when the most complicated mathematical procedures can be handled with very little expertise, the important skill becomes understanding the possibilities well enough to wield the tools of the time effectively. And cultivating that skill requires practice.

The old math class was also about practice. I can still remember doldrums of workbook pages completed night after night at the kitchen table. My teachers assigned what Keith calls toy problems, drills and exercises designed to help me memorize certain procedures and protocols. Like a piano player who practices scales to lock intervals into his muscle memory, we practiced executing algebraic operations until we could solve for variables without even thinking. It became second nature. And it was the right way to teach math at the time. But my kids should be solving what Keith calls *real-world problems* using *real-world* data. They need the kind of muscle memory that instantly recognizes how numbers can be dropped into an Excel spreadsheet. They no longer need to know how to do long division, but they'd better have sense enough to understand how it works.

Keith is always talking about "number sense" and "mathematical thinking." He acknowledges the difference between essential math skills and the trendy tools used to solve equations. He knows that humanity's fundamental ways of knowing the world are fairly rigid. They change very slowly, if at all. But after years of researching situation theory, he also recognizes that the networked technologies of a connected world have already transformed the way we need to teach almost everything. Nowadays we're educating cognitive agents. We're preparing people to receive data, to decode it into information, and to exchange it as knowledge.

Our kids' long-term utility, economic value, and sense of personal fulfillment will not be dependent on their flexibility. School is not yoga class. Adulthood is not defined by how far one can bend or how easily one can squeeze into an uncomfortable position. Instead, it's about one's capacity to creatively adapt the pillars of human wisdom so that our collective values remain meaningful even when situated in new contexts.

Takeaways

Teach kids to see themselves as nodes of connection, points through which knowledge is transmitted across time and space.

The old education was structured according to the logic of card catalogs. It taught us to imagine each discipline as a collection of ideas or skills that could be stored in an intellectual repository. Students were like boxes into which teachers packed academic stuff.

The new education needs to cultivate habits of mind for a more fluid, transactional, and nonlinear world. Our children need to understand that math, physics, biology, chemistry, history, poetry, mythology, and literature are all comparable and related ways of taking human experience into account. Academic disciplines are just symbolic languages, or situational constraints that enable us to extract meaning from representative data sets.

In previous technological eras, it was fine to imagine that ideas were "content," a sort of abstract substance contained within books, records, documents, and texts. But now that we use digital bits to transmit coded instructions to machines that can decipher data into sounds, pictures, maps, games, and even 3-D printed objects, students need to be taught how to imagine themselves as web browsers and printers. A child is not a container, but rather a cognitive agent who decodes symbolic systems, adds the constraints of character, puts things in personal boxes, and creates contexts based on values and opinions.

Schools need more interdisciplinary activities that provide students with opportunities to extract information from mixed data sets and turn it into knowledge that becomes relevant in unexpected contexts.

All around the world, educators and policy makers are trying to figure out what kids will need to learn in order to be prepared to contribute to an uncertain economy. Already in 2015, McKinsey and Company estimated that "45 percent of work activities could be automated using already demonstrated technology." Another 13 percent could be automated if a computer's ability to process language were to reach "the median level of human performance."

Folks recognize technology's potential to disrupt economic

norms, and grown-ups are desperate to identify the so-called twenty-first-century skills that will provide children with financial and professional stability. The most common refrain is that children need to develop a capacity for flexibility, adaptability, and creativity — supposedly, these are inherently human competencies that artificial intelligence will never be able to mimic. But this is an inadequate solution to the problem. Actually, it doesn't even seem like a solution at all. Instead, it's just a way for grown-ups to avoid the challenge at hand. They acknowledge the uncertainty, but then outsource the work of imagining the future to our children. It's irresponsible.

The truth is that unpredictability is not unique to our time. The world is always in flux. And the whole purpose of child-rearing has always been to transmit wisdom, ingenuity, and ideas from one generation to the next, while simultaneously managing the difficulties that come from living in an ever-changing world. A grown-up's job is to redesign the rites of childhood so that the values, skills, and concepts that have served humanity so well in the past remain meaningful, relevant, and applicable even in new contexts.

Right now, adults need to focus on modifying well-worn languages, codes, and symbolic systems so that they maintain their status and utility as knowledge. The real solution to the twenty-first-century skills problem involves preparing kids to put old concepts into new information management systems. We must abandon the card-catalog education system and get rid of everyday rites and routines that promote a repository sense of self. Remember that we're educating cognitive agents. We're preparing people to receive data, to decode it into information, and to exchange it as knowledge.

Teachers need to recognize that the old specialized and siloed drill-and-practice "toy problems" are no longer adequate learning activities. They don't represent the way we approach problem solving in a connected world, and they don't prepare kids to meet the demands of the new technological era. Instead, our kids need immersive and interdisciplinary learning experiences. Let them practice on real-world problems that require combining an array of seemingly unrelated ideas. Teach students to recognize what diverse perspectives have in common, how dissimilar concepts can coalesce in useful ways — that information transforms into knowledge when it becomes compatible across a range of intellectual platforms.

Our current education system teaches kids to see themselves as rigid vessels. But the world demands that they be porous membranes.

Old school structures, routines, and curricula promote a segmented understanding of the universe. The monastery model of time privileges episodic focus. The card-catalog view of information promotes a repository sense of self. All the conventions of the school day teach our children to partition their experience of existence into separate areas. That's a problem, because in the future, it won't matter how flexible, adaptable, creative, confident, or entrepreneurial they are if they cannot imagine how skills, ideas, and identity narratives are transmitted across digital, infrastructural, and economic networks using the tools of the time.

We need to abandon our loyalty to the shallow ornaments of obsolete information management systems. We need to stop imagining that the technological remnants of our former unyielding centralized bureaucracies are essential components of the learning process.

In a connected world, success becomes automatically redefined. Protocols and processes are now more valuable than properties. Hence, education can no longer focus on destinations, milestones, or fence posts.

Now, it's all about bandwidth. And therefore, we need to assess children's flow capacity rather than their retention.

PART FOUR

SOCIETY

CHAPTER 10

THE NEW EMPATHY

BACK BEFORE PLATO, before Socrates, before Pythagoras, perhaps even before Homer's *Odyssey,* Greece was already a globalized society. Its globe was much smaller than ours, but the Greeks were making trade deals with foreigners wherever and whenever they could.

Archeologists have evidence of Mycenaean maritime routes as far west as the Atlantic coast, which means that the ancients sailed north around the Iberian Peninsula (Spain). They exchanged wine, olive oil, and pottery for silver and tin from the places we now call France and Great Britain. They sourced grain, gold, and copper from throughout the Mediterranean, including the MENA region (Middle East and Northern Africa). They imported animal hides, timber, and salt fish from the far reaches of the Black Sea, now part of Russia.

Global trade must have felt prosperous to ancient Greek families — at least those few lucky enough to live freely within them. They had access to exotic goods, strong industry, and a high quality of life.

They also had immigrants. People hopped on and off trading

ships. Importers and exporters established offices in every port town. The downtrodden and alienated sought new possibilities and opportunities in faraway places. Slaves and servants were trafficked across the sea.

Migration always goes hand in hand with global trade. Unfortunately, so does bigotry, prejudice, and tribalism. People don't like what they don't understand. Why? Because for those who derive a sense of self through status and power — like every ancient Greek patriarch who owned land and slaves — diversity can feel like a destabilizing threat to their authority. Just think about it: if children grow up seeing that a foreign tribe survives just fine by following an entirely different set of rules, it indicates that their current regime is not absolute. Foreign presence seeds doubt. Immigrants make people ask questions. They disrupt the status quo, bring new ways of thinking, reveal other perspectives. And that's a big problem for top-down hierarchies, which are always maintained on a foundation of faith and terror. The system is only secure when less powerful inhabitants live in fear; the youth need to tremble at the prospect of rebellion. So, the elite try to quash potential resistance. They tell stories that slander everything "other." They cultivate bigotry and tribalism; they teach children that conflicting viewpoints are sinful and sacrilegious. They blame the technologies of the time.

"Stay away from the port," the ancient Greeks might have told their children. Maritime trade connected their world. It was their equivalent of our World Wide Web. ("The docks, the boats: they'll ruin you!")

In the long term, separatist inclinations like these always fail. Resistance is futile. Networks of reciprocity are always destined to unite humans. It started long before the advent of the internet. Irrigation canals, aqueducts, power grids, municipal plumbing, ferries, trolleys, subways, regional rail, interstate highways, oil pipelines, postal routes, the printing press, fiber-optic cable, cell towers, and satellites are all tools of connection. They facilitate humanity's innate desire to link, join, bond, interact, and exchange. We keep building tools that bring us closer together. We can't help it. As Kofi Annan, former secretary general of the United Nations, famously said, "Arguing against globalization is like arguing against the laws of gravity."

But just because something's inevitable doesn't mean that it's easy to accept. Hence, the global community continues to struggle, trying to maintain order and meaning in a world where everyone can now plainly see that no single viewpoint is completely infallible. It's especially hard on our children. They're constantly exposed to a dizzying set of conflicting networked perspectives. And they're confused because they lack the empathetic skills needed to confront the challenges of constant connection.

It's good that we let them go play by the metaphorical docks; it's bad that we didn't teach them the appropriate ways to do it. Exposure to diversity, without guidance or education, is troublesome. It won't lead to a utopian alliance. You can't just put a bunch of different people in the same room and assume that they'll all magically learn to love one another. We can't foster empathy while everybody's inching toward a crisis of identity.

The word "crisis" literally describes the need to make a judgment, a decision, a determination, or a choice — it refers to the moment when one faces an amalgamated set of seemingly incompatible factors and struggles to find a way to resolve the tension.

Our children are facing a nonstop crisis of identity.

Self and Other

Imagine a mound of Play-Doh. I don't know about you, but my kids always get carried away. They sculpt a lump of modeling clay into a turtle, maybe a fish, a house, a car, a spaceship. And with each itera-tion, they add new colors, combining, mixing, and blending until everything becomes a boring shade of brownish-gray. The artwork transforms from one thing to another, but nevertheless, the medium remains Play-Doh.

People are like Play-Doh. We interact with different friends, change schools, buy new styles of clothing, engage in unfamiliar activities. These situations mold us. But nevertheless, we remain ourselves. Bodies grow, skin cells shed, teeth fall out, toenails are clipped, hair turns gray. Physical traits transform us throughout our lives, yet I know that I am still the same *me* I've always been. How can that be? What is this part of myself that stays put even as every-thing around it changes? How do I sustain a cohesive identity even as my avatar and its context both transform? This problem has puz-zled philosophers for thousands of years. It's where we get the con-cept of the soul, the psyche, the self, and personality. Each term is just a way of naming the mysterious and intangible piece of a person that somehow remains constant while everything else is always moving.

At base, the discipline of psychology aims to help people maintain a stable sense of self in the face of persistent vicissitudes. But even our psychologists weren't really prepared for life in a connected world. A networked existence comes with a unique set of emotional and intel-lectual challenges. The globalized economy and its worldwide digital communication systems now expose each of us to diverse ideas, peo-ple, and images. And that makes the ability to cultivate a healthy sense of self more tenuous than ever. Why? Because as many of humanity's greatest thinkers have pointed out, an individual identity depends on one's ability to distinguish an "other." After all, I only know what's *me* because I know what's *not*. You're not me. A turtle is not me. Play-Doh is not me. And I am not Play-Doh.

Some psychologists and social scientists speculate that nationalism, tribalism, racism, and isolationism are all unconscious attempts to strengthen a threatened sense of self by identifying an exaggerated caricature of the "other." Like girls who put a sign on the ladder up to their tree house — NO BOYS ALLOWED!!! — communities sometimes construct walls that aim to reinforce what belongs and what doesn't. When girls keep the boys out, they are embracing a gender identity. When nations keep their neighbors out, they are embracing a geographical sense of identity. Likewise, when folks cling to the Industrial Age division between home and work, they're protecting against a perceived threat to their family identities.

To foster empathy, people need a strong sense of identity. And they also need a reasonable understanding of what's other. But persistent connection without intention makes both difficult. It threatens to turn every one of us into a lump of brownish-gray Play-Doh. And all parents know that kids get frustrated and stop creating sculptures as soon as the colors become indiscriminate. They stop using Play-Doh or choose to play with just one color. Similarly, the digital onslaught of varied voices, ideas, cultures, and images makes it hard for individuals to feel distinct. We're not equipped to be confronted with so many things that fall outside the boundaries of our most familiar and sacred knowledge systems. We haven't learned how to manage the deluge of unfiltered exposure. Therefore, connection can trigger anxiety and frustration — a crisis of uncertainty that can lead to anger and conflict. In response, some people may try to compensate with isolationist or separatist tendencies. We don't want that. So, kids need our help. We must teach them how to leverage the tools of the time in ways that promote a meaningful sense of self and an empathetic approach to others.

But remember that empathy involves a lot more than a mere connection, especially since digital technologies often facilitate fast but discordant interactions. Consider Skype. Before dawn, I log in from Philadelphia. I'm taking sips from a big mug of morning coffee, the orange-yellow sunrise is glaring in through the window to the right of my desk. I'm video chatting with a friend in Sarajevo (six hours ahead). For him, it's lunchtime. He nibbles on "pita." Not the flatbread that my kids and I like to dip into hummus, but a savory pastry pie that's often called *burek*. Information technology has brought the two of us together, but the encoded signals, sent back and forth, do not facilitate an experience identical to being in the same place. Our communications may be quick and efficient, but the affective stimuli, which shape our moods and dispositions — and provide the foundation for empathy — remain disjointed. I'm still picking the rheum (what my kids call sleepy seeds or boogers) from the corners of my eyes, feeling barely alert and speaking softly to avoid waking anyone up. My friend, however, is full of midday energy. His jokes are jovial. His voice is enthusiastic. He even calls out to his wife, who's somewhere on the second floor. His loud, quick, and spontaneous charisma is completely out of sync with my slow, quiet, and reserved intimacy. It may be easy for us to overcome the cultural dissonances — I can just read Wikipedia to learn about the foods he eats — but the lack of affective harmony is more complicated.

When we're just enjoying a conversation between friends, it doesn't seem like a big deal. In fact, the pros easily outweigh the cons. Without Skype, we'd have to wait until the next time we were in the same city to talk. Or, I suppose we could send letters, written with fountain pens, in our best handwriting. But postal delivery takes time. And the lack of temporal simultaneity — he won't be reading while I'm writing — makes it even more likely that our individual experiences of the interaction will be discordant. Separate context situations might lead one of us to decode the words on the page inaccurately. We might misinterpret tone and intention. People often do.

On some level, any communication is always like Broken Telephone, a game kids all over the world play. It's known by a variety of names: Russian Scandal, Chinese Whispers, Gossip, Pass the Message, Whisper down the Lane. But no matter what it's called, it demonstrates how small misunderstandings can quickly accumulate into large errors. Imagine the game from a macro perspective— consider all the images, words, and stories that people now encounter, interpret, and pass on to others. Worldwide, there are more than 4 billion internet users, and each spends an average of six hours a day using devices that enable these oddly dissonant connections. Things can quickly become so entangled that it's easy to imagine that the World Wide Web was spun by a wily and cunning spider. We have metamorphosed into a global community, but we've yet to unravel all the potential intellectual, social, and emotional knots.

This is a challenge that's even more acute when it comes to child-rearing. To live and thrive in this new world—to confront and adapt to its unique frictions and challenges—today's kids will need to develop a capacity for a new kind of empathy.

A History of Empathy

Our kids are playing the world's most complex game of Broken Telephone. And they will need to know that hearing is not the same thing as listening, especially when we're gossiping with hyperconnected digital tools.

To accurately transform whispered data into information and knowledge, they'll need to understand rapidly changing geopolitical climates. To find productive ways to contribute to a globalized economy, they'll need to see themselves as stewards of an interconnected worldwide community. The new context requires them to be open-minded, tolerant, and respectful of diversity. But for that, they need a fortified sense of self—enough confidence to manage the muddy ambivalence of persistent connection. They need to know how to maintain distinct and individual ways of being while simultaneously adopting standardized and uniform means of communication. They need to preserve distinct family and cultural value systems while also embracing the nebulous and vague realities of a connected world. It's about letting the hearth inform the agora. And this is the foundation of a new kind of empathy.

The empathy with which we're all familiar is a twentieth-century invention. The word is derived from ancient Greek roots, but it wasn't coined until 1909. Psychologist Edward Titchener used it as a translation for the German term *Einfühlung,* which means "feeling into." At first, empathy was described in terms of "motor mimicry"—the physical reaction to other people's sensory stimuli. When I cringe because my son skins his knee, or smile when he's happy about an impressive achievement, it's what early philosophers described as motor mimicry. I project my own feelings onto his experience. I observe physical cues, such as facial expressions, and then I imitate his inner state.

Similarly, in the 1990s, neuroscientists working with macaque monkeys discovered that identical brain activity can happen in response to someone else's physical actions. The theory is that if I'm watching you eat hummus and pita, some of my synapses will be identical to yours, even if I'm not eating anything. Mirror neurons will fire for both subjects and observers simultaneously. I don't have to think or try to make it happen; it's automatic. It's not based on my intellectual capacity to recognize and reflect on how we're alike, so it's called prereflective mimicry.

At first, researchers believed that mirror neurons could explain social empathy. They speculated that we were inclined toward species connection because mirror neurons allow us to recognize the essential similarities that make all humans alike. But so far, the evidence is shaky. We're not even sure that humans have the same mirror neurons as macaque monkeys. Neuroimaging has consistently mapped behaviors and responses that tend to be associated with empathy to activity in specific regions of the brain. However, researchers haven't yet been able to reproduce conclusive evidence that the subjective, or first-person, experience of pain actually activates the same regions of the human brain as the objective, or third-person, experience of observing another's pain. So, this evidence is hardly conclusive.

The problem is likely that the concept of empathy cannot be clearly defined. It's dependent on context. Social and cultural factors determine what kinds of behavior we consider to be empathetic. And the most common understanding of empathy continues to draw its philosophical framework from the Industrial Age concept of *Einfühlung,* a notion that was always linked to the predominant technologies of the late nineteenth and early twentieth centuries. Back then, scientists and natural philosophers were gripped by enlightenment ideas that originated around the 1500s, when Newton, Copernicus, Galileo, and Descartes introduced "empiricism." Borrowing the word from the Greek ἐμπειρικός *(empeirikos)* — which means "experienced" — they saw a universe that could be described as consisting of discrete units that interact through observable cause-and-effect relationships: laws of nature that operate in efficient linear sequences, like the cogs in a clock tower.

Empiricism works very well when we're describing physical events. Gravity, velocity, and acceleration are all obvious when we're watching objects in motion. But what about feelings? Like love. Rage. Compassion. Admiration. Desire. What causes the sensations that accompany these emotional responses? One can't see gear-wheels turning in my head when I get a warm and fuzzy feeling while admiring the beauty of a sunrise or a painting at the Guggenheim. There's no direct line to draw between the soloist performing Sibelius's violin concerto and the goose bumps that form on the back of my neck at the end of the second movement. Still, these sensations are just as valid as the pain I feel when someone pinches my arm. Our experience of nontangible aesthetic stimuli is just as real as our experience of physical or mechanical stimuli. Back in 1905, Bavarian philosopher Theodore Lipps wanted to explain how these ephemeral, or affective, sensations could fit into an empirical conception of the universe. So, he wrote about "empathy." He argued that a subject always sees a little bit of herself in the object she perceives, and that leads to a kind of internal or emotional motor mimicry. When I'm standing at the Guggenheim, Lipps theorized, I'm able to appreciate the art because I "feel into" the object and imagine the artist's experience must be like my own.

Our current use of the term "empathy" is still very much akin to Lipps's original. We use the word to describe one's capacity to see, feel, or understand how things might be experienced from another person's perspective. And we continue to look for empirical evidence that Lipps's general framing is accurate. We've also incorporated the presumption that empathy is always good because it supposedly automatically triggers compassion and kindness, a concern for other people's well-being. This is what psychologist C. Daniel Batson calls the empathy-altruism hypothesis. But even this becomes problematic when we take cultural context into account. For instance, research has shown that folks tend to have more empathy for loved ones. And one neuroimaging study even found that Red Sox and Yankees fans feel sadness when their own team strikes out but experience pleasure in response to their rivals' failure. Both are empathetic reactions. One is compassionate, the other aggressive.

Still, the idea that empathy is inherently positive drives a lot of social theories. For instance, Jeremy Rifkin describes empathy as the driving force of human civilization. "Empathic development and the development of selfhood go hand in hand," he writes, "and accompany the increasingly complex energy-consuming social structures that make up the human journey." Rifkin sees empathetic camaraderie, rather than competition and survival, as the primary motivating factor behind social progress, economic development, and technological innovation. He assumes that because I can imagine how your suffering feels, I'm inclined to do what I can to minimize it. Therefore, I contribute to my community because I recognize that cooperative projects might eliminate the pain I can imagine feeling. Rifkin even takes this thesis to an Age of Aquarius extreme, predicting that the technologies of a connected world will eventually catalyze a new form of empathic consciousness — one that elevates species solidarity above national, ethnic, or regional factionalism.

But don't tell that to twentieth-century philosopher Martin Buber, a popular religious thinker, political activist, and educator. He's most famous for his 1923 book *I and Thou*. And even though his work elevated loving, compassionate human interactions and relationships as the foundation of a meaningful existence, he resisted the very idea of empathy. Why? Because for him, the concept still retained too much of its original motor-mimicry meaning, even in its later iterations. Empathy is "the absorption in pure aestheticism," he wrote, by which he means it's all about sensation, about experiencing things the same way another person does, about seeing things through their eyes. "Empathy means, if anything, to glide with one's own feeling into the dynamic structure of an object," Buber explains.

From his point of view, it's not a true interpersonal connection because, in empathy, we leave ourselves behind to occupy the perspective of another. "It means the exclusion of one's own concreteness," he says.

That's his poetic way of describing what I was referring to with the Play-Doh problem. When we try to see through someone else's eyes, we find ourselves in an anxiety-provoking situation. We intuitively recognize that perfect empathy — lauded as an aspirational ideal — requires letting go of our identities completely, forgetting all of our own experiences, suspending a lifetime of memories, and abandoning everything we've learned about situational meaning-making. In other words, it involves momentarily weakening our sense of self. And therefore, it feels inherently destabilizing.

Think about how often this uneasiness manifests itself in a connected world. We are confronted with access to so many different perspectives. We're constantly barraged with opportunities for empathy. All day long there's moral and ethical pressure to abandon ourselves and feel into the experience of others. But by definition, that means we also spend a lot of time being like brownish-gray lumps of modeling clay — dissatisfied, with a vague and indeterminate sense of self. To make matters worse, we're also probably racked with guilt and shame because we've bought into an Industrial Age conception of empathy as altruism that's misaligned with our current technological reality. *Einfühlung* is creating personal anguish rather than reducing collective suffering.

Hence, we need to reimagine empathy for a connected world.

On Hospitality

Once upon a time, the ancient Greeks had a way of preparing their children to live in a globalized economy. They developed a polytheistic religious system. They told stories of many powerful gods.

These were deities with conflicting perspectives, gods who demonstrated a spirit of diversity. They contradicted one another. They fought among themselves. Just like the people, the immortals had conflicting desires. They struggled to cooperate in constructing their world. Ancient Greek narratives were like islands: never bound into a single unit, but always connected. Gods, monsters, and heroes migrated across a sea of stories, arriving suddenly in a new myth with little context or explanation.

At first, the listening children were surely confused. But over time, as they heard more tales of familiar characters, they started to understand. Things became clear. Each character's significance was enriched by the logic of a network, by the connections and shared relationships carried from one story to the next. Think about how children raised on these myths must have imagined the world. What sense of self did the structure of this mythological information management system cultivate? If the ultimate beings are always hopping from one story to another, then connections rule supreme. In this primitive version of networked thinking, individual stories are almost meaningless when standing alone.

Did you ever wonder why so many of today's students hate reading the ancient Greek classics in school? It's not because the stories are old. Nor is it the result of poor or inaccessible translations. Rather, the tales are boring when taken out of their linked context.

I struggled to understand Greek mythology for the first thirty years of my life. All my childhood trips to synagogue had conditioned me to think in accordance with the procedural rhetoric of monotheistic storytelling—one God, one people, one linear genealogy, one chronological history. All the routines of family life taught me to divide the world into discrete categories, so I was more comfortable with unambiguously good guys and bad guys, protagonists and antagonists. The everyday routines of the school day compelled me to enjoy the stories of a clockwork world, where episodes provide answers that can be filed into card catalogs. It was a challenge to make sense of Greek mythology's multifaceted, nonlinear, and dispersed narrative structure. I was used to movies and novels with an isolated dramatic arc, an egoistic underdog's trajectory in which crisis leads to catharsis, revolution, and success. Therefore, like most kids, I suffered through the classical parts of my education, struggling to make sense of Homer, Sophocles, Aristophanes, Plato. It was not until graduate school, when I had finally read enough ancient Greek mythology, that it all suddenly clicked.

When my boys were born, I tried to spare them the same experience. I wanted to give them a head start on the most miserable parts of English class. So, as early as possible, I introduced them to as much Greek mythology as I could. I read them the stories constantly. They learned about Aphrodite, the goddess whose spirit controls you when you're consumed with passion, lust, and desire. "When you feel like you absolutely need candy or ice cream, when you cannot imagine sharing because you love it so completely," I explained, "you can be sure that Aphrodite is nearby." I taught them about Ares, the warrior god of combat and rage. "When you feel self-righteous, ready to smack your brother for wrecking a LEGO spaceship, that is Ares." I taught them about Hermes the trickster, a snake-oil salesman who lurks in the poetry of advertising—he's the clever one who constantly convinces my kids that they *need* each trendy fad: fidget spinners, Rainbow Looms, Silly Bandz. I told them that Hephaestus, the maker, lives in construction paper, scissors, glue sticks, and 3-D printers. I presented each god as if he or she were a line of code, a process that defines our actions and curates our experiences.

I showed my sons how the immortals travel from one myth to the next, creating connections and adding value by building networks of meaning. My version of paganism, reimagined for the internet age, wasn't about a devout belief in figures who lived in the sky; it was about conditioning children to make meaning in a diverse and globally connected world. I wanted their fantasy lives to prepare them for adulthood, to contour their thinking and influence their identity in specific ways. I wanted them to integrate a procedural, almost algorithmic, view of human consciousness.

I don't know if it worked; ask me in about fifteen years.

What I do know is that it probably wasn't necessary. The cultural narratives of the twenty-first century are already beginning to take on structural characteristics similar to those of the polytheistic mythology of ancient Greece.

Consider YouTube. Like most preteens in the United States with a dependable broadband connection, my boys spend a lot of time on this video-sharing website. YouTube claims that more viewers now watch on their platform than watch prime-time television. Three hundred new videos are uploaded every minute, and about 5 billion are viewed every day. It is the most popular and most recognized brand among 6-to-12-year-old children in the United States, surpassing such longtime mainstays as Oreo, Disney, and LEGO. I'm not surprised. My kids watch all the time.

What are they watching? According to Star Network Kids, the most popular videos are about game play, toys, real-life super heroes, Play-Doh, and more. My sons mostly watch the "Let's Play" videos. Originally, this meant that a YouTuber would strap on a headset with microphone, "cast" his or her screen, and play a popular video game. The gamer screamed and giggled into the microphone, offering play-by-play narration, speaking— stream-of-consciousness style— while making in-game decisions.

At first, kids were probably watching just to learn tips and secrets. But soon, the competition for viewers became fierce. YouTubers started making money. Now, channels with more than a thousand annual subscribers and four thousand hours of watch time can earn advertising revenue. And a study published in *Convergence: The International Journal of Research into New Media Technologies* found that just 3 percent of all channels get about 85 percent of the eyeballs. Therefore, YouTubers who wanted the cash that comes from more views needed to create better content. They started producing skits, scripting the game play, inviting cohosts to join their adventures. Open sandbox games like *Minecraft* provided a cheap and easy tool for production. Anyone could build a block-based virtual setting and then effortlessly animate stories within it. Game avatars became like puppets and the games themselves, virtual soundstages. YouTubers created weekly episodes featuring familiar characters (the players) in different settings (the games). Think of it as a hybrid combination of the sitcom and reality TV genres. Imagine if the *Seinfeld* cast showed up in a different location, with different jobs and different tasks every time they started a new episode, yet their personality traits stayed constant, and their character arcs continued to develop. That gives you a sense of what the YouTube entertainment ecosystem is like.

Millions of viewers love it. Now, in addition to play-through videos and skits, there are mockumentaries, informative newscasts, and hundreds (maybe thousands) of game-review magazine shows. However, what's most interesting to me about YouTube is that the characters sometimes hop from one video to another. Popular YouTubers appear in one another's videos, crossing genres and creating a connected network of cultural narratives. In other words, it works just like ancient Greek mythology.

Think back to your high school English class. If you're like me, you struggled to read Homer's *Odyssey*. But in order to pass the exam, you still learned to say that it's an epic about hospitality. The Greek word *xenia* (ξενία) refers to the relationship between hosts and their guests.

Wherever Odysseus washed ashore, he expected to be met by folks who abided by the reciprocal etiquette of *xenia*. The bad guys are all poor hosts—the Cyclops doesn't even offer a meal; he turns Odysseus's men into one. But the good guys always provide the hero with food, shelter, and gifts—even before inquiring about his identity. "Help yourselves! Enjoy the food! When you have shared our meal, we will begin to ask who you are," Menelaus says when he welcomes Telemachus. The conventions of *xenia* may seem crazy to us; after all, we currently teach kids never to talk to strangers, and we're not likely to feed any vagabond who rings our doorbell. But we don't live in a pre-electric maritime culture in which the journey to visit your neighbor could take weeks. Imagine how tired you'd be after a fortnight at sea, and how desperately you'd want a nice bed, clean clothes, and a warm meal. *Xenia* is the ultimate expression of pay-it-forward thinking for a seafaring society. By agreeing to a system that guarantees mutual hospitality, everyone benefits. (Although, to be fair, in the ancient world only the elite free men participated in the rites of *xenia*.) The reason they don't ask a visitor for his name is to avoid the possibility that old baggage might soil the *xenia* relationship. For instance, if your father killed mine during the Trojan War, I might be inclined to leave you outside, hungry and cold. But if I'm unaware of your identity, I will welcome you into my home, accept you at face value, and perform the rituals of friendship.

What would *xenia* look like in the modern world? How can we teach our kids to greet digital encounters as if they were boats washing ashore? Can they learn to ignore the familiar indicators of otherness—to let go of assumptions that are often based on obsolete approaches to ethnic, cultural, and religious difference? Can they suspend judgment long enough to welcome a fresh understanding of the images they confront? Digital *xenia* could be a kind of structural and systemic empathy that's tailored to a networked existence.

And I not only think it's possible; I also think that most of the pieces are already in place. All that's missing is guidance and mentorship from grown-ups. Currently, few of our institutions are designed in ways that prepare kids to see how the old values remain relevant in connected contexts. Why? I suspect it's because we're seduced by the sentimental fantasy that the rituals of *xenia* will spontaneously develop as a result of empathetic encounters. But take a moment to really think about that. Doesn't it seem just as likely that without adult intervention, the winds could blow the new childhood in the other direction? Toward aggression rather than compassion?

Xenophobia is the opposite of *xenia*. It's a fear of *xenoi*/ξένοι (foreigners, strangers) — hostility rather than hospitality. It's an irrational distrust of anything "other." And it often arises in response to a crisis of identity. Therefore, we should above all teach our kids to be confident in their self-expression. They need to know how to articulate a sandbox sense of self using the nonlinear tools of a connected world. Children need grown-ups to show them how to recognize that situated contexts shape interpretations, that gamelike systems create limitations and possibilities. They need to feel anchored in family, not fenced in to a secluded home compound. And they need adults to model a practice of ethical and compassionate communication. They need to see powerful examples of relatedness, conveyed through networked platforms.

This is the foundation of the new empathy, and it's how we cultivate a generation of kind and considerate global citizens.

Takeaways

Cultivate Connected Thinkers

We are connected through more than digital communication technologies. Globalization, worldwide economic interdependence, faster transportation, hyperefficient energy grids, migration, and urbanization are all examples of a networked mindset. Humans seem to have an innate desire to link, join, bond, interact, and exchange. We keep building tools that bring people closer together.

But better connections come with new psychological, emotional, and intellectual challenges. It can be difficult to maintain a stable sense of self in the face of constant access to contradictory ideas and images. Folks need help adjusting. So far, we've introduced them to a multicultural and pluralistic world without providing the empathetic skills needed to deal with it. We seem to be seduced by a utopian fantasy that all contact among people eventually leads toward understanding, compassion, and kindness. Unfortunately, that's not necessarily so. We're quickly discovering that persistent exposure to diversity without sufficient preparation, guidance, and/or mentorship can just as easily lead toward prejudice and isolationism.

To avoid conflict, uncertainty, and political unrest in the future, we will need to be more intentional about how we prepare kids to live together in a connected world. Let's make sure that children have a strong sense of identity and that they don't feel threatened by cultural diversity. Let's show them how to express their distinct personalities with the networked technologies at their disposal. They need to know how to use new media to articulate their unique sense of self while simultaneously sustaining the dignity and value of global difference and diversity.

Start by teaching your kids to leverage digital tools that encourage creative self-expression. For this, active is better than passive play. Building with virtual blocks in *Minecraft* or coding with Scratch can help kids see that networks provide opportunities to articulate narratives of the self. Drawing and painting on the iPad's screen helps them learn to express who they are, see where they stand, and imagine fitting in and contributing to a connected world.

Digital play lays the foundation for a lifetime's worth of connected habits. So, let's start encouraging kids to perceive the technologies around them as instruments of empowerment. They should recognize that the world is full of tools they can command — not boxes that distribute content to be consumed, or rigid systems that confine the shape of their experiences.

Participating in a Global Community

In addition to understanding themselves, kids need to learn how to live, play, work, and communicate with others. They must develop the capacity to see the world from alternative perspectives. But that involves more than merely recognizing and acknowledging differences. The New Empathy runs much deeper than awareness, acceptance, and tolerance.

Kids need to know how to negotiate respectful interactions without expecting distinction to dissolve into sameness. And this can be difficult, because networks require standardization. Tools must be compatible with one another. Data needs to fit into packets that can be transmitted between shared platforms. Programming languages need to be consistent, file formats congruent. Yet when these technical requirements are combined with social-media sharing, or when we imagine that we're uploading pieces of ourselves and downloading pieces of others, uniformity can be perceived as a threat. It's easy to misinterpret the homogeneity of the systems as an affront to distinction and individual freedom. No one wants to feel like they're being forced to fit their lives into the same old boxes.

Therefore, kids need to know that they are not equivalent to their data. They need to be taught that they are cognitive agents. Yes, connected systems move data, but it's the people who interpret it, exchange it, and use it as knowledge. If kids are not able to preserve their individuality while also embracing the nebulous and vague realities of a connected world, they're bound to find themselves in a crisis of identity.

Encouraging Digital Hospitality

The good news is that we already have most of the tools we need to make the New Empathy a reality. The bad news is that we're not doing a very good job accepting them.

During the Industrial Age, kids learned the skills necessary for prosocial interactions on playgrounds and in sandboxes. Make-believe scenarios offered children opportunities to practice maintaining a sense of self while simultaneously accepting conflicting social contexts. You'll remember, from Part One, that this is called accommodation, and it involves both self-regulation and executive-function skills.

But sliding boards and monkey bars are no longer enough. Today's kids also need to practice these skills in a variety of connected contexts. And grown-ups need to help them acquire the vocabulary with which to make meaning out of these experiences. To understand this, just think about what happens when kids in the schoolyard find themselves in the middle of a conflict. A teacher usually intervenes and helps them "talk it out." Through these conversations, children learn to make sense of what happened. They assimilate language, they adopt new frameworks. The teacher models, guides, and mentors, thereby preparing kids for a lifetime of confrontations, negotiations, and social encounters.

Likewise, asking kids to describe the events of their day teaches them to find meaning in the most mundane social situations. Of course, every parent knows that you'll often have to tease out the details. When I ask "How was school?" they just mumble "Fine." But as I ask a series of qualifying questions, my kids learn that certain specifics matter more than others. They gauge my reactions and integrate an image of maturity. They notice which stories make me laugh and which trigger disappointment. They discover, through subtle cues, that I approve of some friends and disapprove of others.

Unfortunately, very few grown-ups take an interest in their kids' digital play. They don't ask questions about the games, nor do they pay much attention to online playmates. But remember that these are the playgrounds on which our kids are preparing for the future. So, adults should help children make sense out of these connected experiences. Model a practice of ethical and compassionate communication. Show them powerful examples of relatedness.

Digital hospitality needs to be taught with just as much care as real-life hospitality. There's no easy or quick solution; it requires a lifetime of practice, which begins at home, with ongoing parental engagement.

CHAPTER 11

THE NEW MEDIA LITERACY

MY YOUNGER SON is hooked on *Doctor Who*. He's also seen all the *Back to the Future* movies multiple times. And he dreams of becoming a theoretical physicist.

I wonder what causes a ten-year-old to be so interested in time travel. He hasn't been alive long enough to feel the pathos of impermanence, nor the heavy burden that comes with regret or remorse. Perhaps he's just curious about the future, wondering what it might hold.

Recently, I sat down beside him on the living room floor and said, "Listen, you know that building a time machine is easy, right?"

He looked at me skeptically.

My favorite part of parenting is messing with my kids. That's what makes it worth putting up with all the thankless responsibility that goes with being a dad: I get these little miniature people that I can just mess with all day long.

"The only issue is speed," I tell him, "—well, speed, and that you can't ever go backwards…"

His interest is piqued now; visions of the Tardis and the Flux Capacitor must be flooding his mind.

"The problem is that I only know how to build a time machine that works superslow."

He considers this limitation.

"If I set it for ten minutes into the future, it'll take ten minutes to get there," I explain, "and then you're stuck. You've got to move on with your life from there." He looks at me; he's silent, but I can almost hear his eyebrows furling. He's crunching the numbers, jumping to conclusions. If it takes ten minutes to move ten minutes, is it really still time travel? Does it count?

Slowly, a smile forms on his face. "Right, Dad. Duh! We're always time traveling."

Yes! He's got it. We're always moving forward in time, whether we want to or not. "And with video and photography," he adds, "we can even turn it back." He's right. Writing, painting, file cabinets, the internet: these are technologies of memory. And anytime we're thinking about the practice of parenting, or teaching, or child-rearing — when we're concerned with preserving values, skills, and culture by passing them from one generation to the next — we're practicing time travel.

In a way, it's even part of what I'm doing when I ask my kids questions designed to challenge their sense of intellectual stability. My goal is to freak them out — to totally confuse them. It might sound a little cruel, but I do it for a good reason. It's part of how I raise critical thinkers who are prepared to live with the challenges that come with being a media consumer in the twenty-first century. Our contemporary world is so saturated with predictive algorithms and microtargeted advertisements that the majority of news we read just confirms, validates, or reinforces the things we already believe. Consider fake news, insular Facebook groups, and self-selected

Twitter feeds. People never have to have their opinions challenged anymore. And when they're forced to confront opposing ideas, they don't know how to deal with it. Folks have this kind of tunnel vision that is obviously inadequate for a healthy connected society. Grown-ups need to purge that fatheadedness and intolerance right out of the next generation. It's our duty. And it's also an economic and political necessity.

That's why I mess with my kids. It prepares them to confront dissonant perspectives. Research psychologists call it prosocial teasing. Poking, gentle jabs, baiting, and flirting are all ambiguous provocations that can help children develop intellectual humility. Prosocial teasing has been shown to stifle arrogance and curb narcissism. I tease my kids because I want the constant tiny confrontations to provide them with tons of practice accommodating a plurality of viewpoints. And at the same time, I hope they learn to associate challenges to their worldview with parental love, safety, and acceptance. I'm training them not to experience intellectual opposition as a threat, but rather to see vulnerability as an opportunity to grow and explore, to play with ideas, to engage in dialogue, to transform a stagnant sense of self.

I'm cultivating the prerequisite skill set needed for using connected technologies within a healthy marketplace of social capital.

Digital Diaspora

Robert D. Putnam is a political scientist best known for his book *Bowling Alone: The Collapse and Revival of American Community* (2000). He complains about the decline of public social engagement due to "electronic entertainment—above all, television." From his perspective, the modern media landscape is problematic because "a society of many virtuous but isolated individuals is not necessarily rich in social capital."

With the term "social capital," Putnam is referring to the quality as well as the quantity of one's relationships with other people. Those relationships are important because they serve both a private and a public need. For individuals, a strong personal network might lead to more professional opportunities. For a society, networks linked to agoras help maintain equity, citizenship, and collective prosperity. To understand these ideas, first consider the personal benefits of social capital.

My older brother finished law school in 1995. He was immediately offered a job at the elite firm where our childhood neighbor, Toby, was a senior partner. My parents had become friends with Toby's family at block parties and other local events. And when my brother applied for jobs, he didn't send out his resumé willy-nilly, hoping someone would notice. No, he called all the lawyers my family knew and asked them for advice and assistance. Toby was one of many people who helped.

Putnam considers friendships like these to be a form of capital—which is really just a fancy way of saying that these connections have value; they can be considered assets. Because my parents have accumulated so many personal friends and professional acquaintances, my brothers and I have always had access to an enormous amount of social capital. We can use my parents' network almost as if we're withdrawing funds from an ATM.

But that's not the whole story. If you really want to understand the idea of social capital, you also need to consider how my parents came to know such a well-established and influential lawyer in the first place. My father was the son of a chicken farmer. My mother was the daughter of a schoolteacher. They left a small rural town in New Jersey to raise a family in big-city Philadelphia. Neither of them worked in the legal profession, yet they managed to form many close bonds with people who did. That is because they spent a lot of time at public gatherings. They went to block parties, volunteered for local political campaigns, attended synagogue, served on the PTA, coached Little League, and more. Being embedded in these small communities, they constantly interacted with a diverse set of people and therefore had opportunities to make friends with folks outside their professional spheres. They also engaged with people of higher and lower socioeconomic status than theirs. A true agora can function as an equalizer. It brings people together — rich and poor — who share common values, interests, stories, or maybe just a geographic location. It is like a sandbox for grown-ups; it lets local communities gather, exchange, build, and play with social capital.

Putnam provides ample evidence that high levels of social capital create healthier and more equitable neighborhoods, schools, economies, and democracies. But I think he ultimately diminishes his argument by offering a nostalgic iteration of technophobia. He blames electronic media for pulling people away from the physical agoras. It may be true that mid-twentieth-century civic participation fragmented because of the TV hearth. But at the same time, national narratives became more unified. Sure, at first people separated into private family households — they started "bowling alone" — but eventually, many new pathways to social engagement opened up. Now, thanks to technology, folks can assemble into niche communities, interacting with people around the world who share their interests, skills, curiosities, belief systems, cultural histories, and more.

As J. Philipp Schmidt, director of Learning Innovation at the MIT Media Lab, writes, "a small black terminal window with some white text and a blinking cursor became my window to a whole new world." He's reflecting on his personal experience with informal online learning in the 1990s. "Strangers commonly helped each other with technical questions," he says, describing how, in the early days of the internet, "sharing ideas and knowledge was the default."

Schmidt went on to cofound Peer2Peer University and to design BlockCerts, a blockchain-based set of tools for managing digital credentials. He also launched the MIT Refugee Learning Accelerator, a program that supports engineers from the Middle East to create technologies for refugee learners. All of his projects have something in common. They aim to strengthen communities by making it easier for people to connect and share their knowledge and expertise. Schmidt knows that the best learning often happens through unsanctioned, passionate, and messy interactions—at moments when groups of people gather playfully but end up creating things together and exchanging intellectual assets. He has an exceptionally nuanced understanding of how intellectual capital is related to social capital, all thanks to observations he initially made while browsing through the earliest digital agoras. "There was an amazing sense of community," he reminisces, "and I formed friendships that lasted many years with people who, in some cases, I would never meet in person."

To make meaningful connections, we no longer need to sit face-to-face, staring across the table. So, it's futile to point our time machines away from electronic media and back toward Putnam's ideal world where perfect American families gather for perfect suburban potlucks. Instead, we should follow Schmidt's lead and think about how to enable more opportunities to develop useful social capital in a digital diaspora.

At present, a computer with a broadband connection has the potential to function like a boat that I can virtually row to just about every part of the planet. And in theory, digital hospitality should gather more of us together into open communities than ever before. But so far, it isn't working that way. Instead, new media platforms often divide communities into factions. Why? One reason is that today's information streams have been engineered like memory-foam mattresses, the shape always defined by whatever we were interested in yesterday. Thanks to artificial intelligence and predictive algorithms, my mobile phone, laptop, and smart TV all know what I want to view, even before I can articulate it. I see only what I'm interested in.

I never have to be messed with — my thinking never needs to be challenged. A made-to-order, neat and tidy media menu holds me in a tight embrace. It feels great. It's also convenient. But it's problematic because it eliminates everyday opportunities for what Harvard Law professor Cass R. Sunstein calls "serendipity." Using imagery of isolation similar to Putnam's, Sunstein compares the current digital media experience to living in a gated community. He says that people are now shielded from having to interact with images, ideas, or stories that fall outside of their comfort zone. And that's a problem, because "unplanned, unanticipated encounters are central to democracy itself."

Just think about all the people my parents met at those local gatherings. But keep in mind that the serendipity was not only beneficial because it helped my brother draw from a diverse collection of social assets. It also encouraged good citizenship through the exchange of cultural capital. In other words, everyone knew much more about the different people living around them. They were exposed to opposing points of view. And presumably, because they were better informed, they became more tolerant, reflective, and considerate of people who were different from them. The flow of social capital was profitable for both the individual and the collective.

In comparison, the problem with the current digital agora is the lack of social serendipity. It limits potential opportunities for developing a diverse portfolio of relationships and intellectual assets. Think about what that means for today's kids. They may be more connected than ever, but they tend to stick with what's familiar. They get pigeonholed. When I was a preteen, I spent most Sunday afternoons flipping through cable television channels, trying to find something interesting to watch. Back then, there was no such thing as on-demand entertainment. You were stuck with whatever was on; that's how I discovered reruns of *All In The Family, Sanford and Son,* and *Mr. Ed*. My kids, however, have so many choices that they can't even imagine how boring some of my weekends were.

From a multicultural perspective, the sheer quantity and variety of available media is a good thing. My kids' options are less homogenous than mine were; the narrative formulas are more diverse. Unfortunately, however, that doesn't necessarily correlate to more wide-ranging exposure. Most people still end up neglecting a huge swath of the available pathways. But not by choice: most of the content children (and adults) encounter — on Google, Facebook, Netflix, Amazon, iTunes, Hulu, Xbox — is autocurated to keep them engaged. The goal, like flypaper, is to make the platforms sticky. And as a result, kids rarely experience serendipity while online. It might seem to them that they're following a random series of YouTube suggestions, and discovering new favorites. But their choices have actually been predetermined, or at least directed. Algorithms now sort users into precise demographic categories. Then they prod us, like cattle, toward customized "microtargeted" troughs. They pour fine-grained nuggets of information into our "feeds" and reformulate the recipes on the fly, responding and learning from our reactions.

In this way, our exposure to digital content is hypercontrolled while the illusion of serendipity is maintained. For example, children are exposed to a steady stream of embellished stories of underdog entertainers like Justin Bieber, who found fame by uploading home videos to YouTube. His miraculous ascension to superstardom reinforces the myth of a free and neutral media meritocracy. And the kids hearing his story are unaware that the architecture of their media agora limits freedom of discovery. Instead, they continue to believe in uninhibited consumer choices. After all, it seems clear to them that anyone's work can go viral — you just have to get enough "likes." Social media can make you into a celebrity, gamers can become stars without leaving their bedrooms, a good Kickstarter campaign can transform you into a titan of industry, and a strong Tumblr blog can land you a book deal.

It's true that a few lucky outliers may have managed to find success in this way, but mostly the story of serendipitous entrepreneurship serves only to give the impression that new technologies are disrupting existing power structures and creating a "level" and "open" playing field. That's a far cry from the truth. In fact, almost all digital media remains controlled by just twelve corporations (most of which have dominated for decades): Walt Disney, 21st Century Fox, Time Warner, AT&T, Comcast/NBC Universal, CBS, Viacom, Amazon, Alphabet/Google, and Facebook. And when a single entity governs a significant percentage of the distribution channels, virality can be easily engineered.

Digital media has mostly become an instrument to facilitate niche consumption. But it has the potential to be a tool for the serendipitous exchange of social capital if we will only teach our kids how to understand and use it.

Entertainment Consumerism

When I was a kid, media literacy was much simpler than it is now. First, we followed the money. We did some digging to find out who funded our favorite TV shows. We knew that if Tide laundry detergent was an advertiser, we weren't likely to see anything that would damage the brand's reputation. Instead, we'd probably see product placements.

My friends and I became experts at spotting corporate logos

whenever they showed up in our favorite science-fiction films. Picture "Coca-Cola" and "Ford" written in Spencerian script, still clearly legible even in space-age settings. It may be hard to predict the future, but in the movies, one thing was certain: even postapocalypse there's still a strong corporate presence. We realized that although individual writers, musicians, and actors may be in the entertainment game for altruistic reasons — to make us laugh, smile, or experience some kind of emotional catharsis — the distribution channels were ultimately motivated by profit. Programming only showed up on our television sets because network executives thought the work would hold our attention long enough to keep us watching the commercials.

We also considered the creators' motivations. We looked to see who was working behind the scenes. We asked about political positions that the directors or the producers held. Did someone's personal belief system shape the artistic vision? Was the movie trying to persuade us to think a certain way? How did the story reflect the author's point of view? All media is constructed from a particular perspective; it sends messages to the audience. And even if coercion is not the artists' objective, the work will still feature representations of race, gender, sexuality, ethnicity, socioeconomic class, and more. It will also include portrayals of less politically charged things, like family dinners and school-day routines. As a result, young viewers often establish their core understanding of what's "normal" — what's defined as right and wrong, or what constitutes "healthy adjustment" — according to the images they see in the world of entertainment. Thus we learned to recognize and interpret the cultural messaging that was ubiquitous in our lives.

Notice that my friends and I were focused almost entirely on the content itself. For my kids, however, it's much more complicated. In addition to everything we used to think about, they also need to consider the container, the process, the procedural rhetoric. Media literacy is no longer just about ideas and images; it's also about structures, protocols, and rituals that transcend traditional definitions of "entertainment." We now live in a world where most of one's interactions — social, commercial, informational, political, even educational — are mediated through software, apps, games, and smart devices. You may not realize it, but each of these interactions is an engagement with media.

Some of the material we encounter on our devices is clearly produced as "entertainment" and/or "news," but most of it is a lot more nuanced. Consider the "user interface," a term that refers to the way software is designed so that a person can interact with it. Think of the virtual buttons and sliders on your favorite smartphone app, the shape and placement of icons used to navigate through menus. Developers may tell their customers that they make design decisions for the sake of efficiency, ease of operation, or convenience, but they say that only because it gives users the impression that the experience is neutral. It's not. Every swipe, tap, and click is a constructed interaction with media. And users are conditioned to believe that some software features feel more "intuitive" than others.

For example, product development teams put enormous amounts of energy into the "onboarding" process. That's the term they use to describe the consumer's first interaction with a product. Think about the sign-up or registration sequence. Many experts compare this onboarding process to a first date, presumably because they recognize how important it is to seduce users into feeling comfortable with their product from the very beginning. First impressions matter. But often, we're not just inputting our personal information and setting up our user names and passwords. We're also being trained to feel comfortable with a specific software "flow." Next time you download an app, be mindful of the onboarding experience it takes you through. A good app onboards like the first level of a video game, not only because it gets you hooked on a specific objective, but also because it shows you how to operate the superpowers that the code puts at your avatar's disposal.

Are you and your children cognizant of the user-interface decisions that have been made by engineers, entrepreneurs, and powerful corporations? Facebook, Snapchat, Instagram, WhatsApp, Twitter, Gmail, Photoshop, and even Microsoft Office products each have their own procedural rhetoric. Just like video games, these applications demand ritualized engagements. And hiding in almost every process is a structure that not only prefigures how you use the software, but also only allows for certain ways of thinking about the content.

The new media ends up wrangling our thoughts so that ideas can fit only into certain situated contexts. That's why children need adult mentorship that teaches them not to surrender blindly to ritualized digital actions. They need to recognize that software is almost always designed with an agenda. They need to consider the way a tool set can shape their choices.

Personality Brands

Today's kids also need to understand the role that they inadvertently play in the production of digital media. Each time a child downloads a new app, she may feel like the customer but she's actually becoming part of the assembly line. Social platforms depend on the content that users manufacture for one another. This makes the term "onboarding" even more appropriate, since software designers borrowed it from human resources departments.

Onboarding originally described the progression a new employee follows to learn the ropes. It's the orientation process at a new job. Since social media companies profit by selling the data that their users provide, onboarding is the perfect term to describe the way users are being trained to participate in what Julian Küchlich calls playbour. He combines the words "play" and "labour" (he uses the British spelling) to signify the increasingly unclear distinction between leisure and production as digital media turns creative play into a commodity. But don't get distracted by the fancy jargon he borrows from the academic field of political economy. There's nothing especially complicated about what he's trying to say. It's basically just the observation that every time my boys post a photo on Instagram or update their status on social media, they're providing content that other users will enjoy.

Remember that without their contributions, there is no product, no advertising space to sell; we'd all leave Facebook if our friends stopped posting. Similarly, YouTube is like a television channel on which all the programming is produced by the audience. And when my kids modify *Minecraft* code and upload new variations on the game — what gamer geeks call *modding* — they're actually increasing the overall value of someone else's intellectual property. Yes, my children are just having fun, but Mojang and Microsoft, who own *Minecraft,* benefit financially from my kids' unpaid playbour.

Unfortunately, most people give very little thought to the unpaid playbour they contribute to online platforms. Nevertheless, they learn to see themselves as part of the product because they're always performing, always presenting images from their lives as if they need to offer a "value proposition," the term start-ups and investors use to describe why someone should purchase their product. What distinguishes my widget from a competitor's? What makes it stand out? How is my solution to an existing problem unique and therefore worth spending money on?

To understand value propositions, just imagine you're trying to start an umbrella company. You're probably not going to redesign the curved Paragon frame that Samuel Fox developed around 1850 when he replaced whalebone ribbing with curved steel stays left over from ladies' corsets. But in 1929, Slawa Horowitz added a new value proposition. Her umbrella, called the Flirt, was portable because it introduced the compact folding mechanism with which we're now so familiar. Collapsibility was an improvement that added value. If you want to distinguish your new umbrella company, you'll need another new value proposition. Perhaps you'll add some fancy synthetic fabric, a carbon-fiber handle, or a Bluetooth connection. The point is, you'll need to show that your product has a unique value.

Likewise, when kids (and adults) post on social media, they're trying to turn the mundane moments of everyday life into valuable content. And it's not easy. We all go out to eat, hang out with our friends, attend cultural events, and go on vacations. But online, we need to compete to share our story in a way that's more engaging than everyone else's. We're trying to build a better umbrella. And likes, retweets, and followers become the currency with which a personal network endorses our value propositions.

Of course, there's nothing necessarily wrong with communicating a public identity narrative full of value propositions. It may just be part of living in a connected world. But we do need to make sure our children are equipped with adequate digital media literacy skills. They need to recognize that the online performance is only one part of the self — the part that fits into specific kinds of containers, pathways, and boxes designed to create profit for corporate media conglomerates.

Also, consider how this value proposition mindset relates to concerns about online privacy. To be online is to be under constant surveillance. Even when we feel like we're not performing, our web navigations and internet behaviors are being documented, interpreted, and analyzed. Our actions, beliefs, and ideals are imagined as com-modities that should be tracked, measured, and exchanged.

Privacy issues raise some major red flags around digital media literacy. Kids need to learn the etiquette of online discretion for both practical and emotional reasons. From a practical standpoint, they need to be aware that almost everything uploaded to the inter-net has the potential to endure. Nothing is temporary. If you thought, like my ten-year-old, that 8mm home movies or video cam-corders were like time machines because they preserve memories and allow folks to relive important moments from their past, just contemplate how much data about our lives is currently documented online.

Nowadays, there's a lasting trace of every digital interaction. And it's horrifying to imagine being a middle schooler at a time when anything and everything you say can end up on your permanent record. At forty years old, I'm often embarrassed when I pull out old journals, sketch pads, and notebooks from when I was younger. I read the things I scribbled on the pages, and I'm appalled by my own naiveté. Luckily, these documents aren't public; they're hidden in boxes at the back of my closet.

For today's kids, however, everything is public. And the digital residue of online engagement is regularly accessed not only by col-lege admissions departments but also by future employers. One sur-vey, by Kaplan Test Prep, found that almost half of college admissions officers regularly check applicants' social media profiles. Another survey, by CareerBuilder, found that 70 percent of employers use social media to screen potential candidates. What image of them-selves are your kids projecting online? How will it impact their futures? Oddly, many parents haven't even considered the fact that their kids are inadvertently cataloging snapshots, memes, and

Boomerang videos into haphazard resumés. Just think about how the web now plays a part in your own adult life.

I know that whenever I meet a new business associate, the first thing I do is look her up online. Prior to arriving at a meeting, I try to learn as much as I can about the colleagues who will be in the room. I use Google, Facebook, LinkedIn, and Instagram to piece together biographies. This means that before I sit down at the table, I know quite a bit about all the people around me. It's not really the ideal *xenia* hospitality I described in Chapter Ten. Nowadays, most of my real-life encounters lack spontaneity, open-mindedness, and serendipity. Often they're calculated and transactional. If I don't intentionally make an effort to listen carefully and be present with all the individuals around me, I'm bound to direct most of my attention toward folks whose online profiles best articulated a value proposition.

With this sad reality in mind, I do what I can to make sure my kids understand the difference between public documentation and private memory. Physical keepsakes — videocassettes, photo-booth snapshots, love letters, and old diaries — work like time machines. I pull them from the back of my closet and recollect feelings, sensations, and thoughts in a way that reveals the general spirit of another time in my life. It's a private interaction with the physical relics that catalyze memories. I'm taken back in time, led to an internal, emotional encounter with a past sense of self.

Alternatively, the digital artifacts that now define our public profiles are not memories at all. The data is collected once and permanently left in place. Nothing is re-collected because it's never been shoved into boxes. Our online selves are built like cement pylons rather than sand castles. There's nothing to remember because the ambiguous reinventions of identity that once marked a childhood experience are now superseded by iterative pivots — life lived through the determinate possibilities of a software flowchart. We may debug our online pasts, but the old code never goes away.

That's not good for kids. They need opportunities to maintain their private memories and, by extension, their capacity for transformative personal development. Everyone is entitled to change the course of life's ongoing psychological journey, to give their identity a costume change. Therefore, grown-ups must teach kids to be cautiously aware of the permanence that goes with public online documentation. In the same way that behaviorists see the ability to distinguish appropriate conversation topics as a key social skill for face-to-face encounters, the ability to modulate between suitable online and offline sharing is now a key element of digital media literacy.

Talk to your kids about the kind of online encounters that are appropriate. Show them that some posts can permanently damage a reputation and curtail the possibility for personal reinvention. Help them understand how the difference between public and private manifests within the current technological paradigm.

Takeaways

Niche casting threatens critical thinking.

Consider the challenges today's kids face as media consumers in a connected world. Digital technology has transformed the way information and entertainment are distributed. Microtargeting makes it almost impossible to distinguish between marketing and journalism — so much so that in the media business, they use the term "advertorial" to describe paid advertising that's delivered as if it were unbiased editorial content.

In addition, predictive algorithms offer everyone a personalized news stream, and therefore most of the content we encounter has been tailored and customized to keep us engaged. All the information we receive tends to confirm, validate, or reinforce things we already believe. We rarely have meaningful encounters with opposed ideas. And therefore we're never required to practice the kind of intellectual humility that's at the core of good critical thinking.

To be kind, thoughtful, open-minded, and hospitable, our kids will need to recognize that their viewpoints are fallible. As Socrates famously explained almost three millennia ago, true wisdom lies in knowing what you don't know, recognizing how little you can be certain of, and demonstrating a willingness to ask yourself the hardest questions.

Our children will grow up to be nodes in a worldwide network and contributors to a global economy. Their ability to be comfortable with intellectual, social, and cultural diversity will be one of the primary prerequisites for success and fulfillment. But the media to which they're currently exposed often promotes the opposite attitude. Therefore, grown-ups need to equip kids with the adequate media literacy skills for a connected world.

Teach kids to think about how media is constructed.

At this point, digital media has mostly become an instrument to facilitate niche consumption. But it has the potential to be a tool for the open and democratic exchange of information and ideas. To achieve this ideal, however, grown-ups will need to teach the next generation how to recognize that all interactions with digital devices involve some sort of procedural rhetoric.

Apps, websites, games, and even smart speakers like Google Home and Alexa force users to engage in certain kinds of rituals and routines. Today, most of an individual's interactions — social, commercial, informational, political, even educational — are mediated through software and smart devices. And each encounter is an engagement with media. Hence, we need to show children that they can do more than just swipe, click, and tap. They can also think critically about digital experiences, approaching them as things to be analyzed, interpreted, and evaluated.

Teachers can promote this kind of thinking by using video games as texts. Add them to the curriculum. At the moment, there's far too little critical examination of video games happening in school. We take it for granted that we should teach our students how to read books interpretively, how to analyze movies, and how to read the newspaper critically. But all too often we overlook video games as a meaningless triviality. There are plenty of serious games that are intentionally created to provoke thought, designed so that they force players to ask questions. These are often called social impact games. They are essentially the new nonlinear equivalent of essays and social commentaries. To see them in action, check out the annual award winners at the Games for Change Festival website (www .gamesforchange.org) or read through the Guide to Digital Play for Global Citizens that I produced at Sesame Workshop (joanganz-cooneycenter.org/digitalplay). Resources like these can help teachers show kids how to think critically about the images, stories, and technologies that surround them.

Parents can help kids interpret digital media during the new family time. When you turn on Netflix or Amazon Prime, you can talk about the way these platforms are designed not only to personalize choices, but also to push certain kinds of content into your home—presumably, the service providers want you watching the things that are most profitable for them. Show your kids that even smart TVs involve user interfaces that encourage them to make certain kinds of decisions. Talk to them about how television menus work in the same predictive way as YouTube, the App Store, and just about every other media and shopping experience.

There's also a lot about media literacy that kids can learn through playing video games with their parents. It's not hard. Just talk to your kids about in-game elements while you play. Draw their attention to the soundtrack, remind them that someone had to write it, perform it, and record it. Discuss the story, ask them how they imagine the author. Evaluate the quality of the controls, point out that developers decided how avatars would jump, run, and shoot. Each question you ask is an opportunity to show your kids that their interactive experiences were constructed with an agenda.

Online Self and Online Other

On social media and video/photo-sharing platforms, kids often create the content themselves. And there are both practical and emotional reasons why it's important that they understand issues around digital privacy and surveillance before uploading anything.

From a practical standpoint, they need to be aware that there's an enduring trace of every digital interaction. Nothing online is private; everything is public. A child's digital footprint can last a long time. College admissions departments and employers now check social media profiles regularly. So, even at a very young age, kids might be posting things that will end up on a permanent resumé.

Teach your kids what should be shared and what shouldn't. Often, discussions around digital discretion focus on preventing predators, fraud, and identity theft. And while these are certainly important issues, it's also worth considering that grown-ups need to teach kids simple judgment and tact. Just as we teach them to distinguish appropriate conversations for different contexts — you don't talk to your teacher using the same swear words you'd use with your friends — we also need to teach them appropriate social modulation skills for different kinds of online interactions.

Grown-ups also need to recognize that the dangers associated with a permanent record are not only about outward appearances. The lack of privacy can have a destructive impact on kids' internal psychological experience, too. Part of growing up involves reinvention. We try on different personas with different social groups, and we often change the way we choose to show up in specific social situations. Think about all the times a teenager adopts new fashion styles, haircuts, or nicknames. Each time she's experimenting with ways to incorporate vulnerable parts of herself into an authentic public persona. This is a crucial part of personal development. The more times an individual reinvents herself, the clearer it is that today's most sacred beliefs can easily become tomorrow's absurdities. That's how one learns about intellectual humility.

CHAPTER 12

THE NEW CHILDHOOD

LIKE MOST SIBLINGS, my boys sometimes call each other names.

"You're such a nub," one says to the other.

They both laugh.

"Nub" rhymes with pub, grub, and tub. It's what the kids say these days. "Nub" has a connotation similar to "dork" and "loser." The language children use changes over time.

My older brothers and I called each other names back before Silicon Valley millionaires reclaimed "geek" as their own. In those days, the word was negative. We kept "geek" as a weapon in our arsenal of insults. And now that we're adults, it shows up whenever the polite discourse over a holiday dinner devolves into verbal jousting. For us, the old playful slurs are like lances made of pillows. They simultaneously function as nonaggressive terms of endearment and as hostile manifestations of our semiconscious competition for parental recognition.

"Butthead. Doofus. Dweeb."

Even fully grown, we spar. It fortifies our psychological armor, builds up protection against the outside world. Name-calling is defensive; it shields our insecurities. Yet it also provides a sense of identity. Through these playful interactions, we project an image of the self. We demonstrate confidence. And when my brothers and I were young, we must really have needed a boost, because scuffles seemed to erupt every time we were together. Things were never frictionless.

In fact, most of what we played on our Atari 2600 video-game console was just simulated skirmish. Our favorite was *Combat* — a two-player shootout between pixelated tanks, biplanes, or jets. We played it so often that I can almost still hear the soundtrack: a constant purr of electrostatic white noise interrupted by shooting blasts. The battles were slow and uneventful, not hyperchaotic like *Super Smash Bros: Melee* or the 3-D online battle royale games that my kids log on to daily. When they play today's shooters, the boom mics on their headsets curve around their cheeks and they howl at their friends with the same frenzy I once used when my older brothers were sitting right next to me. Their heated spirit is familiar. But the mechanics and graphics of video games have gotten so complex that my kids barely recognize that they're essentially playing souped-up, high-spectacle derivatives of the same old duels.

"Staged fights" have been around forever. One-on-one battles were fought for honor, glory, trophies, and treasures long before my brothers and I ever slid the *Combat* cartridge into Atari's slot. In Hellenic times, the victor of a duel often ended up wearing the pilfered armor of his defeated opponent. During the fourth century BCE, Celtic warriors hung the severed heads of conquered rivals from their belts. Heroes have always collected what sociologist Randall Collins calls "tokens of honor." In his exhaustive study of violence, Collins explains that "the general pattern is to build one's reputation — and one's fighting confidence, or emotional ascendancy — by taking a commemorative emblem and publicizing it." This is why gamers have been competing for *Donkey Kong*'s high score ever since the early days of shopping-mall video arcades. It's hard to resist the appeal of a leaderboard that publicizes the best of the "geeks."

Similarly, in many of today's popular online games, players accumulate weapons, special powers, and access to restricted levels; these features function as indicators of achievement, proof of a player's in-game status. A duel is not really about rage or dominance. Instead, whether fought with fists or joysticks, it's an opportunity to prove you're part of the in-crowd. It connects you to opponents by demonstrating your familiarity with all the implicit rules and regulations of a fair fight. It lets others see that you're privy to the intricate terms of an elite social contract. Only the cool kids know the honor code, the rites and etiquette of high combat. Think of the martial arts, the chivalry of knighthood, or even the stereotypical school playground fistfight: just being able to compete is already a signifier of rank.

Recently, I attached an Atari Flashback console to one of the six HDMI inputs on the back of my television set. The inexpensive retro-style device comes preloaded with 120 8-bit video-game classics. I called my kids into the room so they could experience the legacy game play of my youth. I turned on *Combat,* excited about an evening of the new family time and found they didn't have the patience to tolerate the clumsiness of old-school gaming. They were bored after just a few minutes of battle. My younger son took the lead a little too quickly. He challenged the hierarchy of age by racking up significantly more points than his older brother.

But it wasn't until the game was over that he moved in for the real hit.

"You nub!" he taunted.

"Nub" literally means neophyte, novice, or rookie. It's like pointing out and laughing at warriors who don't have enough severed heads hanging from their belts. The word fascinates me because even though it communicates an ancient and essential element of competitive sport, it emerged in a way that's unique to its current technological context.

At first it was "newbie," a term that longtime members of internet forums employed to haze recent additions; it made their lack of social standing explicit. Then, in the chat streams of the first online games, it got spelled phonetically: "noob." And finally, by the time my son was building in *Minecraft*'s block world, both the spelling and the vowel sound had been shortened to "nub."

Similarly, my boys vocalize "LOL" so that it rhymes with null and dull. And "YOLO"—which was originally an acronym for "you only live once"—has become an ordinary exclamation among tweens. It's more likely to be voiced with two hard *O*s than it is to be written as an abbreviation.

All of these pronunciations developed from online text into a spoken dialect unique to my kids' era. It's a specialized vernacular, shaped by tools of the time. It's also a language all their own. They never hear grown-ups say these words. We couldn't have taught them to our children. We're an entirely different generation.

In a connected world, the adults are the nubs.

Talking about Their Generation

It's popular to group people by generation: the baby boomers, GenX, and the Millennials. At this point in time, almost all grown-ups have been conditioned by a monastery model of education. They've been trained to file everything into categories that align with a clockwork view of the universe. So, it's hardly surprising that our understanding of cultural history follows the same pattern.

It's telling, however, that we haven't yet landed on a good name for my kids' generation. Lots of people have tried to come up with one. "Generation Z" commonly appears in media headlines, but I doubt it will stick because it doesn't say anything about the kids it's trying to describe. The baby boomers were named when the birthrate soared after World War II. Gen X was meant to signify an entire generation's resistance to being defined. And Millennials (briefly called Generation Y) came of age at the beginning of the twenty-first century. By comparison, Generation Z is an entirely referential name. It harks back to X and continues the sequence of alphabetic variables. In other words, it just means that my kids were born two generations after X — and that's not very descriptive. Moreover, it feels so final. If they're Z, what comes next? Presumably something that transcends the inclination to organize things into episodic cohorts.

In 2013, Howard Gardner and Katie Davis published a book called *The App Generation*. In it they wrote, "The apps arrayed on a person's smartphone or tablet represent a fingerprint of sorts — only instead of a unique pattern of ridges, it's the combination of interests, habits, and social connections." They argued that kids were learning to see themselves according to the workflow of a mobile operating system. Just think about how highly curated children's leisure time is these days. They move from soccer practice to piano lessons, to psychotherapy sessions, to dance classes, to math tutors, to coding clubs, and so on. Extracurricular activities and social cliques have become just like apps. Life is experienced as an aggregate collection of disjointed single-purpose pursuits. As a result, kids may not want to "hang out" just for fun or without an objective in mind. Hence, they struggle to experience the self as something greater than the sum of all parts.

I like how this idea emphasizes the relationship between technology and consciousness, even if it is a tinge too technophobic. But ultimately, despite Gardner's high profile as an influential education theorist—he pioneered the idea of multiple intelligences—the term didn't stick. My kids are not part of the App Generation.

Another potential moniker came from research psychologist Jean M. Twenge. She called them "iGen" in her book by the same name. But her reasoning wasn't as nuanced as Gardner's and Davis's. She picked the term mostly because this generation "grew up with cell phones, had an Instagram page before they started high school, and do not remember a time before the Internet." In addition, she explained that the "I" also stands for "individualism" and "income inequality." But I'd argue that at least since the beginning of the Industrial Age, individualism has been a part of every generation's sandbox sense of self. And while it's true that the consequences of income inequality may be manifesting in new ways, the phenomenon is not at all unique to our times. Worse still, Twenge claimed that my kids "are at the forefront of the worst mental health crisis in decades, with rates of teen depression and suicide skyrocketing since 2011." She suggested that by and large, today's kids are unhappy because they are using digital technology in inherently shallow, narcissistic, and unhealthy ways. Certainly, many experts agree, but I object to the philosophical and psychological framing—it would take me an entire book to explain all the reasons why, but luckily for you, you're already reading the final chapter.

One refreshing attempt to name the generation born from 2005 onward makes no explicit reference to digitally networked technologies. William Strauss and Neil Howe, who authored the 1991 book *Generations: The History of America's Future, 1548 to 2069* (in which they named the Millennials), settled on "Homeland Generation." Why? Because my kids were born in the aftermath of the 9/11 World Trade Center attacks, when the U.S. government established the

Department of Homeland Security. In an article Howe wrote for *Forbes*, he pointed to "a worldwide cultural movement towards nationalism, localism, and an increased identification with one's roots." He also connected the term "Homeland" to research that suggests that current parenting styles offer today's kids much less freedom than previous generations; they literally spend more time at home. Of course, I've already explained how this "homing" impulse is actually a reactionary attempt to locate a stable hearth within a hyperconnected digital agora (see Part Two). Therefore, I also doubt that Homeland Generation will be a lasting term. It may accurately describe the way grown-ups are dealing with the anxieties of constant connection, but it says little about how my kids actually live and learn.

Their experience will be characterized by the messy duel between intimacy and scale. This is the universal dilemma that everyone living in a connected world now faces. It manifests in the tension between online privacy and transparency—which can also be framed as a battle between the conveniences of personalization and the terrors of surveillance. We feel the struggle between local and global economies. We see border walls strengthened even as migration swells. Intimacy and scale also clash at the eroding boundary that once separated home and work. And it's the pendulum that swings between innovation and orthodoxy, haste and prudence, disruption and tradition, modernity and legacy. It's where Amazon's mass distribution meets Etsy's artisanal craftsmanship. And where the exploitation of Uber's piecemeal labor rubs up against the freedom of individual entrepreneurship.

Of course, there's nothing new about this quandary. Since the beginning of recorded history, people have been choosing between monotheism and polytheism, one and many, unity and partition, individual and collective. But nowadays, it's impossible to know which side you're on. All the lines are ambiguous, all the boundaries vague.

Philosopher Edward S. Casey explains that "*vague* itself means 'wandering or straying.'" It shares a root with *vagrant* and *vagabond*. And in French, it means "wave," like water crashing against the indefinite border between beach and sea. There is no such thing as a rigid coastline. Not only because tides ebb and flow, eroding the shore, but also because, as Casey writes, "it is of the very nature of water to wander — to find its way through the places of least resistance." His description is poetic and abstract, but not complicated. It just tells us that our quest for clarity is ultimately Sisyphean. Things will always seep through the pores. Our rigid categories and precise measurements may enable the standardization on which scale depends, but they are also dams that attempt to thwart fluidity. And because we crave intimacy and connection, we'll continue to bore pathways in the very bulwarks we build.

This contradiction characterizes the essential challenge of the New Childhood. And it's the duel for which grown-ups need to prepare their children. We must teach them the values, rules, and etiquette necessary to referee a fair fight between scale and intimacy, to maintain an honor code and reinforce the chivalrous ethics of participation.

We also need to recognize that the biggest obstacle to successful child-rearing is our sanctimonious commitment to the ritualized engagement with obsolete technological ways of thinking. We grown-ups are accustomed to staking out our territory, hoarding our treasures, drawing lines in the sand, and protecting our castles. Hence, we gravitate toward parenting strategies that divide things: an on/off switch approach to screen time, a commuter's view of the family, a monastery model of education, and a card-catalog conception of information and knowledge. We pass these ways of thinking on to our children because they have served us so well.

But our nostalgic loyalty to what's already past does a disservice to the future. As author Parag Khanna points out in his book *Connectography: Mapping the Future of Global Civilization,* "there's no better investment than connectivity." Of course, he's talking about it in geopolitical terms, suggesting that nations should focus on developing the infrastructure that links economies. But it's easy to apply the same idea to child-rearing. Your kids need you to do everything you can to help them cultivate the capacity to connect. They need to see themselves as nodes in a network, resolving and interpreting data, creating meaning and value by articulating and redistributing information on- and offline. The issue is not developing a practical skill set; humans are tenacious and resourceful, and will always figure out how to operate the tools around them. But without adequate modeling and mentoring—without sufficient opportunities for social and imaginative digital play—they can't learn to open emotional pipelines or make use of compassionate conduits.

A Global Playdate

During the summer of 2017, my children traveled with me to an annual symposium that takes place in the Greek islands. It was an international gathering of economists, politicians, leaders of NGOs, and thought leaders. We spent four or five days working, talking, eating, and swimming together.

All day the adults sat around a table that looked like the casual, beachy version of the United Nations: we had gooseneck microphones, official name placards, and printed agendas full of data and metrics. We discussed politics, migration, impending economic trends, technology, and twenty-first-century skills.

Meanwhile, our children ran around outside: laughing, playing, and splashing in the Aegean Sea together. Every adult there understood what a privilege it was that our kids were able to engage with a multicultural and international cohort of peers. My boys made friends from Bosnia, Kosovo, Britain, Turkey, Syria, Belgium, France, Tunisia, South Africa, and Germany. Talk about a global sandbox!

Each night at dinner, while the grown-ups continued our serious conversations over food and libations, the kids congregated at their own table. I looked over occasionally, when their voices seemed too loud or when their laughter became suspiciously intense. I discovered that they were all being sneaky. Just like the students in my college classroom, they were looking down at their laps because, despite their parents' insistence that they leave their devices in the hotel room, every one of them had smuggled a smartphone or a tablet to the table.

They tried desperately to conceal their touchscreens beneath the tablecloth, often looking over their shoulders to make sure none of the parents noticed. Of course, it didn't work. Kids can't really whisper; they are never as discreet as they think. The grown-ups spotted the transgression almost immediately, but we all chose not to say anything. Why? Because we realized very quickly that our initial objections were unjustified.

We had worried that the presence of digital devices would cause our kids to be antisocial. And at an event that provided them with such unprecedented exposure to a diverse peer group, we wanted to encourage them to make the most of their time. They should've been talking to one another, not staring into the bezels of their smartphones. In other words, we imagined that video games and social-media apps would divide them. But we discovered that our concerns were misguided. The technology ended up providing the common ground that enabled our children to form friendships. The kids giggled with joy as they shared their favorite apps and games, as they tried to swap phones and tablets undetected.

This happened night after night, all week long. And then, a few days later, when we all returned to our respective countries of origin, we adults went back to our everyday routines. The kids, however, continued to play together. Perhaps they intuitively understood something that their parental nubs didn't: intimacy can be achieved through scale. In fact, as the technological animal, that's what the human does — builds tools that standardize experience and facilitate the kind of connections that can transcend the limitations of time and space.

Almost a year later, the kids continue to chat on Skype, they play online games together, and they share ideas, photos, and stories.

This is the New Childhood.

ACKNOWLEDGMENTS

If not for Tracy Behar, I doubt you would have read all the way to the end of this book; you would have stopped in the middle of Chapter Four, in the section about forks (which, thankfully, we cut from the manuscript). She edited this book like a master teacher: saying so much but using very few words.

I cannot adequately express how grateful I am for superagent Bonnie Solow, who called me out of the blue after hearing me on NPR connecting online cat videos to the ancient Egyptian goddess Bastet. Bonnie recognized that I had things to say even before I knew how to say them.

Thank you, Rebecca Winthrop, for being an ongoing sounding board; so many parts of this book began as conversations with you. Roxanne Partridge sometimes pulls me out of psyche's depths and other times throws me back down — it depends on what I need, and she always seems to know. Robert Granat is often the audience in my mind, hopefully laughing at each witty turn of phrase, not rolling his eyes in disappointment. George Papandreou is perhaps the most genuine person I know, and it's thanks to him, and the entire Symi Symposium community, that I became macrominded. An extra special thanks to Jane Laties: your classroom provided many of the examples in this book, but more important, I will always be appreciative that you taught both my boys to read, count, tell time, and measure.

Thank you to Michael Levine, Catherine Jhee, and everyone at the Joan Ganz Cooney Center and Sesame Workshop. To Doug Greenfield, Dan Berman, Sheryl Sawin, Emily Carlin and all the folks at Temple University. Thanks to Alicia Cunningham-Bryant, who keeps a cuneiform tablet on her desk and worked tirelessly along with me to build Temple's Intellectual Heritage Online Learning Program. To Wendy Urban, without whom I never would have developed a philosophical approach to digital literacy. To Bart Kessler, Chris Willis, and everyone at Air University's eSchool: I come home from every encounter inspired and provoked.

There are so many other people who either read early chapters of this book, shared in thoughtful discussions, provided general support, or shaped my thinking in indispensable ways: Lucy Lake, Vikas Pota, Zlatko Lagumdžija, Frederikke Tømmergaard, Bo Stjerne Thomsen, Mitch Resnick, Keith Devlin, Jean-Baptiste Huynh, Robert Gehorsam, Charlie Campbell, Anthony Salcito, Kari Sherrod, Meghan Gaebe, Kathy Hirsch-Pasek, Jack Shonkoff, Jim Gee, Greg Toppo, Jessica Lahey, Meghan McDermott, Gregg Behr, Sarah Biemuller, Sophie Schrader, Alison Cutts, Frankie Tartaglia, Ben Lee, Avi Kaplan, Tresa Grauer, Lisa Pack, Roni Anton, Donna Allender, Dolly Oberoi, Michael Stipe, Jennifer Selig, Ed Casey, Ben Lee, Jack McDavid, Bruce Upbin, Richard Rosso.

To Irv, Sharon, Mathieu, Jessica, Seth, Courtney, Shelly, David, Melissa, Peter, Jennifer, Erik — even Jane, Paul, Julian, and David:

all together, and in more ways than one, you comprise my enduring flame, a temple to honor the goddess Vesta.

To Dylan and Maya: you will probably never realize how many of the ideas in this book were inspired by you.

To Sergey and Niko: thank you for putting up with me; it can't be easy to live with a dad who's always testing new child-rearing theories on you.

Most of all: Amanda. Saying thank you is not nearly enough. I can no longer imagine this journey without you.

BIBLIOGRAPHY

Batson, C. Daniel, et al. 1991. "Empathic joy and the empathy-altruism hypothesis." *Journal of Personality and Social Psychology* 61 (3): 413-426.

Bers, Marina Umaschi. 2018. *Coding as a Playground: Programming and Computational Thinking in the Early Childhood Classroom.* New York: Routledge.

Bettelheim, Bruno. 1989. *The Uses of Enchantment: The Meaning and Importance of Fairy Tales.* New York: Vintage.

Bogost, Ian. 2010. *Persuasive Games: The Expressive Power of Videogames.* Cambridge, MA: MIT Press.

boyd, danah. 2015. *It's Complicated: The Social Lives of Networked Teens.* New Haven, Connecticut: Yale University Press.

Buber, Martin. 2002. *Between Man and Man.* New York: Routledge.

Bush, Vannevar. 1945. "As We May Think." *The Atlantic*, July. Accessed September 2, 2017. https://www.theatlantic.com/magazine/archive/1945/07/as-we-may-think/303881/.

Carlson, Stephanie M., and Rachel E. White. 2013. "Executive Function, Pretend Play, and Imagination." In *The Oxford Handbook of the Development of*

Imagination, edited by Marjorie Taylor, 161-174. New York: Oxford Univeristy Press.

Carrol, Abigail. 2013. *Three Squares: The Invention of the American Meal*. New York: Basic Books.

Casey, Edward S. 2017. *The World on Edge*. Indiana: Indiana University Press.

Chui, Michael, James Manyika, and Mehdi Miremadi. 2015. "Four Fundamentals of Workplace Automation." *Digital McKinsey*. November. https://www.mckinsey.com/business-functions/digital-mckinsey/our-insights/four-fundamentals-of-workplace-automation.

Collins, Randall. 2008. *Violence: A Micro-Sociological Theory*. Princeton: Princeton University Press.

Coontz, Stephanie. 1992. *The Way We Never Were: American Families and the Nostalgia Trap*. NYC: Basic Books.

Crudden, Michael. 2001. *The Homeric Hymns*. New York: Oxford World's Classics.

Cushman, Philip. 1995. *Constructing the Self, Constructing America: A Cultural History of Psychotherapy*. Cambridge, MA: Perseus Publishing.

Devlin, Keith. 2001. *InfoSense: Turning Information into Knowledge*. New York: W. H. Freeman and Company.

Eichenbaum, Adam, Daphne Bavelier, and C. Shawn Green. 2014. "Play That Can Do Serious Good." *American Journal of Play*. Volume 7 (Number 1): 50-72.

Engelhardt, Tom. 1991. "The Primal Screen." *Mother Jones*, May/June: 68-69.

Fass, Paula S. 2016. *The End of Childhood: A History of Parenting from Life on the Frontier to the Managed Child*. Princeton, NJ: Princeton University Press.

Freie, Paulo and Donaldo Macedo. 2018. *Pedagogy of the Oppressed 50th Anniversary Edition*. Bloomsbury USA Academic.

Freud, Sigmund. 1961. *Civilization and Its Discontents*. New York: W.W. Norton & Company.

Gardner, Howard, and Katie Davis. 2013. *The App Generation: How Today's Youth Navigate Identity, Intimacy, And Imagination In A Digital World*. New Haven: Yale University Press.

Gee, James Paul. 2007. *What Video Games Have To Teach Us About Learning Literacy*. New York City: Palgrave MacMillan.

Gillis, John. 1996. "Making Time For Family: The Invention of Family Time(s) and the Reinvention of Family History." *Journal of Family History* (Sage Publications) 21 (1): 4–11.

Gillis, John R. 1996. *A World of Their Own Making: Myth, Ritual, and the Quest for Family Values*. Cambridge, Massachusetts: Harvard University Press.

Gray, Peter. 2013. "The Educative Value of Teasing." *Psychology Today*, January 13.

Guernsey, Lisa. 2007. *Into the Minds of Babes: How Screen Time Affects Children From Birth to Age Five*. New York City: Basic Books.

Hall, G. Stanley. 1904. *Adolescence: Its Psychology and Its Relations to Physiology, Anthropology, Sociology, Sex, Crime, Religion, and Education, Volume 1*. New York: D. Appleton and Company.

———. 1897. *The Story of a Sand-Pile*. New York, Chicago: E.L. Kellogg & Co.

Harris, Malcolm. 2017. *Kids These Days: Human Capital and the Making of Millennials*. New York: Little, Brown and Company.

Harvard, Center on the Developing Child at. 2007. *The Science of Early Childhood Development: Closing the Gap Between What We Know and What We Do*. National Scientific Council on the Developing Child.

Heidegger, Martin. 1971. *On The Way To Language*. Translated by Peter D. Hertz. New York: HarperCollins.

———. 1992. *Parmenides*. Translated by André Shuwer and Richard Rojcewicz. Bloomington and Indianapolis, IN: Indiana University Press.

Hillman, James. 2007. *Mythic Figures*. New York: Spring Publications.

Hirsh-Pasek, Kathy, and Roberta Michnick Golinkoff. 2016. *Becoming Brilliant: What Science Tells Us About Raising Successful Children*. Washington DC: American Psychological Association.

———. 2003. *Einstein Never Used Flash Cards: How Our Children REALLY Learn—and Why They Need to Play More and Memorize Less*. Emmaus, PA: Rodale.

Hirsh-Pasek, Kathy, Roberta Michnik Golinkoff, Laura E. Berk, and Dorothy G. Singer. 2009. *A Mandate for Playful Learning in Preschool.* New York: Oxford University Press.

Holland, Dorothy, and William Lachiotte, Jr. 2007. "Vygotsky, Mead, and the New Sociocultural Studies of Identity." In *The Cambridge Companion to Vygotsky*, by Harry Daniels, 101-135. Cambridge: Cambridge University Press.

Homer. 2018. *The Odyssey.* Translated by Emily Wilson. New York: W.W. Norton & Company.

Horkheimer, Max and Theodor W. Adorno. 2002. *Dialectic of Enlightenment: Philosophical Fragments.* Edited by Gunzelin Schmid Noerr. Translated by Edmund Jephcott. Stanford, CA: Stanford University Press.

Huizinga, Johan. 2014. *Homo Ludens : A Study of the Play-Element in Culture.* Mansfield Centre, CT: Martino Publishing.

Keltner, Dacher, Lisa Capps, Ann M. Kring, Randall C. Young, and Erin, A. Heerey. 2001. "Just Teasing: A Conceptual Analysis and Empirical Review." *Psychological Bulletin* 127 (2): 229-248.

Kocurek, Carly A. 2016. *Coin-Operated Americans: Rebooting Boyhood at the Video Game Arcade.* Minnesota: University of Minnesota Press.

Kucklich, Julian. 2002. "Precarious Playbour: Modders and the Digital Games Industry." *fiberculturejournal.org*, April 16.

Kurlansky, Mark. 2016. *Paper: Paging Through History.* New York: W.W. Norton & Company.

Manyika, James, Susan Lund, Jacques Bughin, Kelsey Robinson, Jan Mische, and Deepa Mahajan. 2016. "Independent Work: Choice, Necessity, And The Gig Economy."

McKnight, Katherine. 2018. *Leveling the Playing Field with Microsoft Learning Tools.* RTI International. http://edudownloads.azureedge.net/msdownloads/ Learning_Tools_research_study_BSD.pdf.

McLuhan, Marshall, and Quintin Fiore. 1996. *The Medium is the Message: An Inventory of Effects.* Berkeley, CA: Ginko Press.

Merleau-Ponty, Maurice. 1987. *Signs*. Evanston, IL: Northwestern University Press.

Mintz, Steven. 2004. *Huck's Raft : A History of American Childhood*. Cambridge, MA: Belknap Press of Harvard University Press.

Moore, Gordon E. 1965. "Cramming more components onto integrated circuits." *Electronics* 38 (8).

Mumford, Lewis. 2010. *Technics and Civilization*. Chicago: University of Chicago Press.

OECD. 2017. *PISA 2015 Results (Volume III): Students' Well-Being*. Paris, France: OECD Publishing. doi:http://dx.doi.org/10.1787/9789264273856-en.

OECD. 2017. *PISA 2015 Results (Volume V): Collaborative Problem Solving*. Paris, France: OECD Publishing.

Papert, Seymour. 1980. *Mindstorms; Children, Computers, and Powerful Ideas*. Basic Books.

Papert, Syemour and Cynthia Solomon. 1971. "Twenty Things To Do With A Computer." Cambridge: Massachusetts Institute of Technology, Artificial Intelligence Lab, June.

Paris, Ginette. 1986. *Pagan Meditations*. Woodstock, Connecticut: Spring Publications, Inc.

Paumgarten, Nick. 2007. *There and Back Again: The Soul of the Commuter*. April 16. http://www.newyorker.com/magazine/2007/04/16/there-and-back-again.

Plato. 2005. *Phaedrus*. Translated by C.J. Rowe. New York: Penguin Classics.

Puchner, Martin. 2017. *The Written World: The Power of Stories to Shape People, History, Civilization*. New York: Random House.

Putnam, Robert D. 2007. *Bowling Alone: The Collapse and Revival of American Community*. New York: Simon & Schuster.

Rainie, L. and K. Zickuhr. 2015. *Americans' Views on Mobile Etiquette*. Pew Research Center. http://www.pewinternet.org/2015/08/26/americans -views-on-mobile-etiquette/.

Resnick, Mitchel. 2017. *Lifelong Kindergarten: Cultivating Creativity Through Projects, Passion, Peers, and Play*. Cambridge, Massachusetts: MIT Press.

Rideout, Victoria. 2017. *The Common Sense Census: Media Use by Kids Age Zero to Eight*. San Francisco, CA: Common Sense Media.

Rifkin, Jeremy. 2009. *Empathic Civilization: The Race to Global Conciousness in a World in Crisis*. New York: Penguin.

Ross, Dorothy. 1972. *G. Stanley Hall: The Psychologist as Prophet*. Chicago: University of Chicago Press.

Rybczynski, Witold. 1986. *Home: A Short History of an Idea*. New York: Penguin.

Schmidt, J. Philipp. 2014. "From Courses to Communities." *dmlcentral: Digital Media + Learning: The Power of Participation*. October 13. Accessed March 21, 2018. https://dmlcentral.net/from-courses-to-communities/.

Seidenberg, Mark. 2017. *Language at the Speed of Sight*. New York: Basic Books.

Shonkoff, Jack P. and Deboarh A. Phillips. 2000. *From Neurons to Neighborhoods: the Science of Early Child Development*. Washington, DC: National Academy Press.

Snyder, Gary. 1990. *The Practice of the Wild*. New York: North Point Press.

Sontag, Susan. 2011. *On Photography*. New York: Farrar, Straus and Giroux.

Spock, Benjamin and Robert Needleman. 2012. *Dr. Spock's Baby and Child Care*. New York: Gallery Books.

Stueber, Karsten. 2017. "Empathy." In *The Stanford Encyclopedia of Philosophy*, by Edward N. Zalta (ed). https://plato.stanford.edu/archives/spr2017/entries/empathy/.

Sunstein, Cass R. 2017. *#Republic: Divided Democracy in the Age of Social Media*. Princeton, NJ: Princeton University Press.

Taylor, Mark C. 2014. *Speed Limits: Where Time Went and Why We Have So Little Left*. New Haven: Yale University Press.

Thornton, Tamara Platkins. 1996. *Handwriting in America: A Cultural History*. New Haven, CT: Yale University Press.

Trubek, Anne. 2016. *The History and Uncertain Future of Handwriting*. New York: Bloomsbury.

BIBLIOGRAPHY

Twenge, Jean M. 2017. *iGen: Why Today's Super-Connected Kids Are Growing Up Less Rebellious, More Tolerant, Less Happy—and Completely Unprepared for Adulthood.* New York: Atria.

Visser, Margaret. 1991. *The Rituals of Dinner.* New York: Grove Weidenfeld.

Vygotskii, Lev and Michael Cole. 1978. *Mind in Society: The Development of Higher Psychological Processes.* Cambridge, Massachusetts: Harvard University Press.

Vygotsky, Lev. 1986. *Thought and Language.* Cambridge, Massachusetts: The MIT Press.

Winnicott, D.W. 2016. *Through Paediatrics to Psycho-analysis.* Routledge.

Wolf, Maryanne. 2007. *Proust and the Squid: The Story and Science of the Reading Brain.* New York: Harper.

INDEX

INDEX

INDEX

INDEX

INDEX

ABOUT THE AUTHOR

Jordan Shapiro, PhD, is a world-renowned American thought leader. He's currently Senior Fellow for the Joan Ganz Cooney Center at Sesame Workshop and Nonresident Fellow with the Center for Universal Education at the Brookings Institution. He teaches in Temple University's Intellectual Heritage Program, and he wrote a column for *Forbes* magazine on global education, digital play, and family life from 2012 to 2017. He lives in Philadelphia with his two sons.

books to help you live a good life

Join the conversation and tell
us how you live a #goodlife

 🐦 @yellowkitebooks
 ⓕ YellowKiteBooks
 ⓟ Yellow Kite Books
 📷 YellowKiteBooks